SHAPER NATIONS

Shaper Nations

Strategies for a Changing World

EDITED BY

William I. Hitchcock

Melvyn P. Leffler

Jeffrey W. Legro

HARVARD UNIVERSITY PRESS

Cambridge, Massachusetts

London, England • *2016*

Second Printing

Library of Congress Cataloging-in-Publication Data
Names: Hitchcock, William I., editor. | Leffler , Melvyn P., 1945– editor. |
  Legro, Jeffrey, editor.
Title: Shaper nations : strategies for a changing world / edited by William
  I. Hitchcock, Melvyn P. Leffl r, Jeffr ey W. Legro.
Description: Cambridge, Massachusetts : Harvard University Press, 2016. |
  Includes bibliographical references and index.
Identifiers:L CCN 2015032634 | ISBN 9780674660212 (hc : alk. paper)
Subjects: LCSH: International relations. | World politics—21st century. |
  Security, International. | National security—United States. |
  International organization.
Classification: LCC JZ1313 .S534 2016 | DDC 327.101—dc23
LC record available at http://lccn.loc.gov/2015032634

CONTENTS

INTRODUCTION
Making National Strategy in the
Twenty-First Century

WILLIAM I. HITCHCOCK

T HE ESSAYS in this book analyze the national strategies of key nations that are shaping the global politics of
our century. The nations considered here—Brazil, China,
Germany, India, Israel, Russia, Turkey, and the United States—of course vary
a great deal. Some are geographically and demographically huge and some
are small; some are global powerhouses and some are rising regional powers; some are transparent democracies while others are governed by opaque,
authoritarian regimes; some possess nuclear weapons and some do not; some
face serious security threats and others are less threatened. But they all share
one major characteristic: in our multipolar and interdependent world, these
states will have a decisive influence on their geopolitical "neighborhoods"
and perhaps on international relations the world over. Since these nations
will shape the future world order, policymakers and scholars need to be attuned to the factors that are most influential in the making of their national
strategies, from geopolitical ambition to ideology to threat perceptions and
historical identity. The more we know about what is driving the making of
strategy, the better informed we will be to manage the desires, expectations,
and fears of the world's most powerful states.

This book aims to evaluate both the sources of national strategy in these
nations as well as the impact that the pursuit of such strategies is having
upon contemporary world politics. It is important to note that the contributors to the volume were chosen for their scholarly expertise as well as their
national origin: each author lives and works primarily in the country about

which he or she is writing, and this is by design. Rather than rely on U.S.-based scholars, the editors of this book wished to learn about the making of national strategy from experts who have a keen "feel" for the debates and politics of their own countries. We have asked them to address the same set of questions with a specific aim. Rather than simply offering a collection of individual country portraits, we hope to illuminate their similarities and differences and what they can tell us about the sources and impact of strategies in the world ahead.

Our selection of these shaping nations needs some brief explanation. In our view, these eight countries are already having a significant effect on the politics, economic development, and security of their immediate geopolitical neighborhoods and will likely shape the future course of the global system. Earlier exercises in identifying such a list of key nations have used different criteria from ours. A 1996 study of "pivotal states," for example, argued that American policymakers ought to take special care to examine certain nations "on the brink"—that is, nations whose internal and regional troubles were so great that, should they collapse, the ripple effects would be enormous. This was an argument for focusing attention on troubled states whose principal impact on the world order would be associated with *failure*.[1] We have taken a different approach. Our focus is on increasingly powerful and influential states whose current policies are already shaping key geopolitical zones in Asia, Latin America, the Middle East, and Europe. It is because of their geopolitical prowess that these states have the capacity to shape regional outcomes. Our selection of countries is not meant to be comprehensive or complete. We are well aware that important countries like Japan, Iran, Indonesia, and Mexico, as well as Nigeria and South Africa, though not included here, have geopolitical significance. Our intent is not to consider every country that might potentially be a "shaper" of the future international order. Rather, we examine how national strategy is made in a representative range of these "shaping" countries, and, by doing so, we hope to illuminate the factors that influence shaper strategies as well as the kind of world these shaping nations will create.

Therefore, we include Israel because it has large conventional military capabilities, a nuclear arsenal, significant economic power, and the technological sophistication to hugely influence regional dynamics and international politics. Indeed, for the last sixty years, its employment of military force, its territorial expansion, its rejection of a nuclear nonproliferation regime, and its settlement policies have all shaped the politics of the Middle East and greatly influenced world politics. By contrast, the large African nations do not possess these characteristics. Nigeria is beleaguered by civil strife, an insurrection it cannot suppress, and endemic corruption that has sapped the strength of its military establishment and hampered its economic potential. Nigeria might be a pivotal state, in that its failure would be a disaster for Africa, but it is not a "shaper" nation because its current policy choices are not altering world politics. Nor did we include South Africa. It does not have the military power, economic strength, technological sophistication, and political and social cohesion to be among the most important shapers of international politics in the years ahead. In terms of total GDP, it ranks around thirtieth in the world, far below Brazil and Turkey; its GDP per capita places it around eighty-fifth in the world.[2] In terms of national power index, which combines GDP, defense spending, population, and technology, South Africa is projected to decrease or remain at the same level of power, whereas the United States, Russia, China, Germany, Brazil, and India already constitute the top six, and Turkey and Israel are projected to increase in national power.[3] None of this is to say that South Africa is unimportant. Rather, we believe that South Africa is unlikely to shape international relations globally in anything like the manner of our selected countries.

Having identified our key shaping states, we zero in on the making of national strategy in each. What do we mean by strategy? We do not limit ourselves, as Clausewitz did, to thinking of strategy as "the art of using battles to win the war."[4] Like a number of scholars and theorists, we have adopted a much more capacious definition. "A strategy," Lawrence Freedman has written, "is much more than a plan," which is simply a linear procession of steps one might take toward a goal. Strategy is more demanding. In a complicated world that is dynamic and unstable, national strategy must account for constant change, the possibility of conflict and war, and the unpredictable consequences that pursuit of one's strategy might trigger. Developing a strategy to achieve national ends requires thoughtful consideration of all aspects of national power, from military capabilities to economic potential, diplomatic influence, and considerations of ideology and domestic politics, as well as strong national leadership. Strategy must be both proactive and reactive, for it must account for the cost of pursuing a set of goals that may appear detrimental to others, thus leading to possible conflict. Furthermore, wise strategy integrates the need for diplomacy, since the pursuit of national interests usually requires support from allies and the cultivation of coalitions. Finally, strategy must take into

consideration popular support for the ends that the government has identified. As Basil Liddell Hart put it, "a good cause is sword as well as armor";
it can augment national strength. But a poor cause can be disruptive and
erode national effectiveness. For all of these reasons, strategy-making is a
constantly adaptive process that ranges across military, political, and economic policy. National strategy must respond to ever-changing internal,
geopolitical, economic, and even moral circumstances.[5]

Typically, scholars of "grand" strategy—that is, strategic action on a national and global scale rather than in an operational, military sense—have directed their attention toward the actions of "great powers." Since Thucydides,
the study of strategy has examined nations or empires that have emerged as
preeminent and that face a series of challenges to that preeminence. To study
the fate of Periclean Athens, or Philip II's Spanish Empire, or nineteenth-
century Britain, or even the United States since 1945, is to explore the behavior of polities that are at the apex of a particular configuration of power and
are anxious to hold their position.[6] By contrast, the essays in this volume are
not limited to the study of one or two hegemonic states. Rather, the authors
have tried to pull back the curtain to reveal the strategic thinking and policymaking in states which, while indisputably powerful, are nonetheless still
searching for their place in the twenty-first-century world order. These nations are riding a wave of historical change that may lift them into positions
of regional or global preeminence. We seek to understand how their strategic
cultures will guide them as they shape international politics.

Strategy, however, is not crafted in a laboratory under controlled conditions. The strategies of these states are not merely expressions of preferred
ends, with means to match. On the contrary, specific context matters, as does
the centrality of ideas that are seen as core values for each nation.[7] What
makes the analysis of these states so compelling is that we can observe the
making of strategy in a national context that is in flux: as these states rise
in influence, they are forced to adjust and adapt their strategic thinking and
behavior to match their new circumstances and to contend with the shifting configurations of power. For the nations we have studied here—nations
whose economies, domestic political arrangements, and security environ-
ments are rapidly changing—making strategy is like skeet-shooting from
the stern of a ship on a foaming sea: you may see your target clearly only for
the briefest of moments before your environment has shifted and your calculations must be adjusted. In the contemporary world, the strategy-making
process is one of flux, dynamism, revision, and improvisation.

This is not to suggest that these states are simply reacting in a hasty, ill-conceived manner to a series of short-term crises. On the contrary, strategic choices, however improvisational they may seem, are usually framed by a number of powerful forces that direct or restrict strategic behavior. Williamson Murray and Mark Grimsley argue that the most significant ingredients in the evolution of national strategy include geography, history, ideology (and/or religion), economic capabilities, form of government, and individual leadership.[8] While policymakers may at times appear to be acting rashly or impetuously, careful examination usually reveals that national strategy is strongly shaped by such long-term environmental factors, lending a coherence and predictability to the actions and choices of states. It is the purpose of this book to highlight the ways such long-term background factors influence the making of strategy in these key nations.

In these eight nations, we find a number of common patterns that apply across the whole group and which contemporary policymakers must bear in mind if they are to make sense of what is driving national strategy in the contemporary world. The common factors that are shaping today's strategic thinking include the nonnational nature of most security threats, the importance of domestic politics in shaping national strategy, the powerful and distorting effects of history and national identity upon national strategy, and the economic capabilities and ambitions of each nation; finally, there is the sheer difficulty, in the face of so many powerful internal and external constraints, to shape and pursue an effective national strategy. Let us consider briefly each of these interpretive categories.

Most Security Threats Are Nonnational

One striking feature of the early twenty-first century is that security threats have become deracinated from a national context. For most of these "shaping" powers, the central security threat is not the prospect of war with one or two neighboring states. Security challenges are more diffuse than ever, leaving states to contemplate a broad range of shifting threats. Strategy therefore requires a more sophisticated calculation about the importance of relative threats presented by a combination of problems. These might include terrorism (Israel, India), a worsening of the "neighborhood" as a result of failed states (Turkey, India), rival bids from competitors for regional economic hegemony (Brazil, China), ethnic tensions along geopolitical fault-lines (Russia), or the weakening of international institutions and agreements that have held a certain favorable order in place (Germany). The United States, as the world's dominant power, has an even greater challenge: it must prepare for both conventional military rivals as well as nonstate threats—terrorism and Islamic radicalism, global economic turmoil, ecological and public health crises, cyber-attacks, and so on. For the states analyzed here, with the possible exception of India, a state-to-state war with a rival nation or coalition is among the least urgent of threats. Instead, these nations view their main strategic challenges coming from disruptive nonstate forces that may persist for a long time precisely because their origins are diffuse and resistant to traditional security countermeasures.

Strategy Starts at Home

Because the chief security threats are diffuse in nature and often resistant to easy quarantine, most of these states worry about internal instability and fractiousness as much as they do about direct external challenges. In states like India, Russia, China, and Turkey, the main threats to national security lie in the disruptive power of regional and global forces—whether ideological, religious, ethnic, or economic—and the way those forces threaten to inflame domestic politics. Many of the leaders examined here understand that their foreign and security policies are in many ways being driven by domestic politics precisely because domestic politics has become a "front" in the battle of ideas over how to shape foreign and security policy. If they wish to "keep their state," in Machiavelli's phrase, national leaders must shape their foreign policies in ways that either appease domestic criticism or unite the polity through a shared sense of grievance and hostility toward an external rival. This is a dangerous move, for an environment in which domestic political power struggles are driving choices in foreign and security policy tempts leaders to adopt radical policies in order to achieve a rally-round-the-flag effect, even as they trigger a security dilemma that leaves them more vulnerable.

For example, Yaprak Gürsoy (in Chapter 7) shows the powerful influence of domestic politics on Turkish national strategy. Turkey's foreign policy of late is characterized by wary relations with the United States, bad relations with Israel, hostility toward the West, and a search for regional partners to quell Islamist unrest. These remarkable departures from many decades of Turkish pro-Western orientation have derived from calculations of domestic politics, most notably the bid by President Recep Tayyip Erdoğan to consolidate the power of his Justice and Development Party. In Russia, as Fyodor

Lukyanov shows (in Chapter 6), a failed economic development strategy and a lack of domestic political rewards have led Vladimir Putin's government into striking out at Crimea and Ukraine, partly in a bid to reassert regional influence but mainly, perhaps, in an effort to mask the failure of his regime to produce economic growth and good governance. Consolidating "lost" Russian populations in neighboring Ukraine while blocking the perceived "threat" of an expanded European Union into the former Soviet Union seems to Putin to be a successful strategy for mobilizing popular support for his otherwise much-embattled regime. And democratic states, too, play this game, though perhaps less brazenly. In Brazil, for example, as Matias Spektor shows (in Chapter 1), even political leaders who have sharply differing philosophies about economic development nonetheless join in adopting a rhetorical stance that stresses a "bullying," interventionist United States and directs attention at the threats of neoliberal economic policies in an effort to shore up domestic political support. Other examples in this book illuminate how the quest for domestic political consensus shapes the making of national strategy, and the trend is worrisome, to say the least.

History and Identity Matter

Because the audience for strategic choices is as much internal as external, leaders of these "shaping powers" are eager to present their national strategies as flowing from the natural course of history. This is obvious for example in Russia, where Putin has constructed a national ideology that is premised upon the past—a past filled with glorious achievements, centuries-long expansion into Eastern and Southeastern Europe as well as Asia, heroic responses to external threats and aggression, the rapid modernization of the homeland, and its rise to great power status, all serving to transform Russia into a world power. It stands to reason that no rival or coalition can or should ever turn Russia away from her rightful place among the great powers, nor deny Russia the right to impose its will on small neighbors who threaten that historical destiny.

But the appeal to history and national identity is a powerful force in many states examined here. China has an acute awareness of its recent geopolitical weakness, having been a target of rapacious imperialism and humiliation at the hands of outsiders from the mid-nineteenth to the mid-twentieth centuries. The terrible years of World War II, the revolution and the civil war, when as many as twenty million Chinese perished, deeply influenced China's strategic culture. Ever since, China has felt a need to develop sufficient military power to control its own territory and extend influence along its periphery. Nor should the persistence of conflict in the region after 1945 be forgotten. At various times since the war, China has been engaged in military encounters with Taiwan, Tibet, the United States, the Soviet Union, India, and Vietnam. Clearly, Chinese leaders, when they ponder recent history, may have every reason to be kept awake at night by the same "*cauchemar des coalitions*" that haunted Bismarck and Wilhelmine Germany in the 1880s.[9]

Perhaps no country is more engaged with its history and identity as is Israel, and the public debates about these matters directly shape national strategy. Ariel E. Levite (in Chapter 5) reminds us that Israel's founders looked to biblical history to lend legitimacy to their claim for the creation of *Eretz Israel*, and ever since 1948, politics and security strategy have been governed by the need to sustain the legitimacy of that claim. The question of identity has also become a battleground in Israel: what kind of society and nation does Israel wish to be? Should it be a Jewish or a multicultural nation? Should it be a secular or a religious society? Should it keep faith with the socialist traditions of its founders or embrace market capitalism? Can it be democratic and yet maintain Arab Israelis in a second-class status? The answers to these questions strike at the heart of Israel's national identity and, therefore, its strategy, because so many of the thorny questions that bedevil Israel's relations with its neighbors are overlaid with historical claims: the status of Jerusalem, the right of return for Palestinian refugees, and the issues of borders and national sovereignty.

But the implications of "history" for the countries discussed in this book go beyond the shaping of strategic ambitions. Powerful framing narratives, premised on a reading of the past, can close off opportunities for collaborative action in the international arena. If one nation chooses to place long-standing grievances or claims of "national destiny" at the center of its public debates over strategy, leaders may quickly find themselves unable to uncouple their strategic interests from their ideologies. As a consequence, we find that states with shared interests are often unable to overcome the polarizing forces of national identity. Consider the goals that might pull key states together into collaboration: Russia and the United States both wish to stamp out Islamist radicalism, China and the United States wish to contain nuclear proliferation in Asia, Israel and Turkey both want to quell insurgencies throughout the Arab world, Germany and Russia would like to nurture economic ties especially in the energy section, and India and China both desire global economic development. Yet these powerful forces of attraction are often undermined by the enduring power of nationalist historical narratives that stress grievances, threats, and old animosities. Not only do history, memory, and identity matter in shaping strategy; they have the power to trump even the most basic of national interests.

Economic Capabilities and Ambitions

Students of grand strategy know that economic capabilities are an essential ingredient in the projection of power, and indeed economic growth in one major country will tend to shape the responses of its neighbors. It is the oldest lesson of international politics, taught by Thucydides: "what made war [between Athens and Sparta] inevitable was the growth of Athenian power and the fear which this caused in Sparta."[10] Ever since, scholars have looked to shifts in relative economic power to predict, or explain, military-strategic rivalry between states. Paul Kennedy in *The Rise and Fall of the Great Powers* considered rapid economic growth—and the relative decline this entailed for certain states—to be the chief source of strategic rivalry and war in the modern era. More recent scholarship has pursued this line of inquiry.[11]

The essays in this volume, however, complicate the picture somewhat. If one looks at certain key economic measurements (see Figures I.1 and I.2), one would conclude that China and the United States are on a collision course. China has the world's second-largest gross domestic product (GDP) and is growing at the rate of 7 percent a year (down from 10 percent annual growth four years ago), compared to America's anemic growth rate of 2 percent annually. In 2010, China displaced the United States as the world's largest manufacturer and now holds a 22 percent share of world manufacturing compared to 17 percent for America. Yet are we to conclude that China and the United States are destined to go to war? The issue is a hotly contested one. Certainly, the economic rivalry between these nations has security implications, and there are plenty of other geopolitical flashpoints in the U.S.-China relationship. But Men Honghua (in Chapter 2) argues that China knows its welfare is linked to that of its neighbors. Indeed, China's growth is premised upon finding global buyers for its products and global sellers of raw materials. So it does seem possible that China's rapid growth may serve

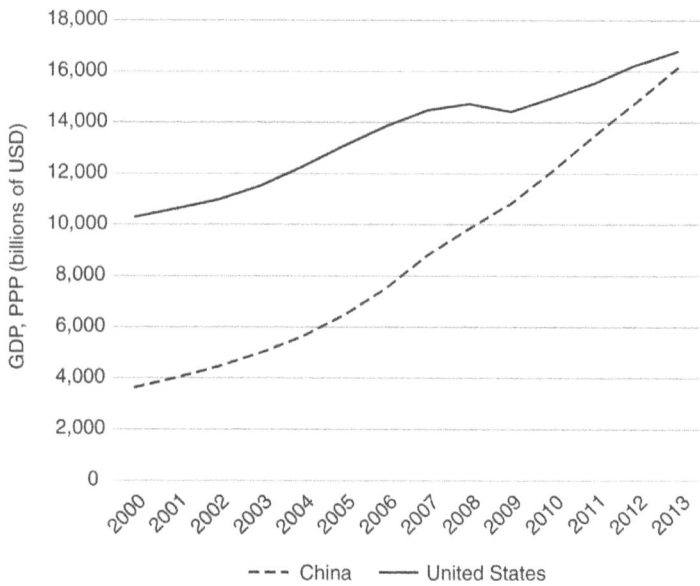

Figure I.1. GDP and PPP (purchasing power parity) in China and the United States (current USD).

as a force for further global cooperation rather than conflict. Because the relationship is so important and also so fragile, James Steinberg, one of the contributors to this volume, has argued for a policy of "strategic reassurance" designed to fend off the security dilemma and guide the U.S.-China relationship along a productive path. Even so, other analysts anticipate a much more fraught and dangerous future for this relationship.[12]

Rapid global economic shifts typify our epoch—up to a point. China's rise is astonishing, while Brazil and India have climbed to take the eighth and ninth positions, respectively, in the global manufacturing rankings. But what is perhaps of more significance, and less discussed, than the sudden rise of the global South is the persistence of the older modernized states at the top of the pile: the United States, Japan, and Germany today rank second, third, and fourth, respectively, among manufacturing nations, and they were also the top three in 1990—twenty-five years ago.[13] This would suggest that there is a certain stability built into the global economic system such that the sudden rise of China need not be seen as an existential threat to other status quo powers. If so, this is surely good news.

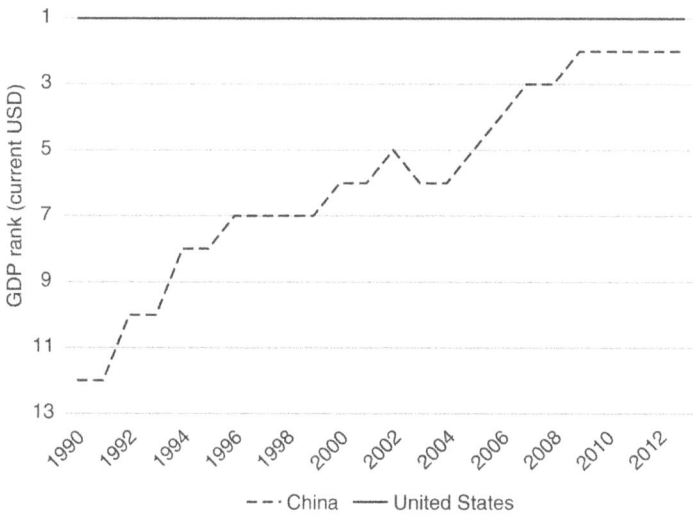

Figure I.2. GDP rankings of China and the United States (current USD).

In another way, too, economic factors may drive these states toward policies of restraint rather than aggression. Many of the countries we examine here (with the important exception of Russia) know that the legitimacy of their political systems depends upon delivering greater prosperity to their peoples. The imperative to sustain economic growth at home has a decided impact upon a range of policy choices among these states, in areas as diverse as defense spending, education, social welfare, and health care. Srinath Raghavan (in Chapter 4) shows that internal economic growth continues to be the "core objective" of the Indian state and that India's external policies are evaluated through the prism of this chief goal. Similarly, Matias Spektor demonstrates that Brazil's national strategy is fundamentally shaped by a desire to insure fiscal stability (after long stretches of economic mismanagement), enhance the welfare state, and integrate Brazil's economy with the world. There is an interesting strategic challenge visible here: economic growth may make the projection of power possible, but the projection of power can cause conflict and thus threaten internal economic development. Such a calculation suggests that the imperative for economic growth may tend to encourage cooperation rather than rivalry.

The Challenge of Crafting National Strategy

One alarming conclusion that emerges from these essays is that these "shaping" states are not always competent, or confident, in crafting national strategy. Consider Barry Posen's definition of "grand" strategy: it is a logical chain of arguments—in essence, a theory—about how a state can best secure its interests. To be effective, however, a grand strategy "must identify likely threats to the state's security and it must devise political, economic, military, and other remedies for those threats. Priorities must be established among both threats and remedies because, given an anarchical international environment, the number of possible threats is great . . . and resources are scarce."[14] Identify threats; establish priorities to meet them; then deploy sufficient and available resources in ways that are carefully adjusted to achieve those goals while not creating additional security threats. This is the essence of grand strategy. But if we try to assess the effectiveness of strategy-making among the states analyzed here, we find a spotty record at best.

On a spectrum from good to bad, we might place China near the top. As Men Honghua shows, China knows what it wants: internal political stability, the continuation of economic growth, and a free hand to project its growing power across Asia. China is also clear in what it considers threats: chiefly, any restriction on its economic expansion, any direct military threat to its sphere of influence in East Asia and the Pacific, and any hint of internal subversion. China has shown that it knows how to achieve these ends without exhausting its national resources. Economically, it has maximized opportunities for industrial and economic development, and militarily it has kept its robust defense buildup just short of triggering a security dilemma with the United States. Even so, China has adopted a risky strategy: its internal political stability is dependent upon rapid economic growth, and any significant fall-off of that growth might undercut the implicit bargain the Chinese government has struck with its people: prosperity in return for obedience. Further, its economic and military growth has been so rapid that the United States has undertaken a "pivot to Asia"—a reorientation of its security strategy that assumes a long-term rivalry with China.

Brazil has managed to emerge from a period of dramatic change and economic growth with opportunities to shape its region as never before. Yet even so, Brazil has had little experience of expressing its national interests in terms of "grand strategy." Its recent democratization and its rise to global economic power have compelled a debate in the country about how best to frame its interests, and that debate, as Matias Spektor shows, continues to rage, making the strategy process difficult indeed. At times, Brazil has seemed to desire a close accommodation with the United States, riding along the wave of globalization in order to increase prosperity and ease inequality at home. At other times, Brazil has seemed to want to pursue a power-balancing strategy against the United States, pushing back against global economic arrangements dominated by the United States and even pursuing a maverick foreign policy in the Middle East and Arab world. While Brazil's regional policies, such as the pursuit of a South American Union, have more coherence, Brazil has not been able to project its power across the region in a fundamental way. Nor has it been able to leverage its ties to other "BRICS" (Brazil, Russia, India, China, South Africa) into genuine global power. In short, Brazil remains an economically powerful state in search of a coherent national strategy.

India, for all its internal and external security problems, has done reasonably well in articulating a national strategy. Its principal goal, as Srinath Raghavan argues, is to sustain its internal economic transformation, thus enabling India to address crippling domestic social problems while also strengthening its regional influence. After experimenting with a variety of economic policies in the post-independence years, India has largely embraced high-growth and pro-business policies that reflect its urgent need to create employment and promote prosperity. In its security policies, however, India has not been able to transcend its intense rivalry with Pakistan. Since their partition, these two states have been locked in a fierce struggle with one another; as both are armed with nuclear weapons, the stakes of the struggle are high. Moreover, the launching of terrorist attacks out of Pakistan against India has intensified the tension. Attempts to manage the relationship expose leaders in both countries to charges of appeasement. Both states are locked in a security dilemma and there seems to be no clear path out. And with the rise of China to global power status, India faces an even more important potential rival in the region. India's strategy, therefore, is wedded to its economic policies: rapid growth may mask some of these unresolved security problems, but not indefinitely.

A bit lower down the spectrum of effective national strategies comes Germany. Germany's national strategy is adrift and in need of remediation. Constanze Stelzenmüller (in Chapter 3) points out that Germany has not really developed the habit of developing grand strategy because for decades after 1945 its sovereignty was circumscribed. After 1990, when a reunited Germany did regain de jure sovereignty, it remained constrained by the institutions which were deemed central to regional and global stability, such as the European Union, NATO, and the United Nations. In its economic strategy within the EU, Germany has managed to alienate states that are demanding more inflationary monetary policies and has won few allies by championing fiscal retrenchment. Austerity has not reinvigorated the EU, raising the question of whether Germany, despite its economic power, really has the ability to save Europe and secure the Continent's future stability. Without success on that front, Germany will be unmoored at a time when Russian aggressiveness has made European unity more important than ever.

Israel, as Ariel Levite shows, has achieved a number of major strategic successes over its history. In a constant state of war and facing daily threats, it concentrates its resources on security. In this narrow sense, Israeli strategy has succeeded. But at what cost? Here the flaws with Israeli strategy become visible. Diplomatically, Israel has increasingly lost friends and allies; the United States now is Israel's only consistent great power supporter. Moreover, each step Israel takes to increase its security—whether building walls in the West Bank, using military force to fight Hamas in Gaza, or arming itself against threatening states like Iran or Syria—inflames anti-Israeli sentiment in the region, thereby reinforcing the security dilemma in which Israel finds itself. Equally worrisome are the profound cleavages that the pursuit of this strategy has opened in Israeli society. The disagreements are not so much over security policies, which are largely uncontroversial, but over the issues of identity that have been stirred up by the pursuit of its security policies: what kind of nation does Israel aspire to be? Can it become an Athens of the Near East, with an open, vibrant, and tolerant culture, economically prosperous and socially equitable, as its founders had hoped? Or is it destined always to be a Sparta, a militaristic society whose sole purpose is to organize its resources for war? In this environment, the making of national strategy has become increasingly fraught.

At the lowest end of the spectrum sit Turkey and Russia. These states have pursued risky national strategies that seem unlikely to succeed in the long run. Turkey has fallen under the sway of a powerful leader whose grip on power has grown. In the quest to consolidate his authority, Erdoğan has inflamed nationalist opinion, worsened ties to the West, and pursued regional deals with Arab regimes that share Turkey's strategic goals. Turkey has nursed its wounds since its rebuff by the European Union and now has sought to become a regional power, downgrading its Western orientation. It is a high-risk strategy, especially in light of the turmoil triggered by Syria's civil war, in which Turkey has taken sides but cannot exert a decisive influence. In a similar manner, Russia's actions on the world stage reveal a state that has no national strategy. Russia's strategic thinking has been clouded by conspiracy theories and raw national memories of mistreatment by the West. The result has been a sequence of daring gambles and strategic mistakes that have left Russia isolated and the target of economic sanctions. An angry and embittered Russia, governed by a backward-looking autocrat, fueled by nationalist fury, and armed with nuclear weapons, creates a dangerous situation indeed.

Finally, how has the United States managed its strategy in this new world order? James B. Steinberg (in Chapter 8) suggests that for all of the troubles that have beset American national security policy since 9/11, the global configuration of power today presents significant opportunities for the United States. We may live in a multipolar world, but even so, the United States is uniquely powerful and has greater military and economic capabilities, as well as credibility, to shape the world order than any other single nation. Moreover, its ambitions are not territorial: the United States seeks global economic growth, prosperity, and stability because those goals foster its own national interests. With little to fear in the short run from the other shapers and acknowledging many overlapping interests, U.S. strategy would be wise, says Steinberg, to focus less on purely military preeminence and more on implementing a multipart diplomatic and economic strategy. Washington, he argues, should nurture multilateral institutions, support the rule of law, preserve existing alliances, and engage and coopt potential rivals. These policies will be most effective, Steinberg suggests, if they also take into account the particular historical and economic circumstances that drive strategy inside each of the major powers.

Certainly, the "shapers" will need the United States to play a positive role in constructing a stable world order. The essays in this volume suggest that strategy-making is very difficult when, as is the case for most of these shaper nations, it is hobbled by institutional weaknesses, internal political divisions, and ideological modes of thinking. These essays show that in many of these shaper states, domestic politics clash with geopolitical interests, regional struggles endanger national economic ambitions, and government leaders deploy ethnic arguments and exploit memories of historical grievances at the expense of collaborative initiatives. The lack of effective and consistent strategy-making in these states, as Jeffrey W. Legro argues in the conclusion to this volume, has made world politics less orderly and predictable. Shaper states, seeking short-term opportunities, focused on regional influence, and led by powerful individuals catering to domestic audiences, are unlikely to provide a firm foundation for international stability. It is our hope that the more we know about the sources of strategy for these emerging nations, and the more we take into account the hopes, fears, ambitions, and anxieties of this dynamic but uncertain group of countries, the more able we will be to manage a world filled with both promise and danger.

CHAPTER 1

BRAZIL

*Shadows of the Past
and Contested Ambitions*

MATIAS SPEKTOR

WHAT IS Brazil's strategy to cope with the emerging world order? The question has come up time and again in scholarly writings as analysts try to project whether Brazil is bound to be a "responsible stakeholder" or a spoiler of the emerging system.[1] Answers, however, are not readily available because generations of Brazilian statesmen have rarely couched their foreign policies in the language of "grand strategy" that is common in American scholarly discourse.

In this chapter, I examine what Brazil wants in the world and how it hopes to get it by putting its foreign policy frameworks in context. First, I focus on three underlying factors that have shaped the evolution of Brazilian strategy: domestic politics, ideology, and the intersection between geopolitics and economics. The chapter then turns to the substance of Brazilian strategies, with reference to four core strategic themes that recur in national conversations and in the making of foreign policy—namely polarity, regional order, membership in international institutions, and global justice. The pages that follow frame these issues in a historical perspective; even if my chief concern is with the contemporary period, Brazilian attitudes regarding global order are profoundly shaped by shared national grievances about the past and by the widespread perception that the country remains at the receiving end of a highly unequal and discriminating international system. Across the political spectrum, there is a persistent national historical narrative of relative weakness and dependence that influences behavior.

While critics often point out that a Brazilian foreign policy community bounded by historical tropes risks walking forward while looking backward, the fact remains that shadows of the past must be integrated into any account of Brazil's behavior in the world today.

Core Constraining Factors

Three core factors have shaped the evolution of Brazilian strategy: domestic politics, ideology, and the country's relative position in the international system.

Domestic Politics

Of the three factors shaping current Brazilian strategy, domestic politics is the most salient. Unlike three decades ago when an authoritarian regime ran the country, democratic Brazil defies careful, calculated foreign policy-making by elites. Brazil is as vibrant and messy a democracy as any other: Brazilian presidents preside over an often-fractured governing coalition and they face the challenge of managing a vast federal state with an unruly set of bureaucracies and semi-independent agencies operating within it. Candidates for the Senate and the Chamber of Deputies are chosen on the basis of a highly competitive open-list, proportional electoral system and coexist with twenty-seven powerful state governors and legislatures. Members of the gargantuan judiciary branch are staunchly independent from executive control, and so is the free press. Private lobbies and organized interests seek to and do exert influence at all levels, further complicating the ability of leaders to conduct foreign policy according to a rationally constructed notion of "national interests."[2]

Domestic factors have been critical in the foreign policies of the last three presidencies: Fernando Henrique Cardoso (1995–2002), Luiz Inacio Lula da Silva (2003–2010), and Dilma Rousseff (2011 to the present). Facing different domestic circumstances, all three presidents invested in grand strategies that they thought would best serve their ability to govern successfully and retain power. Their individual skill, rhetoric, and experience must figure prominently in any detailed account of their respective foreign policies, but the focus here is on the incentives emerging from the domestic political system that they faced.

For the past twenty years, intense electoral competition between center-right and center-left coalitions have dominated the political scene. For all of their divisions, however, these two poles came to frame national politics around a set of shared priorities: consolidating democratic rule through free, competitive elections and an independent judiciary; securing financial stability after years of hyper-inflation and economic mismanagement; building an incipient welfare state to assist the poor who still comprise over half the population; and embracing many of the benefits of a liberal global order, like norms governing human rights, free trade, and nuclear nonproliferation.[3] But the differences in these coalitions are reflected in the two political leaders—Cardoso and Lula—who emerged on the national political scene as opponents to dictatorial rule and who went on to govern Brazil from 1995 to 2002 and from 2003 to 2010, respectively. The parties they commanded fought for the presidency in 2010, with Lula's anointed successor Dilma Rousseff winning the election that year and gaining reelection in 2014.

Both Cardoso and Lula thought of themselves as statesmen set to transform Brazil's position in the international system. The two of them traveled extensively around the globe and actively used foreign policy to build their authority at home. Perhaps more importantly, each couched his own vision for the future of Brazil in terms of wider changes in the global context. Let us look at their views in turn.

Cardoso took office in the mid-1990s believing that unipolarity was not a fleeting moment but a structure of world politics that was likely to endure. As an academic sociologist years earlier, he had written extensively about global inequality and the dependence of nations from the postcolonial world on the major industrial countries of the North Atlantic. As president, his core conviction was that countries like Brazil had little policy space. Either they had to adapt to the rules of the game or they would be left behind. According to this view, Brazil's ability to shape the international system was limited, and the best foreign policy was one that avoided conflict with the major centers of power and sought to adapt to the dominant regimes and institutions. Normatively, it was the duty of leadership to ensure that Brazil took part in the prevailing wave of globalization, with a view toward stabilizing the economy, consolidating democracy, and transforming one of the most unequal societies in the world into a middle-class nation.[4]

Lula held a very different view as he took office in 2003. He believed a significant transition of power was under way in the world that would benefit countries like Brazil. This was partly the result of changes in the global economy, but also a consequence of what he saw as the failures of neoliberalism under Ronald Reagan and Margaret Thatcher, as well as Bill Clinton and Tony Blair. Lula saw the anti-globalization protests erupting in Seattle in 1999 as a signal that the global political mood was about to shift and the international system would become more malleable for a country like Brazil. In his estimation, there was policy space to reform existing regimes and institutions with a view to secure a better place for Brazil, a newfound position that would offer Brazilian authorities more "autonomy" to pursue policies consistent with growing the economy, reducing poverty and inequality at home, and producing a middle-class society.[5]

Even if their ultimate goals were similar, Cardoso and Lula developed very different causal logics. Their thinking shaped two alternative ways of conceiving of polarity, regional order, membership in international institutions, and global justice. Before turning to these in the section below, let us first look at the domestic political incentives influencing the foreign policies of each president.

Cardoso was elected in 1994 on the promise to end the cycle of hyperinflation that had haunted Brazil for the better part of the fifteen years prior to his arrival in power. He launched a major program to reform the state, open the economy to foreign trade, privatize large state-owned companies, modernize public services, and construct for the first time ever a fairly basic but nonetheless impressive welfare state to nurture the poor, who accounted for about half the population, but who had been denied the vote until 1989 (when illiterates first got the right to vote).

Accordingly, Cardoso did not have a major incentive to invest his time and attention in foreign policy. He only assumed a more active interest as his first term came to an end in 1998. This occurred as a response to a more ominous international environment, as financial crises systematically threatened his economic stabilization policies (1995, 1997, 1998, 1999, and 2000). He focused on global financial reform and on fortifying South America against the instabilities of global capitalism, realizing that public opinion was turning markedly against "neoliberalism" in the wake of the anti-globalization protests in Seattle in 1999. When Osama bin Laden attacked the United States on 9/11, Cardoso, who was at the peak of his foreign policy activism, was inclined to emphasize that "terror equals barbarianism, but so does unilateralism."[6] In spite of his fast-declining popularity ratings, he knew he had built a major coalition in Congress that would support him.

Lula won office in late 2002 under very different circumstances. The economy was stable, state reform was in process, and a welfare state for the poor was in place. Lula had a clear mandate from the electorate to challenge the neoliberal orthodoxy and to denounce George W. Bush's foreign policies, but the economic climate was good as the commodity super-cycle saw the value of Brazilian exports (increasingly to China) soar. A favorable global economy allowed Lula to amass unprecedented popular support without having to challenge global capitalism or to confront the United States. Within a decade, Brazil underwent rapid change in its class structure, with some forty million people moving from poverty or extreme poverty up the social ladder.

In this context, Lula and his foreign policy advisors thought they had the material resources and the political space to embark on an activist foreign policy. Overseeing a massive party coalition in Congress, his administration launched an expansive set of international initiatives not so much to challenge the existing global order as to secure for Brazil a better position in that order. By the time Lula's tenure in office came to a close, his critics accused him of overreaching. None of his major foreign policy initiatives had paid off: there was no trade agreement at the Doha world trade conference, no reform of the UN Security Council, and no nuclear agreement brokered between the West and Iran. But supporters highlighted a list of successes: the formation of a coalition of the BRICS countries (Brazil, Russia, India, China, and South Africa); the development of a Union of South American Nations (Unasur); the engagement with Africa that saw trade from Brazil boom; the protection of democratic rule in neighboring countries like Bolivia, Ecuador, and Venezuela; and the strengthening of the G20 as a prime forum for global economic management.[7]

Dilma Rousseff succeeded Lula in 2011 in a domestic and global context that gave her far less leeway to conduct an activist foreign policy. None of the core elements that had undergirded Cardoso's and Lula's activist turns were present anymore: the economy slowed down in the aftermath of the 2008 global financial crisis, the coalition supporting her administration showed widening cracks, and the public was far less supportive of expansionist foreign policies in the aftermath of Lula's time in power. For the first time in twenty years, there were renewed fears of inflation and recession. Even if Rousseff enjoyed sufficient popular support to secure reelection, the political climate had changed.

Rousseff's opportunity for an activist foreign policy further diminished in the aftermath of massive protests that erupted around June 2013 and then recurred intermittently. Demonstrators demanded better public services, a curb on government corruption, and political reform to offset the impunity of the powerful that is a hallmark of Brazil's public life. These expressions of public anger were leaderless and did not translate into benefits for any one single political party. They reflected a widespread malaise about the state of the country, even if economic growth had climbed, social inequality had declined, and public services had improved, however slowly. The malaise illustrated a widespread phenomenon across the developing world—the disruptive nature of international ascent.

Whereas Brazilians throughout the early 2000s saw the world as a place of opportunity for an ascending Brazil, the mood turned to caution in view of an international system that presented Brazil with many obstacles. Rousseff retrenched, scaling back the high profile that Lula accorded to foreign policy. This reduction in Brazil's geopolitical footprint remained relative—military expenditures stayed pretty high, and so did the range of international issues Brazilian diplomats engaged.

For the emerging countries that had benefited from transformations in the global economy over the prior fifteen years, climbing the international rankings came at the price of unsettling old ways of doing things at home. Critics felt empowered to demand better services from their governments, making it more difficult for governments to achieve their goals.[8] Becoming an "emerging power" and moving up the ranks did not simply expand Brazil's options. On the contrary, it brought a whole new set of constraints on the conduct of foreign policy.[9]

Ideology

The Brazilian view of global order vastly differs from that of the United States. Take for instance people's perceptions of "international threats." Polls show that the average Brazilian worries little about terrorism, radical Islam, or major international war. Brazilians are more fearful of climate change, poverty, and infectious disease. Odd as it may seem, many Brazilians fear the United States itself—the perceived threat it poses to the natural richness of the Amazon and the newfound oilfields under the Brazilian seabed.

Perceptions may be wrong, but they matter enormously. It is no wonder that Brazilian military officials spend a chunk of their time studying how Vietnamese guerrillas won a war against far superior forces in jungle battlefields. Nor should it be a surprise that Brazil is now developing nuclear-propulsion submarines that, its admirals believe, will facilitate their ability to defend oil wells in open waters against the eventuality of an attack from an unnamed industrial power "from the North."

Brazilian leaders who govern the country today came of age in the 1960s and 1970s, the period when foreign policy was closely aligned with that of the Group of 77 (G77) developing countries. That this should be the case today is not obvious; Brazil is the seventh-largest industrial economy in the world, it is an urban society, and it shares few commonalities with most members of the G77. But alignment with this group remains a major force shaping what Brazil does in the world. This is partially about self-interest, as the G77 affords Brazil a prominence that it would not otherwise have. It is also about the power of major Brazilian interest groups that rely on government subsidies and prefer to delay the incorporation of liberal norms in areas like human rights, environmental protection, and nuclear nonproliferation. In these respects, the G77 remains an appealing organization.

But the Brazilian view of international affairs is also powerfully about ideology. The memory of colonialism remains influential in a country that was an object of empire or semi-empire in various forms under Portugal, Spain, Holland, France, Great Britain, and the United States. In most areas of foreign policy, the division of the 1960s between North and South retains its purchase in the Brazilian worldview. Ideology and experience especially influence Brazilian attitudes towards the United States. Any thought of alliance or bandwagoning with Washington never gets serious consideration, notwithstanding the fact that Brazil and the United States share several interests. Scant experience with collaborative engagement along with entrenched bureaucratic resistance in both capitals limit the pace and the scope of strategic cooperation. Even if it were in the interest of Brazil to keep its hotline with Washington functional at all times, a working partnership—if it were to exist at all—would need to be nurtured carefully. Any effort to sustain cooperation would have to dislodge deeply ingrained ideological predilections and emotional sensibilities.

Relative Position in the International System

Brazil is a prime example of a country that enjoys "geopolitical slack"—the absence of an immediate threat to its physical security and low probability of finding itself a target of aggression by a major power. Because the country is geographically distant from the major centers of global conflict, there is little reason for worry in Brasília, even when global conflict erupts. Brazil's gift from geography is that the benefits of its international security situation are plentiful rather than scarce.[10]

This grants Brazilian leaders plenty of room for conducting a foreign policy that is "capricious," to use the famous expression by Kenneth Waltz.[11] While there is no doubt that the international system constrains Brazil in several ways, local authorities enjoy levels of leeway that others simply do not. It should be no surprise that in the early 2000s, Brazilian leaders expanded the range of their foreign policy ambitions and their power-accretion initiatives. During this period the regional hegemon, the United States, was occupied elsewhere, while material conditions at home improved quickly. During the years of the U.S. intervention in Iraq, Brazil moved from the fourteenth to the seventh position in the world economy and extreme poverty fell by a factor of 25 percent, leading the way for a "new middle class" to arise and transform Brazilian society.

The fact that Brazil is only loosely constrained by major-power competition does not mean that the international system is irrelevant. In fact, the contrary is the case when we look at the issue from the prism of the global political economy. Brazil has always been, and remains, profoundly dependent on the movement of global capital. Its prosperity in the 1970s was tightly linked to the global spread of manufacturing away from the North Atlantic toward the east and the global South. Its prosperity in the early 2000s cannot be dissociated from the rise of Chinese demand for Brazilian soy, meat, minerals, and iron ore. Likewise, the prevalence of desperate poverty for just over 15 percent of Brazil's total population is a function, too, of Brazil's position within global capitalism. If Brazil remains among the most unequal societies in the world—with crime rampant in all major cities—causes are to be found in the perverse connection between an unequal international system and its impact on domestic politics.

Crises of global finance have strategic significance to Brazil; a prolonged recession abroad can have major redistributive effects at home. Brazilian leaders, therefore, believe they have a stake in preserving some of the core principles that have underwritten its recent emergence. Accordingly, they have not tried to overturn existing norms and practices; instead, they have tried to adapt them to suit their own national interests.

Global Order through Brazilian Eyes

Ideas about how power and influence work in international relations have been key elements shaping Brazilian foreign policy strategy in the past few years—namely, polarity, regional order, membership in international institutions, and global justice.

Polarity

"Economic globalization is the new global order," wrote Cardoso as he took office and embarked on a massive program of economic deregulation.[12] As he did, the president developed closer diplomatic ties with the United States. His analysis was straightforward. "The United States is the only superpower," he said to his advisers. He went on to say that "our dependence on them is high. Our economic policy depends on the approval of the U.S. Treasury . . . [and] our access to technology depends on the U.S. Congress, the Pentagon and the State Department. Europe is no alternative. Other developing states aren't an alternative either." The resulting policy orientation was obvious: "Under these circumstances any fight with the United States would be lost."[13]

Cardoso's foreign policy in the first term (1995–1999) focused on getting closer to the United States. Brazil passed a patent law, adhered to the Missile Technology Control Regime and the Non-Proliferation Treaty, and opened up its economy. The two countries began to consult on Latin American affairs on a regular basis, and Cardoso was the first Brazilian president ever to criticize Cuba's human rights record publicly.

Cardoso's policies were criticized at home for being subservient to the interests of the United States, a claim that gained a great deal of purchase across Brazil. However, seen from the United States, Cardoso's moves fell short of a policy of "bandwagoning." Argentina, Chile, and Mexico at the time were all moving faster toward good relations with the United States. According to the dominant view in the administration of President Bill Clinton, Cardoso was well-intentioned and committed enough to the globalizing project to be invited to take part in meetings sponsored by Third Way (a centrist Washington think tank). But in the Beltway around Washington, Brazil was still seen as a "laggard," a country that moved slowly and reluctantly toward economic reforms and a better working relationship with Washington.

When he began his second term in office in 1999, Cardoso changed his approach toward the United States. A string of financial crises originating in Russia, Mexico, and East Asia hit Brazil hard and pushed it to the brink of economic collapse. As a result, Cardoso became more critical of market liberalization, as promoted by the U.S. Treasury, and he increasingly ridiculed U.S. trade policy.[14] He also grew more frustrated with the failure to reform the International Monetary Fund (IMF), the World Bank, and the United Nations. He argued for a new global conversation on financial governance.

But he never developed a plan to get this done, nor did he receive support from fellow heads of government around the globe.

After 9/11, Cardoso quickly pledged support for the United States and activated the largely symbolic Rio Pact of 1948, whereby Latin American states declared terrorist attacks on the United States as attacks on themselves. But shortly afterward, Cardoso criticized the "War on Terror." Speaking before the French National Assembly, he denounced the Bush administration as "fundamentalist." By the end of his tenure in power, Cardoso's Brazil was distancing itself diplomatically from the United States.

Cardoso began to say that it was not good to be on the U.S. "radar screen." American attention posed two challenges. It raised expectations in Washington that Brazil would work as a "responsible stakeholder," according to some arbitrary criteria of what "responsible" meant. And it turned Brazil into a target of U.S. pressure when the interests of the two countries did not coincide. As a result, he eventually came to prefer a policy of "ducking"—hiding your head underwater when the hegemonic eagle was around.[15]

Starting in 2002, Lula campaigned not so much on an anti-American ticket as he did on the argument that Brazil did not need to align its foreign policy with that of the United States because the international system was more malleable than Cardoso had thought. Lula's foreign minister optimistically repeated that the chief goal of foreign policy was to "increase, if only by a margin, the degree of multipolarity in the world."[16] The United States might well be the only superpower on earth, but its ability to translate raw power into political influence was faltering and a major factor eroding U.S. power was the emergence of key countries from the postcolonial world.

Among Lula's advisers, the focus on multipolarity was implicit rather than explicit—it was not apparent in official documents. But throughout the early 2000s, the new emphasis on multipolarity did set the tone of the conversation in the Brazilian foreign policy community. Imbued in this discourse was a powerful normative belief that multipolarity was morally superior to any other distribution of global power. Lula's advisers nonetheless were aware that it would be difficult to govern Brazil and ensure financial stability without the assistance of the United States. In their eyes, Brazil's rise was deeply intertwined with the perception in Washington that Brazil was a potential partner—one that was moving upward in the global hierarchy.

In terms of actual policy, there were four key outcomes. First, Lula wanted to build up South America institutionally through Unasur. He also hoped to expand Mercosur (the South American Customs Union) and include new members in order to protect the region against U.S. military and anti-narcotics policies. Second, his administration quickly moved to design a new Middle East policy. He made high-profile visits to Bashar al-Assad in Syria and Muhammar Gaddafi in Libya, and convened a South America-Arab League summit. In addition, he nurtured closer ties with Iran, a strand of policy that subsequently led to the Brazil-Turkey attempt to broker a nuclear agreement between the West and the regime in Tehran. Third, Lula revived Brazil's leadership within the G77 in the United Nations and in the UN Human Rights Council, and with India within the World Trade Organization (WTO). Fourth, Lula worked hard to institutionalize the G20, hoping to use it to reform the World Bank and the IMF, while also seeking to turn the BRICS group into a coalition with a shared agenda and a formal calendar of high-level meetings.[17]

In all these initiatives, Brazil distanced itself from the United States and risked compromising the relationship. However, Lula's behavior was not an attempt to revolutionize the international system. Rather than balancing U.S. power, these policies were seen by the Lula administration as under-cutting unipolarity without necessarily confronting the United States. In fact, Lula made it a habit to consult with George W. Bush on a regular basis. His time in office coincided with the best moments in the bilateral diplomatic relationship since World War II.[18] In other words, Brazilian officials were not seeking to break with the Western order as they knew it. On the contrary, they hoped to improve their relative position within the core institutions that comprised that order: the UN, the WTO, the IMF, and the World Bank.

There was no sense inside Brazil that the country was willing or able to be a spoiler. There was no desire to attack the existing order with a view to design an alternative one. Inside Brazil, Lula and his advisers were viewed as moderate reformers who were willing to assume a greater share of responsibility for managing global order in exchange for a seat at the major tables and a recognition of special rights. Brazilian officials remained very sensitive to the accusation that they operated as shirkers, who sought the privileges of power without paying any of the associated costs.[19]

Lula's efforts to secure the approval and support of the United States, while keeping some distance, were fraught with difficulty. He made it clear to the United States that Brazil would not become an ally like Australia, South

Africa, or even Turkey. He did not seek a too-close relationship; he desired to retain Brazil's independence. As was the case with India, Brazil accepted the core values and basic institutions of the world order that had emerged out of the Second World War, but wanted to carve out a better position for itself.[20]

Regional Order

Starting in 2000, Brazil set out to turn South America into a cohesive region in world politics. This was a conscious attempt to counter U.S. hegemony in the region by transforming Brazil's "near abroad" into a distinctive regional formation where Brazil could exert some degree of international political authority and secure markets for its own industries. At a time when American foreign policy in the region focused on negotiating a Free Trade Area of the Americas (FTAA) and a war on drugs centered in Colombia, Brazil sought to resist U.S. encroachment in its immediate neighborhood.[21]

The policy began with Cardoso and survived the political transition from his center-right coalition to the center-left alliance under Lula and later on Rousseff. In September 2000, President Cardoso hosted the first meeting of South American heads of state, and without the presence of a U.S. delegation. He also extended invitations to third parties to join Mercosur, the customs union binding together Argentina, Brazil, Paraguay, and Uruguay.

When Lula ran his presidential campaign in 2002, he accused Cardoso of being too soft on U.S. policies for market liberalization under the FTAA. Lula presented his plans for South American integration as an effort to promote shared social goals within the regional community. For the first time, a Brazilian head of state spoke of the South American regional space as a place to critique U.S.-style globalization and to resist the FTAA.

Lula's first term saw a flurry of regional initiatives to build up institutions in South America. Brazil accelerated negotiations to extend formal Mercosur membership to Venezuela. In 2004, Brazil agreed to a dispute-resolution tribunal for the Mercosur bloc (Tribunal of Appeals) and to the establishment of the office of secretary general to run Mercosur headquarters in Montevideo and to represent it at international meetings. In 2006, Brazil supported the creation of Parlasur, in theory Mercosur's top community institution, and the Mercosur Convergence Fund (FOCEM), a financial mechanism through which Brazil and Argentina could lend money to Uruguay and Paraguay for infrastructure projects.

In 2004, Lula pushed for Unasur. The original plan closely resembled Cardoso's in that it sought to foster infrastructure cooperation among neighbors. But early in his new administration, Lula also argued for a South American Defense Council to promote dialogue among military establishments and to deepen the levels of political consultation within the group.

Unasur was designed as strictly intergovernmental, with no supranational organization. There was no emphasis on the emergence of a new, shared South American identity among its members. Decision-making was kept in the hands of national authorities, capital cities retained veto power over any community initiatives, and no tools were put in place to push countries toward greater integration. Member state presidents—rather than their bureaucracies—set policies. Neither Mercosur's headquarters in Montevideo nor Unasur's in Quito was given a mandate to evolve into autonomous institutions.

Unasur gained momentum in ways nobody in Brasília had expected, and U.S. influence in South America declined. In 2005, regional states closed ranks against a U.S.-inspired "democracy monitoring mechanism" within the Organization of American States (OAS) that sought to target Hugo Chávez, Venezuela's leader.[22] Four years later, when news leaked of renewed U.S. military plans in Colombia's "war on terror," regional countries pushed back and extracted concessions on transparency and confidence-building from Colombia's president, Álvaro Uribe. A year later, the incoming Colombian government of Juan Manuel Santos chose not to ratify the agreement with the United States. It launched its own rapprochement with its neighbors.[23]

In the years that followed, with Brazil's implicit or explicit support, Bolivia and Venezuela ejected the U.S. Drug Enforcement Administration (DEA) and the U.S. Agency for International Development; Ecuador refused to renew the lease on a U.S. airbase in Manta; and Argentina, Mexico, and Uruguay decriminalized drugs for personal use. By and large, South American states bolstered their ties with Cuba and insisted that the U.S. embargo should be lifted and that the island should rejoin the inter-American system. Regional governments also provided strong rhetorical support for Argentina's claim on the Falkland/Malvinas Islands, putting them at odds with the European Union as well as the United States.

Unasur's cause was helped by the wave of *neogolpismo* that saw the Lula administration become closely involved with conflict resolution and dialogue facilitation in Venezuela (2002), Honduras (2009), and Ecuador (2010). In 2012, when the Paraguayan Congress impeached the president in procedures lasting only twenty-four hours, Brazil denounced the violation of due process and rallied Mercosur and Unasur to suspend the country's membership in each. In 2008, Unasur played an active role in the crisis in Bolivia; it intervened in the aftermath of Colombia's military incursion into Ecuador; and it offered its good offices in the ongoing conflict between *chavismo* and the opposition in Venezuela. In all these events, Brazil tried—although not always with the same intensity or success—to get South America to frame a common response under the auspices of Unasur. To many observers, this was a conscious effort to displace the OAS.

Even if Unasur had none of the explicit anti-U.S. overtones of the 2004 Bolivarian Alliance for the Peoples of Our America (ALBA), an initiative by Cuba and Venezuela, the region's marked move to the left brought Unasur a far more ambitious agenda than the Lula administration initially had intended. Very quickly, Unasur became a forum in which to debate regional policies for eliminating social exclusion, reducing poverty, providing access to health and social security, and protecting indigenous peoples.

From its very beginnings, however, Brazil's South American project had been tentative and partial. Officials embraced the region in fits and starts, and while Brazilian politicians of all stripes made a *rhetorical* pledge to the idea of a united South America, they remained deeply ambivalent about the implications of such a policy in terms of commitments and resources.

It is perhaps no wonder, then, that today the project shows unquestionable signs of strain. After a decade of high hopes and a plethora of initiatives, the actual results are decidedly mixed. Even the most fervent proponents of the South American strategy now speak of it as an aspiration rather than a reality.

Even while Brazil endeavored to extend its regional influence, it eschewed any significant military buildup. Two fundamental geostrategic factors explain this development. First, after Argentina lost its war against Great Britain over the Malvinas/Falkland Islands in 1982, its military budget shrank, its constitution was amended to limit the range of military actions permitted by officers, and its civilian leaders moved toward greater cooperation and integration with Brazil. They even mandated that all references to Brazil as a plausible military threat be scrapped from the textbooks in their military academies. Without a regional rival threatening attack or seeking to lead an anti-Brazil coalition, Brazilian policymakers had little incentive to develop a robust military presence in South America.[24]

Another factor accounting for the absence of a military buildup relates to the role of the United States as a provider of international security in South

America and the South Atlantic. To a significant degree, Brazil did not need to arm because there was a major regional hegemon—the United States— that was willing and able to defray the costs of providing a safe regional environment for the Brazilian state. When the FARC guerrillas in Colombia took physical command over large portions of the country, the United States sponsored a plan for a regional "war on drugs." When fears emerged that terrorist networks were laundering money in South American countries, the CIA and the FBI cobbled together and paid for an initiative to get these countries to respond. And in the South Atlantic, the key transport route for Brazilian exports, the United States continued to secure the shipping lanes and shouldered the fight against piracy.

Free-riding on the United States for security purposes had served Brazil well in the past and was deemed suitable for the future. This did not mean that most Brazilians thought the United States was a benign protector of Brazilian interests. Hegemons, after all, provide security on their own terms. Brazil, therefore, free-rides and preserves cordial military relations with the United States but remains wary of Washington, even while it constrains its own military expenditures. There is no sense of alliance; there is a great deal of pragmatism.[25]

Membership in International Institutions

A major theme running through the more risk-averse policies of Cardoso and the more activist and expansive policies of Lula was Brazil's quest for a "seat at the major tables" and for recognition as a player deserving special rights. From the Brazilian perspective, the postwar order of 1945 was never about openness, inclusion, and multilateral governance. In Brazilian eyes, American hegemony was palpable and self-serving. Brazilian officials, there-fore, have tried to constrain U.S. dominance.

A cursory look at recent voting patterns in the UN illustrates the point: like the other BRICS, Brazil sought to distance itself from the U.S.-sponsored "war on terror" and from the 2003 invasion of Iraq. The Brazilians voted with the United States fewer times than did the Mexicans, Argentines, Chileans, Canadians, Australians, or Turks; they opposed Washington more often than did France and Russia. Brazilian elites rejected the notion that their country should be an integral part of the U.S. alliance system.

No wonder, then, that some Brazilian officials saw the 2008 financial cri-sis—which hurt Brazil only very briefly—as vindication. For much of the

1990s, magazines and newspapers like *The Economist* and *Financial Times* echoed the views of Washington officials that Brazil was a "laggard" in opening up its economy to global capitalism. In fact, Brazilian officials, led by Cardoso and then Lula, endlessly warned against the dangers of financial deregulation. At the height of the 2008 crisis, Lula said that "this crisis was created by white men with blue eyes," who were stubborn enough to ignore the warnings from critics in the global South.

It would be a mistake to discard this sentence as presidential caprice or racism. Running through the Brazilian view of the world there is the notion that global hierarchy is not merely a function of material power. Like Japan in the early twentieth century, Brazilians believe race is a major criterion for deciding who sits and who decides at the big tables. In their eyes, cultural identity is critical for securing access to power and influence in international relations. Unsurprisingly, Brazilian diplomats at the UN sometimes refer to U.S. and European officials (but also to those from allies, like Mexico and South Korea) as "the whites."

These views reflect Brazil's concern with the role of race in securing countries' membership in the major global-governance clubs. Under Lula, Brazil pushed for a pattern of global governance that looked more like a United Colors of Bennetton advertisement. He believed that those sitting at the table ought not to remain the traditional powers of the North Atlantic; he insisted that membership should be more representative of the world's diversity.

Accordingly, Brazil invested heavily in turning the BRICS into a coalition that could exercise some influence in the international system without disrupting ongoing institutions. Brazilian officials wanted the BRICS to have a summit process, common statistical systems, scientific cooperation, a development bank, and a financial rescue system. But rather than overthrow the Bretton Woods Institutions, they wanted the BRICS to have a greater role in global financial governance and garner more resources to support their international ascent.[26]

Likewise, Brazil responded to talk in the United States of a "League of Democracies" in the early 2000s by sponsoring regular meetings of the IBSA (India-Brazil-South Africa) group. In Brasília, this was conceived as an explicit effort to show that democracy at home did not necessitate alignment with the United States or the wider Western formation. Emerging democracies, the argument went, could very well operate independently from the United States and its European allies, drawing on their shared experience of colonialism.[27]

Brazil's thinking about membership in international organizations was never articulated as traditional nonalignment or standard Third-Worldism. Brazilian officials sought to avoid the rhetoric of "The West versus the Rest." This was because Brazil's self-identity sat at the intersection between the West and "the rest." As a result, Brazil did not seek assimilation into the greater West, but neither did it defy Western norms in any significant way. Firm commitments to economic orthodoxy and democracy at home and a willingness to have a seat at the big tables did not exclude a self-identity based on the image of a non–status quo power committed to challenging existing norms and institutions.[28]

When Brazilian leaders look back, they think they benefited greatly from sitting on the periphery of the great Western liberal formation. They were never isolated from it (like China under Mao), but they never fully participated in it. They remain firmly committed to keeping this position. In their view, picking and choosing paid off, and they have little desire to alter this orientation.

Justice

Read a Brazilian foreign policy textbook and you will be surprised: global order after 1945 is not described as open, inclusive, or rooted in multilateralism. Instead, you learn big powers imposed their will on the weak through force, strict and often arbitrary rules, and international institutions that mostly served the interests of the most powerful architects of the postwar order. From this perspective, collective security was not really that collective after all. International law was less about great-power binding and self-restraint than about strong players controlling weaker ones. Consequently, the liberal international order was not as benign as its proponents believed.[29]

These views bred a sense of ambiguity toward the set of liberal ideas, norms, and institutions that Brazilians associated with the Anglo-Saxon West. On one hand, Brazil has benefited enormously from existing patterns of global order. A modest rural economy in the 1940s, it became an industrial powerhouse less than fifty years later thanks to the twin forces of capitalism and an alliance system that kept it safe. But on the other hand, the world also has been a nasty place for most Brazilians. Today, it remains one of the most unequal societies in the world; millions still live in poverty and violence abounds: in 2009, there were more homicides in the state of Rio de Janeiro alone than in the whole of Iraq. No doubt a fair share of the blame is

attributable to successive generations of Brazilian politicians and policymakers, but some of it is a function of the many perversities that prevail when a
country is located on the "periphery" of a very unequal international system.
A stable system governed by rules and norms that represent the interest
of a community of nations depends on predictability. But from the Brazilian
perspective, upon the end of the Cold War, the United States became the
single greatest threat to the status quo. Its pattern of interventionism, its use
of force, its extraterritorial application of U.S. laws, its emphasis on regime
change, its conditional embrace of the norms of sovereignty, and its eagerness to differentiate between "civilized" states and "barbarian" threats made
the United States seem especially menacing to international order in the
aftermath of 9/11.

U.S. talk of "responsible stakeholders," therefore, rarely struck a responsive
chord in Brazil. What was meant by "responsible" seemed arbitrary. U.S. expectations varied from administration to administration and often seemed
unreasonable. The United States itself appeared unable or unwilling to share
and devolve power. Domestic politics made it difficult for Brazilian diplomats to strike deals with U.S. negotiators on climate change, financial regu-
lation, and trade. These factors made "gradual assimilation" for Brazil into a
U.S.-led formation highly unlikely.

Brazil's leaders have never articulated their own coherent vision of a global
order beyond voicing their abstract aspirations for an international system
based on "benign multipolarity" that "promotes peace and development for
all." But there is a powerful sense that unipolarity is morally wrong and ought
to be substituted with multipolarity. The core belief is that the United States
and its European allies should treat non-Western states with greater respect
and some degree of "equality." In the Brazilian view, U.S. behavior is often
imperialistic, unilateral, and dismissive of third countries and of the United
Nations—in sum, illiberal.[30]

Hence, Brazilian officials want to "democratize" international relations. They
do not seek to eradicate hierarchy in the international system, but they do want
the United States to accept pluralism, a sovereignty-based world order, and
strict adherence to the UN Charter. In the Brazilian view, it is the UN that
represents the best bet for a system of "benign multipolarity." Consequently,
most, if not all, Brazilian officials endlessly insist on maintaining the authority
of the UN—and the need to reform its Security Council, assigning new permanent seats to large emerging powers, including Brazil itself.[31]

Brazil's normative vision has a strong economic element to it as well. The expectation is that the global North should do more to accelerate the improvement of economic conditions in the global South by engaging in some form of redistributive justice: opening up their markets, transferring financial and technical support, offering debt relief, or conceding that there are shared responsibilities over climate change, with the pace of adaptation set to reflect levels of development and past levels of pollution.

❋ ❋ ❋

Brazil's core strategic concern in the emerging global order pertains to accruing power and influence—and to moderately reform the institutions of global governance in the process—in order to compensate for the country's structural dependence on an unequal international system. However, there is no clear-cut grand strategy. Successive Brazilian administrations have shied away from offering an explicit and comprehensive vision of the reformed global order they claim to want to create.

The essential ingredients of Brazilian strategy are extrapolated from the ideas and debates among policy elites over polarity, regional order, membership in formal and informal institutions, and global justice. But the core factors shaping Brazilian attitudes toward strategy are domestic politics, ideology, and the country's relative position in the international political and economic system. Filtered through the prisms of personal experience and historical memory, these factors establish the parameters within which Brazilian leaders develop their vague notions of global order.

Looking forward, Brazilian leaders are likely to come under increased pressure from within their country and from abroad to make their understandings of global order more explicit and systematic. Domestically, this pressure might arise from a civil society that has undergone rapid change and is becoming ever-more demanding, as the massive protests of June 2013 illustrated. Internationally, pressure might come from those countries that recognize Brazil as one of the major emerging countries of our era. To such countries, Brazil is likely to become a more important player in areas such as global finance, trade, climate change, and poverty alleviation. Because Brazilian leaders and diplomats now have the clout to facilitate or complicate collective action as never before, grand strategic talk is likely to become more frequent among Brazilian officials, scholars, and commentators.

CHAPTER 2

CHINA

Security Dilemma and "Win Win"

MEN HONGHUA

S TRATEGY is the art of summarizing the laws of the past, evaluating the situation of the present, and making choices for the future. Countries always face decisions at every historical moment, and strategy plays a key role in giving direction to these choices. However, history does not follow a straight line; it is fluid and contingent. Nevertheless, at crucial moments, strategy matters as it shapes key decisions that could lead to disaster or victory.

Strategy is the science and art by which a country wields its resources to achieve its overall objectives in national security and international relationships.[1] Countries use their resources and capabilities, including political, economic, military, cultural, and ideological capabilities, to safeguard and expand their national security, cultural values, and vital interests.

Since 1978, China's rise has accelerated under the general policy of "reform and openness" (*gaige kaifang*). China has focused on economic reform and economic growth. It has abandoned its ideological impulse and no longer constitutes a challenge to the international system. In fact, China seeks to integrate itself into international society and to participate in the evolving international order as a responsible stakeholder. It understands that its own prosperity is linked to the prosperity of others. The economies and publics of other countries have benefited from China's rise, and China's development would have been much more difficult without a peaceful and supportive international environment. As China's economy has grown, it has become more interdependent and globalized and naturally seeks a secure periphery and a dissemination of its civilizational values.

The basic principles of China's strategy are clear, but the situational application varies over time and, as in all countries, there are different opinions about what should be done. The basic principles are laid out in the 2013 Defense White Paper: "It is China's unshakable national commitment and strategic choice to take the road of peaceful development. China unswervingly pursues an independent foreign policy of peace and a national defense policy that is defensive in nature. China opposes any form of hegemonism or power politics, and does not interfere in the internal affairs of other countries. China will never seek hegemony or behave in a hegemonic manner, nor will it engage in military expansion. China advocates a new security concept featuring mutual trust, mutual benefit, equality and coordination, and pursues comprehensive security, common security and cooperative security."[2]

Even though China's rise is generally beneficial to others, China puts defense and realism at the core of its strategy. China realizes that its rise raises doubts, even fears, in its neighborhood and beyond. It seeks to allay those fears, yet recognizes that it must develop its own military capabilities to thwart challenges to its rise. These military capabilities are for defensive purposes, but they are indispensable. China believes that peace requires national power and an "active defense."[3]

The dialectic of popular welfare and military power has been a key theme of China's strategy from its origins. Jiang Taigong, an ancient strategist (1128–1015 BC) and principal advisor to the sage kings Wen and Wu who created the Zhou Dynasty (1059–256 BC), said that "a warlike state, however big it may be, will eventually perish." It will perish, he argued, because the welfare of the people is the root of a strong and stable state. But Taigong also noted that "if a state totally forgets the threat of war, it will face a grim crisis."[4]

Six hundred years later, during the Warring States era (475–221 BC), the classical philosophers and strategists of China elaborated this dialectic. Sun Zi, the most famous Chinese strategist, said that "warfare is the greatest affair of state, the basis of life and death, the way to survival or extinction." However, he also claimed that "no country has ever profited from protracted warfare."[5] Confucius and his disciple Mencius were even more pointed in emphasizing that the welfare of the people was the purpose of the state and its strength.

In the imperial era (221 BC–AD 1911), the focus of strategy shifted from relations among Chinese powers to the external interactions of the empire.

Although strategies differed from dynasty to dynasty and from ruler to ruler, it could be said that, except for the Yuan (Mongol) Dynasty (1271–1368), the primary use of military power was to defend border areas. The Yuan Dynasty was the exception that proved the rule. Its expansionism was frustrated in Southeast Asia and in Japan, and its excessive reliance on force led to its replacement within a hundred years by the Ming Dynasty (1368–1644). The founder of the Ming Dynasty, Zhu Yuanzhang, drew the following conclusion:

> The overseas foreign countries like Annan [Vietnam], Champa, Korea, Siam, Liuqiu [Ryukyu Islands], [the countries of the] Western Oceans [South India] and Eastern Oceans [Japan], and the various small countries of the southern *man* [barbarians] are separated from us by mountains and seas and far away in a corner. Their lands would not produce enough for us to maintain them; their peoples would not usefully serve us if incorporated [into the empire]. If they were so unrealistic as to disturb our borders, it would be unfortunate for them. If they gave us no trouble and we moved troops to fight them unnecessarily, it would be unfortunate for us. I am concerned that future generations might abuse China's wealth and power and covet the military glories of the moment to send armies into the field without reason and cause a loss of life. May they be sharply reminded that this is forbidden.[6]

China's century of humiliation under imperialist dominance reinforced the conviction that military power was necessary for the defense of national interests, but it should be remembered that the key to the success of the Chinese Revolution in 1949 was primarily the mobilization of hundreds of millions of peasants in rural China. The leaders of the first generation of the People's Republic of China (PRC) were more than successful practitioners of people's war; they were the creators of its strategy and tactics. Mao Zedong especially had to face the challenge of survival in the countryside against overwhelming odds and then apply the techniques of guerrilla war in resistance against Japan (1931–1945) and finally in the civil war with the Guomindang (KMT, 1945–1949). As Mao put it in 1934, "What is a true bastion of iron? It is the masses, the millions upon millions of people who genuinely and sincerely support the revolution."[7] Since China's population was 90 percent rural then, surrounding the cities from the countryside could be a successful revolutionary strategy.

Rural revolution gave the PRC such a solid foundation that no enemy could mount a mortal challenge to the Communist Party of China (CPC).

However, revolutionary people's war was a low-technology, land-only form of military power. Although the core values of people's war remained important, modern conditions required the PRC to raise its level of military technology and to expand its air and sea power. The American success in the Gulf War (1990–1991) was a sobering lesson that high-technology weapons could render older weapons useless on the battlefield. Moreover, as China's global presence grew, its security needs expanded as well. During the first decade of the reform era, military modernization took a back seat to maximum economic growth, but ultimately defense had to keep pace with development.

Military power and popular welfare remain intertwined, and, with globalization, China's welfare became interdependent with its neighbors. Consequently, China believes it must enhance its national power, yet at the same time seek security cooperation with its neighbors alongside economic ties. This is how it defines its positive defense requirements—a policy that it regards as a "win-win" for itself, its neighbors, and the international community. "Countries are increasingly bound together in a community of shared destiny," says the Defense Ministry's White Paper of 2015. "Peace, development, cooperation and mutual benefit have become an irresistible tide of the times."[8] Illustratively, despite differences with Vietnam concerning sovereignty in the South China Sea and anti-Chinese disturbances there in May and June of 2014, comprehensive military delegations from both sides met in October.[9]

China's strategy can be clarified by a closer look at how it sees itself in the world, how it makes decisions, how it defines its main goals and the challenges ahead, and how it hopes to achieve those goals and overcome its challenges.

World Transformation and China's New Identity

China's rise influences the fate of the world. In the first half of the twentieth century, China was at the bottom of the international system, the easy prey of predatory powers. It struggled to regain the independence, autonomy, and sovereignty that it had lost in the nineteenth century. But by the end of the twentieth century, China embarked on a new trajectory. Since 1982, it has sought to open its economy to the world and embrace globalization.[10] It acknowledged the importance of regional integration and regional cooperation as prerequisite to its own economic vitality. In the early 1990s, China grasped that its rise to become a regional powerhouse and global player was part of a world transformation and represented a huge shift in the global distribution of power that was linked to the rise of the BRICS—Brazil, Russia, India, China, and South Africa.

China realizes that shifts in the distribution of power are part of a larger global process.[11] Developing countries are now growing more rapidly than developed countries, and because of urbanization and technology transfers this trend is likely to continue.[12] Meanwhile, globalization is increasing interdependence, though at the same time causing feelings of insecurity. Along with these trends, the world population is aging, intensifying the need for stronger welfare systems in all states.

New problems stemming from technological innovation and the global movement of people, goods, and capital require new institutions, new initiatives, and new solutions. Terrorism, drug traffic, and arms smuggling are formidable challenges; so are the public health problems stemming from increased migration.[13] Resources are being depleted worldwide, and environmental degradation and climate change compound the security and economic problems that China and the rest of the world face. Meanwhile, state failure has international reverberations and creates international responsibilities.[14] These nontraditional security threats invite regional and global collaboration because they are beyond the individual capacities of even great powers.[15] The need to address global challenges and nontraditional security threats makes power relations between and among countries look less like zero-sum games and more like opportunities to create positive-sum or win-win solutions.[16] China seeks to cooperate in shaping regional solutions. It wants to cooperate with the Association of Southeast Nations (ASEAN) and other neighboring countries through the Regional Comprehensive Economic Partnership (RCEP) and shows a flexible attitude toward the Trans-Pacific Partnership (TPP) and other regional cooperative initiatives.[17]

For example, in May 2014, China hosted the fourth summit meeting of the Conference on Interaction and Confidence Building Measures in Asia (CICA), an organization with twenty-six member states and eleven observer states, including the United States. Thirteen heads of state and UN Secretary General Ban Ki Moon attended the meeting. In his keynote address, President Xi Jinping emphasized that security in the new era must be universal, equal, inclusive, comprehensive, cooperative, and sustainable.[18]

Another important initiative has been the launch of the Asian Infrastructure Investment Bank (AIIB) in 2014–2015. Most observers agree that the funds available from existing multilateral institutions are insufficient for development needs, so China has put a fifty-billion-dollar stake in a new lending institution. The AIIB has attracted founding members both from developing countries such as India, Indonesia, and Vietnam and from developed countries such as South Korea, the United Kingdom, Germany, and France.[19]

In the era of globalization and all its accompanying changes, the central challenge for a country seeking to safeguard its national interests and to achieve its historical mission is to develop a distinct identity that promotes national integration and helps determine its proper position in the international community.[20] Since 1982, China's position has been in the process of transformation, from a traditional large country to a modern power, from a closed country to an open global power, and from a country with a modest international role to an important player. This transformation has taken shape gradually and is reflected in four main areas:

1. In its political system, China is a new type of socialist major power, the only one among current great powers. It has gradually enriched the basic concept of socialism with Chinese characteristics, including the inheritance of Chinese tradition, an understanding of world trends, reflections on the history of other socialist countries, and the pursuit of its national development goals.[21] It is a country that is open in all areas under the leadership of the CPC, and it has devoted itself to developing a socialist market economy and pursuing common prosperity.[22]

2. In its economic system, China is a large developing country. China is no longer a typical developing country. It is neither a developed nor an underdeveloped country but has traits of both, with the trend heading toward development.[23] In the aggregate, China is the world's second-largest economy, but in per capita terms it has a long way to go. Therefore, dealing with China's issues based on the concept that it is a typical developing country is not practical and has many drawbacks. China is trying to pass through the "middle point" in its primary stage of socialism at a rapid and steady pace. It is imperative for China to complete the transformation of its development path from unsustainable to sustainable, from inequitable to equitable, and from uneven to balanced. "Its national strategic goal is to complete the building of a moderately prosperous society in all respects by 2021, when the CPC celebrates its centenary; and the building of a modern socialist country that is prosperous, strong, democratic, culturally advanced and harmonious by 2049 when the People's Republic of China (PRC) marks its centenary."[24]

3. In terms of culture, China is a country with a rich heritage. Chinese cultural modernization, however, lags behind its economic modernization and the reform of its cultural system is still in its infancy. In the twentieth century, "modernization" tended to be identified with "westernization," and this has led to a neglect of China's own cultural resources and potential.[25] Its cultural security is the most profound security threat currently facing China. In recent years, China has started to establish a strategy of using its culture as a tool to transform itself into an international power. This strategy includes adherence to its cultural traditions, the promotion of those traditions, the deepening of its reform of culturally rooted industries, the further development of China as a cultural power, and the advocacy of dialogue between different cultures.[26]

4. In international politics, China is a responsible great power focused on the Asia-Pacific region. Taking on international responsibilities has become a requisite for any country in the era of globalization, and being a "responsible great power" means to embrace this trend. Looking ahead, China will assess its own international position calmly, actively involve itself in taking on international responsibilities, increase these responsibilities according to its own capabilities, promote its common interests with other countries, strike a balance between its capabilities and its responsibilities when dealing with international issues, and continue actively to seek more international rights. For example, in Africa, China is building on its existing medical presence there to help combat the spread of the Ebola virus. By October 2014, it had already contributed $200 million in aid, and it was shipping large quantities of an experimental treatment developed by Chinese military doctors.[27] As another example, in December 2014, China sent a 700-member peacekeeping force to South Sudan as part of a UN mission.[28]

China is an Asia-Pacific power with a large global influence. For most of its history, China has been a significant country not only in the East Asian region but more broadly across Asia. Traditionally, it has been East Asia's center of population and production. The ideas of *Tianxia* (all under heaven), which was the traditional Chinese perception of world order, and *Chaogong Tixi* (the tribute system), which provided both an administrative framework along with priority trading status for affiliated countries, reflect the splendor of Chinese history. However, China has never been a world power in its 5,000-year history. Despite its accelerated economic growth since 1978 and its growing projection of power in neighboring seas, it still faces many challenges, including shortages of resources on a per-capita basis, uneven economic development, the limited influence of its cultural values around the world, and a lack of adequate overseas capabilities as well as internationally recognized privileges stemming from its traditional emphasis on military defense. Hence, it defines itself as an Asia-Pacific regional power with aspirations to exert a larger impact on world affairs.

Overall, China's strategy is based on the concept that it is a new type of socialist power. It seeks to embrace the global economy and serve as a new developmental model. China wants to revive its traditional values, shape them for the modern world, reconcile them with Western mores, and help create a new global culture. It wants to grow its power yet reassure its neighbors. However, there is a big gap between strategic aspirations and contemporary realities, and there are differences of opinion on how to achieve these goals in a complex world order. Yan Xuetong, the dean of the Institute of Modern International Relations at Tsinghua University, argues that China should shift from Deng Xiaoping's nonalliance policy and his advice to "keep a low profile" and instead form alliances and "strive for achievement."[29] Others, including Qin Yaqing, the president of China Foreign Affairs University, argue that continuity in a middle course (*zhongyong*) is the key to the Chinese culture of decision-making and that a shift to assertive diplomacy would isolate China.[30]

Strategic Decision-Making

The challenges China faces require new decision-making machinery, which will in turn affect policy. Its procedures and mechanisms are intertwined with its pursuit of reform and its embrace of the information age and technological innovation in the quest for economic growth and a desire to exert influence and power. The decision-making community has expanded over time, in the process becoming more open-minded and innovative. Recent changes have seen more centralized policymaking and improved coordination.

Deng Xiaoping played the preeminent role in Chinese foreign policy decision-making in the first stage of the reform era, but as external relations became more complex the institutions and mechanisms dealing with foreign affairs necessarily expanded.[31] Early initiatives, such as the Shenzhen Special Economic Zone, established in 1980, were started as experimental targets of opportunity and were broadened as they proved successful.[32] By the mid-1980s, the leadership had expanded international contact to all coastal areas and every dimension of the economy began to feel the impact of global markets.

China's reform entered a new stage at the fourteenth CPC National Congress in 1992. Building a socialist market economy became the overriding goal. Integrating China's economy into the world market constituted the key task of policymakers. An important example was the creation of the Pudong Special Economic Zone across the river from central Shanghai. Instead of being a tentative experiment on the edge of the Chinese economy, this was a dramatic and high-profile move to put globalization at the heart of economic life.[33] In the 1990s, China pursued a good neighbor policy, welcoming international investment and actively participating in multilateral organizations. Chinese officials determined that the national interest must be reconciled and harmonized with the interests of its neighbors and global partners. China joined the World Trade Organization (WTO) in 2001, a major step in global economic integration. China's strategists sought peace and cooperation, as such goals were indispensable to China's interests. All of these new directions required management of a complex foreign policy.

More ministries and institutions participated in strategic decision-making. Every ministry developed an international department to deal with foreign affairs. Decision-making concerning international issues, therefore, was no longer the exclusive right of the Ministry of Foreign Affairs, the Ministry of Commerce, and the Ministry of Defense. David M. Lampton has characterized the evolution of foreign policy decision-making in terms of "four -izations": professionalization, corporate pluralization, decentralization, and globalization.[34] While these developments make the policy process more complex, and at times bewildering and confusing, they also contribute to its stability.[35]

In addition, many more think tanks play a role in shaping strategy and influencing decision-making. These think tanks exist inside the party apparatus and also within local and provincial governments. At the same time, universities have created many research institutes. They sometimes have access to important information and to important decision-makers. They invite individuals of different ministries to attend conferences or seminars, and a kind of benign interaction between the bureaucracy and academic circles has emerged.

The interaction between experts and political leaders also occurs at the highest levels. Since 2002, the Politburo has held frequent collective study sessions that feature presentations by leading experts on topics important to domestic and foreign policy, such as global warming and changes in the international system. The materials and discussion summaries are then circulated throughout the CPC.[36]

Meanwhile, social media and the Internet are becoming more active in influencing public opinion about international matters of concern. In the past, the official media was virtually the only source of information and viewpoints regarding foreign affairs. However, now the opinions of "netizens" are increasingly vocal, and the government takes public opinion into account.

Local governments have also begun to influence the process. Chinese central government and CPC officials realize that local governments are essential to the sustainable development of the whole country. Different provinces and even counties have their own special circumstances that require attention from the central government. This kind of interaction reshapes their relationship and allows local governments to matter in policymaking. For example, local governments play a role in the Association of North East Asia Regional Governments, including six provincial governments in China and sixty-five local governments from Japan, South Korea, North Korea, Mongolia, and Russia. Their aim is to forge mechanisms for regional cooperation, development, and peace. Similarly, Yunnan Province plays a major role in the Greater Mekong Subregion, organized by the Asia Development Bank in 1992, while Guangxi Province provides leadership in economic cooperation with Vietnam in the Tonkin Gulf area.

The Central Leading Group for Foreign Affairs oversees foreign affairs and national security under the leadership of the Political Bureau of the CPC Central Committee. It coordinates foreign affairs and national security matters under the leadership of the Political Bureau of the CPC Central Committee. The president of China, who is also the general secretary of the CPC, is the chairman, and its members include the state councilor in charge of foreign affairs; heads of the ministries of foreign affairs, national security, public security, and commerce; the information offices of the State Council, the Propaganda Department, and the International Department of the CPC Central Committee; and high-ranking generals. The Central Leading Group for National Security was set up in September 2001 to collaborate with the Central Leading Group for Foreign Affairs.[37]

In November 2013, the CPC Central Committee decided to set up a National Security Commission (NSC) to improve its national security system and strategy.[38] The buildup of the NSC has been based on the institutionalization and professionalization of the Central Leading Group for National

Security. It focuses on crucial issues concerning territory, territorial waters, diplomacy, the military, resources, the economy, and people's livelihoods. It shapes decisions, supervises the implementation of national security strategy, and helps to orchestrate responses to emergencies both inside and outside of China.

Strategic Challenges

China takes development as its core goal and seeks cooperation as the primary means to achieve its objectives. It wants to consult with other nations and hopes for a peaceful and stable world order. Meanwhile, transformative changes are shaping the international arena. The comparative strength of nations is swiftly changing.[39] The relative superior power of the developed countries is waning, and developing countries are emerging quickly and pursuing strategic coordination among themselves. They grasp their mutual interdependence and the common need for global governance. They seek a multipolar, peaceful, and democratic world. Yet formidable challenges present themselves. These tendencies are signs of impending changes in the existing international landscape, with tensions and complex interactions among strategic powers.[40]

As Figures 2.1 and 2.2 demonstrate, China's growth is so rapid that it arouses fears abroad.[41] The contrast between China's continued economic growth and the difficulties faced by the world economy since 2008 has been particularly striking. China's gross national income (GNI, roughly equivalent to GNP) grew much faster than those of developed countries, and its inflation rate and currency control were much better than most developing countries. Although China also suffered from the 2008 financial crisis, it is portrayed more and more as a fierce competitor and a strategic challenger. Neighbors fear its growing power and often protest its military deployments. China believes the fears and suspicions about its rise are not rooted in hostility, but come from misperceptions and misunderstandings. Foreign observers have also noted an exaggerated sensitivity to China's actions since 2008.[42] In the past, China tried to dispel those misgivings, but now realizes that they are part of a natural process. The fears and doubts originate from historical memory, conflicting interests, and strategic imperatives. Solving these problems will depend on China's conduct and the passage of time, so China will be patient and adjust its strategy accordingly.

Other powers are trying to adjust to China's rise. Japan and other neighbors seek to protect their own interests and to hedge against China's ascent

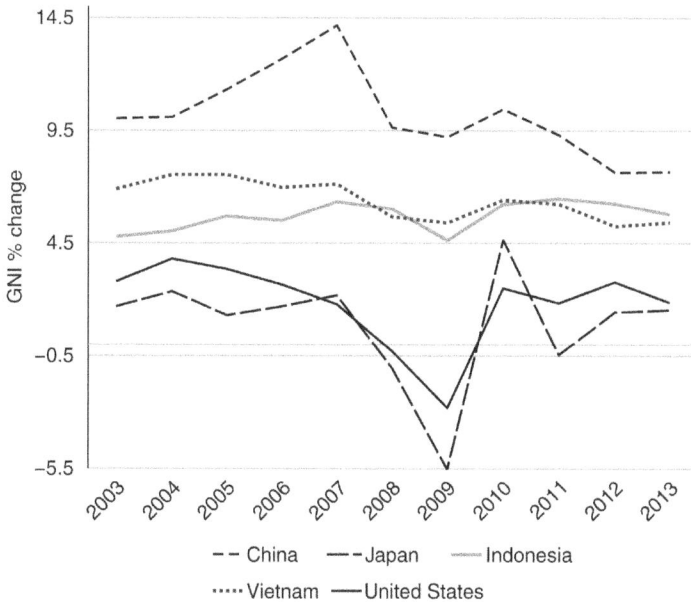

Figure 2.1. GNI growth rates, 2003–2013 (data from World Bank Development Indicators).

to world power. Sometimes they collude with internal dissidents and secessionists. The possibility of foreign collusion with domestic unrest has been a traditional key concern of Chinese policy. Those who are afraid of China want to block its development, contain its growth, and stifle the peaceful change that China seeks.

China is emerging from a world where one superpower and several great powers collaborated with one another. These powers are finding it difficult to adjust to China's mounting capabilities. Their fearful reactions complicate China's national security decision-making. In fact, China faces a series of volatile issues around the globe as it expands its own political, economic, and security interests. It sometimes clashes with the United States in Latin America and with Europe and the United States in Africa.

Only a few years ago, U.S. policymakers and scholars debated whether China constituted a strategic competitor. No longer! Now, the United States adheres to a "congagement" policy, seeking to contain and engage Chinese power.[43] It aims to establish a containment belt around China by cooperating

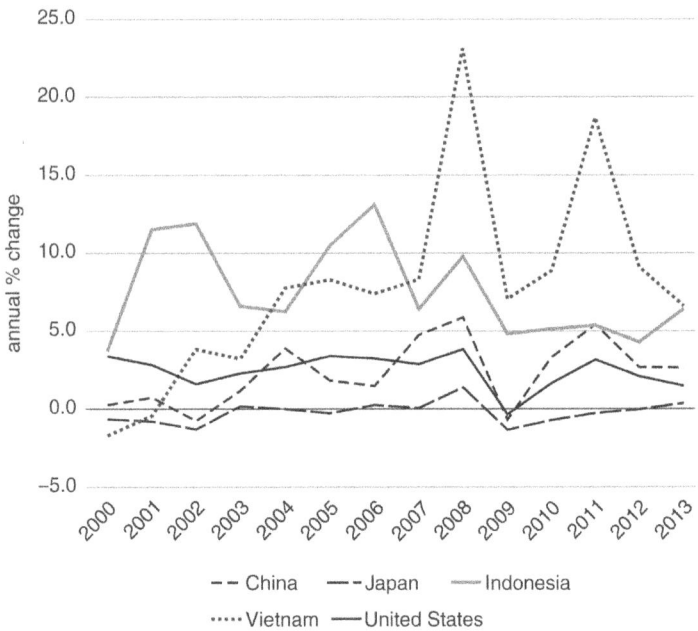

Figure 2.2. Inflation, 2003–2013 (data from World Bank Development Indicators).

militarily, economically, and commercially with China's neighbors. Such initiatives pose threats to China's security and economic ambitions. Likewise, U.S. economic and cultural engagement in China, resulting from economic interdependence, has implications for China's economic and financial security and political stability.

China faces an increasingly complicated and ominous situation in Asia, especially in East Asia. Its remaining boundary issues have evolved into border disputes regarding the sovereignty of offshore islands and maritime rights, and these are complicated by growing U.S. meddling. Although China's territorial frontiers in the north and northwest are secure, the situation in the southwest is less certain. From South Asia to the Persian Gulf, geopolitical competition pulsates among China's neighbors. In the Korean Peninsula, Japanese-U.S. cooperation raises anxieties as does their collaboration over the Diaoyu Islands and over maritime routes and airspace. China also worries about its ability to resolve the Taiwan issue on its own terms and fears

U.S. collaboration with antagonistic neighbors in Southeast Asia and the South China Sea. Everywhere, China worries about its maritime security, especially as its dependence on imports grows.[44]

As external challenges mount, fear of internal subversion also increases. Chinese officials believe that outside forces foment secessionist tendencies, exploit China's economic vulnerabilities, and subvert China's cultural values. Although no major government recognizes the Republic of China on Taiwan, the United States continues to sell it advanced weapons in contravention of the 1982 Joint Communique.[45] Using the pretext of Tibet, several countries attempted to disrupt the carrying of the Olympic Torch to Beijing in 2008. Organizations funded by foreign governments have actively tried to influence politics in the Hong Kong Special Administrative Region (SAR).[46]

Responding to Challenges

China's strategy involves an effort to nurture a regional and global environment conducive to its economic ambitions, domestic needs, cultural sensibilities, and strategic vulnerabilities. More than anything else, China seeks economic growth and development. It embraces economic globalization and wants to be a leading regional economic power, aspiring to be a major catalyst for global modernization. Chinese officials view the nation's economic development as integral to its national renewal, and economic openness serves that renewal. They want to garner a larger share of the global market through technological innovation, managerial expertise, and shrewd investments. As China becomes a global economic presence, Chinese officials also want to create a unified national market at home. They want to push industry into the interior and far west of China and they invite foreign investors to expedite the process. They seek balanced regional growth at home and global penetration abroad.

Yet Chinese officials believe their country's economic growth should be reconciled with the economic needs of current and prospective partners. They do not want to challenge the existing international economic order. They want to be a responsible stakeholder in that order. During the 1997 Asian financial crisis, China maintained the stability of its currency, extended monetary support to its Asian neighbors, and won accolades from the international community. Eleven years later, in 2008, when the international financial order was tottering, China again played a responsible role. It maintained a stable currency, developed its domestic infrastructure, and

consumption, and increased its international investments. China has be-
haved responsibly during economic crises and has participated cooperatively
in global economic governance.

China does not want to be a free-rider. Voluntarily undertaking appropriate international responsibilities is a positive step for a rising country, and
China is prepared to assume a new role in the international arena as a public
goods provider. For example, "China's armed forces," says the Ministry of
Defense, "will continue to take an active part in international disaster rescue
and humanitarian assistance, dispatch professional rescue teams to disaster-
stricken areas for relief and disaster reduction, provide relief materials and
medical aid, and strengthen international exchanges in the fields of rescue
and disaster reduction."[47] Over time, China has changed its attitude toward
UN peacekeeping operations from objection to passive acceptance and then
to positive support. In the 1970s and early 1980s, China regarded UN peacekeeping operations as superpower interference. But in the late 1980s, China
began to participate in some operations. Now, China deploys the largest
peacekeeping police force and provides the greatest financial support among
the five permanent members of the UN Security Council. In recent years,
China also has provided more and more foreign aid. It grew at an annual rate
of 29.4 percent from 2004 to 2009, and the amount for the years 2010–2012
reached 89.34 billion yuan ($14.41 billion).[48] Compared to the $1.7 billion it
pledged in 2001 for foreign aid and government-sponsored investment activities, the figures were $124.8 billion in 2009, $168.6 billion in 2010, and
$189.3 billion in 2011.[49]

While focused on its own economic development, China seeks to play a
global role commensurate with its actual strength. It rejects isolation and desires economic collaboration and policy coordination with other great powers. China has strategic partnership relations with fifty-nine countries and
many international organizations such as the EU and ASEAN. It supports
ASEAN and RCEP, and hopes for a peaceful and just regional commercial
and economic order. China's role in maintaining and renewing the Six-Party
Talks with Korea has drawn attention from around the world. Chinese officials seek to forge new institutions that accommodate the needs and coordinate the policies of emerging nations in East Asia and beyond, as illustrated
by its participation in the BRICS (Brazil, Russia, India, China, South Africa) Summit, a new kind of South-South cooperation. In July 2014, a new
BRICS financial facility was created, headquartered in Shanghai, to which
China contributed $41 billion.[50] Besides new financial institutions, China is

proposing coordinated regional infrastructural development, most importantly the "new silk roads," one overland to Europe and the other a maritime
route to Africa and the Mediterranean.[51]

Yet, acutely conscious of the countermeasures its growing economic power
arouses, Chinese officials believe that they must also nurture military capabilities. For too long, they believe, China sacrificed its military potential in
order to focus on economic priorities. It did not develop a strategic vision or
a maritime strategy, thereby allowing its East Asian and South Asian neighbors to collaborate with the United States in a mounting strategic encircle-
ment. In other words, China has been slow to develop the military strength
it must have to deter adversaries, protect its maritime lines of communication, secure trade routes, and nurture the types of collaboration it prizes. It
now seeks to redress those deficiencies and "to develop a modern maritime
military force commensurate with its national security and development interests."[52] Nonetheless, in 2013, according to independent estimates, the U.S.
military budget was three-and-a-half times that of China's, and its percentage of gross national income devoted to military expenditures was 185 percent of China's.[53] While China has one aircraft carrier, the United States has
twenty, including ten nuclear, and Japan and India each have two.[54] While
China has begun to put multiple warheads on its ballistic missiles, it does
so in response to vast advances in U.S. ballistic missile defenses.[55] Overall,
China's defense expenditures have grown rapidly, from about $35 billion in
2006 to approximately $141 billion in 2015. These expenditures, however, pale
in comparison to the 2015 U.S. defense budget of $560 billion.[56]

Other challenges remain. In pursuit of regional primacy and global influence, China needs to preserve its "cultural security." China has been regarded
not only as a country, but a civilization with distinctive traditional values as
its core. How to modernize traditional culture and carry on its rich tradition
remains a major strategic problem that has not yet been solved. The main
internal risks to Chinese culture are the serious social problems caused by the
erosion of traditional social ethics. China almost lost its traditional morality
to excessive materialism. Currently, efforts are under way to encourage not
only traditional moral principles but also the revolutionary ethics of the mass
line that were crucial to the creation of the PRC.

China has tended to ignore the promotion of the distinctive features of its
own national culture and international influence while actively absorbing foreign civilizations. However, it also realizes that once a nation loses its cultural
distinctiveness, it loses its sense of self. Foreign experts agree that China's

culture has much to offer the contemporary world. For example, Daniel Bell argues that East Asia needs to look to its own roots for political order, and Peter Nolan suggests the same for economic development.[57] Moreover, in external affairs, culture can play an important role in international relations. Since 2004, China has built 475 Confucius Institutes in 125 countries all over the world to teach Chinese language and culture. They serve as platforms for cultural exchanges and as bridges reinforcing friendship and cooperation.[58]

In support and defense of economic development and its national autonomy, China wants to augment its military and maritime capabilities, achieve regional primacy, "and protect the security of strategic lines of communication and overseas interests."[59] It seeks regional integration and aspires to create regional institutions favorable to the entire East Asian economy as well as to itself, willingly offering other countries free-riding opportunities.[60] In an interdependent world, China supports diplomatic policies and takes measures of a military, economic, and cultural nature to resolve disputes and conflicts among countries, which is the normal practice for a mature major country.[61] On the other hand, China lacks diverse strategic capabilities and has difficulties leveraging them for maximum effectiveness.

※ ※ ※

China seeks a strategy commensurate with its economic goals and civilizational values. It does not want to overturn the global order because it realizes how that order has nurtured China's interests. But China wants to assume a larger role in refashioning the multilateral institutions that uphold the global order. It is aware, moreover, that its growing strength and military ambitions engender anxieties abroad and provoke countermeasures to contain its ambitions. This realization impels Chinese officials to augment their military capabilities to deter adversaries and fashion a regional environment conducive to their goals and values. Those values are not those of hegemonic domination, which Chinese officials have always condemned, but rather peace, cooperation, and development. This is what constitutes their vision of realism, a strategy that postulates they can enhance their security and interests while reassuring prospective antagonists that they intend to do no harm to others. Whether such a strategy can succeed depends on whether Chinese efforts to reassure will be as bold as their efforts to enhance their security.

CHAPTER 3

GERMANY

Between Power and Responsibility

CONSTANZE STELZENMÜLLER

G ERMANY'S recent rise to power—only fifteen years after being described as "the sick man" of Europe—is a phenomenon of postwar Western political history.[1] It is no exaggeration to say that within the European Union, Germany's stature now appears rather like that of the United States in NATO: in terms of economic size and political influence, at least, it is a hegemon. The global financial crisis that began in late 2008, and which Germany has so far weathered relatively unscathed, has reinforced Germany's exceptional stature on the continent. The interest with which China, Russia, and other non-Western powers are pursuing special partnerships with Germany demonstrates that its magnetic pull operates on a global scale. Even the United States now treats Germany as a major power.[2]

The conundrum at the core of Germany's rise is whether all this power is underpinned by a strategy. To no small degree, this question is motivated by a desire for greater clarity and predictability from a country whose every action (and inaction) has consequences for others, but which has so far, and unlike most of its Western peers, eschewed a formal national security strategy process. German policies are not made any more intelligible at home or abroad by a leadership culture that is ambivalent about public diplomacy and a chancellor who, like her predecessors, depends on, and takes advantage of, ambiguity.

Above all, this latest iteration of the German Question seeks to understand where the Berlin republic is heading. Is it following an egotistical strategy that seeks to maximize German national interest at the expense of its neighbors, allies, and partners? Or is it engaged in an altruistic approach that sees benefit in shaping and underwriting a European and global order that maximizes freedom, prosperity, and security for the world, and is it willing to pay a price to do so? More bluntly, is Germany's new power about power for its own sake—or about responsibility?[3]

Germany pursues a mostly coherent set of strategic goals and with some determination, even if its record on consistency, or success, is mixed. It continues to bear the bulk of the responsibility for the management of the European crisis. Its elites (together with most of the media) are arguing that Germany needs a robust, responsible, and forward-leaning posture in response not just to its new power, but to the shifts in its strategic environment; and they want a public messaging to match.[4] Nonetheless, the tension at the heart of German strategy—between short-term (often economic) interests and crisis management on the one hand and long-term global order concerns on the other—is structural in nature and thus ultimately unresolvable. The essential question is not whether Germany can abolish or avoid it, but whether it will be able to create and sustain a balance between the two. Another, related way of asking the German Question is: can Germany augment its unquestioned tactical skills with the strategic thinking and planning capacity required for a long game?

This chapter describes core challenges and paradoxes of German power and examines how those play out in four main policy arenas: international order, European policy, partnerships, and security policy.

Germany's Strategic Goals

Postwar German strategy is unique in Europe, and among the greater Western powers, in that the fall of the Wall neatly divides it into two historical phases: one of strategy under occupation and one of strategy as a sovereign country. Each is defined by its own power paradox.

Before 1990, limited sovereignty meant that the Federal Republic of Germany was legally not at liberty to conceptualize, much less implement, a full-spectrum national strategy commensurate with its growing economic might. Nonetheless, it had two long-term strategic objectives which it pursued vigorously: integration into the West as a means of overcoming the legacy of two world wars as well as the Holocaust and keeping the option of reunification open. But *Westbindung* and *Ostpolitik* were by no means harmonious goals to many German citizens, or to its allies.

In the end, Germany attained both goals, and even brought them into alignment. Luck, fate, and the enlightened attitude of others had a hand in this outcome, of course. Yet it is also true that the pre-1990 Federal Republic was very skillful at playing on limitations and tensions to its advantage and at leveraging power through membership in international institutions and alliances. Deliberate ambiguity, combined with an imaginative and not infrequently covert exploitation of the sovereignty limitations imposed by occupation, became a habit and a hallmark of German strategy.

For a country with such a past, and such constraints, achieving reunification while remaining firmly rooted in the West was nothing less than a strategic miracle. Certainly, it provided, and still provides, an historical object lesson in maximizing limited options.

The paradox of German power from 1990 onward is a neat reversal of its previous circumstances; Germany regained its full national sovereignty in legal terms, but it did not thereby recover strategic autonomy in the classical understanding of freedom of action. And while the dramatic changes that have taken place in the global operating environment over the past quarter-century have contributed to Germany's success, they also confront it with a host of new challenges.

Many of Germany's current limitations are self-imposed, as it has remained faithful to a tradition of voluntary multilateral integration. A constantly dedicated member of the United Nations, it has also stayed deeply integrated into the European Union (the EU, indeed, is a continuous source of directly applicable law that today touches almost all areas of German citizens' lives); moreover, all of its armed forces remain committed to NATO.[5] It is occasionally suggested that Germany's newly augmented clout, and its trading relations with non-Western powers, ought to make it loosen its commitment to such "traditional alliances."[6] In reality, all three frameworks remain essential to Germany as mechanisms for building consensus and sharing (or evading) responsibility, as well as for augmenting and sharing power. Actually, one of the EU's most important functions today is containing and mitigating German power—which is very much in its own interest.

Yet (and ironically, for a political culture so keen to define itself with regard to external obligations) the UN, the EU, and NATO provide far less normative and institutional definition for German policies than they once did. All three are currently wrestling both with the task of identifying their missions for the twenty-first century and with disagreement among member states about how to keep them cohesive, effective, and legitimate.

Nor are other powers stepping forward to articulate a new framing. The United States, despite its status as the world's only superpower, is increasingly disinclined to be its sole policeman; it is retrenching and rebalancing, and it is hamstrung by the polarization of domestic politics. Britain and France, the two other major European powers with a global outlook, are going through inward-looking spells of their own, putting Germany in a default leadership position. The new era of global multipolarity has not materialized either— and certainly not, as hoped, in the shape of alternate visions of a liberal and peaceful international order, as China's and Russia's aggressiveness in their respective neighborhoods demonstrate.

Meanwhile, globalization and new technologies have provided huge new opportunities for nations—Germany foremost among them—that are mobile, flexible, and innovative enough to exploit them. Yet, these forces have created new risks while at the same time eroding the power of the state to control them. For Germany, which has traditionally maximized its influence through institutions, outsourced its security through alliances, and based its power on trading with Western and non-Western nations alike, these developments are double-edged: they have greatly increased its wealth, but they embody unprecedented new threats to its influence, its security, and its power.

Perhaps most ominously for Berlin, the European project itself is at risk today in ways which endanger the very foundation of German power. Indeed, Germany is sitting astride all three of the major fault-lines which currently divide Europe—and may yet break it: the dispute about the future of European integration; the social, economic, and political cleavages between Europe's northern and southern member states produced by the economic crisis; and the new east-west split created by the conflict in Ukraine and Russia's role in it. Troubled transformations and multiplying crises in northern Africa and the Middle East provide potent additional stress factors and distractions.

As a detailed look at the four key fields of German strategy—international order, European policy, strategic relationships, and security policy—will show, its record in conceptualizing and implementing strategies that successfully address these challenges is somewhat mixed. But that may be the best that is possible in the current environment. The experiences of the United Kingdom, France, and even the United States are sobering object lessons for how globalization, integration, and the erosion of state power hamper the capacity of even the largest and most powerful states for sovereign planning and strategic action.

Germany and International Order

Championing peaceful multilateralism has been one of Germany's strongest postwar foreign policy traditions, and one where German policy elites and public opinion were very much in sync, not least because this helped persuade the world that Germany was determined to break with its twentieth-century history of war and genocide. Germany has, for decades, been a highly engaged champion of the UN and its special organizations, as well as of multilateral diplomacy and norm-setting (for example, human rights conventions, the UN Convention on the Law of the Sea of 1982, and the International Criminal Court in 1998). It is one of the Western world's major donors of development aid; its government agencies, political foundations, and nongovernmental organizations (NGOs) are active in promoting development, good governance, and human rights. The country's political and economic elites are acutely aware that their country's success as a global trading champion and hence its national prosperity depend on a globalization underpinned by a free, open, and peaceful international order.[7]

Yet, crucial as this approach is for Germany, Berlin has in fact become less and less visible as a shaper of agendas and outcomes in multilateral norm-setting or institution-building frameworks, although it remains a major player in some arenas, such as international climate negotiations. Internet governance is the only other area Germany currently appears to be pursuing with any comparable ambitions, where it has been partnering with Brazil to "internationalize" (read: de-Americanize) global Internet governance. Conversely, Germany has been very willing to engage in flexible new formats like the G20, where it occasionally sides with non-Western powers (against the United States) on issues like rebalancing global trade relations.

What is missing is a sense that Germany possesses a vision of its own for what new governance frameworks adapted to recent changes in the global strategic environment should look like.[8] Given a global environment where access to limited resources and common spaces (deep sea, cyber, and space itself) is becoming increasingly contested and conflict prone, it is notable that there is a disturbing overall lack of ideas and proposals from most Western states, including the United States. Nonetheless, the contrast between Germany's vulnerability to global disorder and its absence as a "shaping power" in this regard is marked.[9] For example, Berlin has endorsed the notion that rising powers should be "socialized" into becoming responsible stakeholders, but has not offered constructive incentives—for example, agreeing to a reduction of its voting rights at the International Monetary Fund (IMF).[10]

There are several possible reasons for this contrast between perceived dependency and vulnerability and an action deficit. Leaders' personalities play a role here: Germany's chancellors over the last sixteen years, Gerhard Schröder and Angela Merkel, have shared a reluctance to articulate strategy, much less visions for global order. Germany's compartmentalized politics and the absence of an interagency strategy process that could channel and catalyze thinking also prevent a coherent national approach. Germany's own increasingly keen interest in rare earth minerals and other strategic resources, as well as in global access to resources and transport routes, is potentially at odds with its traditional commitment to the protection of the global commons. Last but not least, most of Germany's strategic energy has, since 2008, been sucked up by the European crisis—which is seen by Berlin as the most existential crisis to confront Germany and Europe in many decades, and one that has shown signs of returning.

Germany and Europe

The European Union is Germany's principal source of power and leverage for several reasons: the euro area is Germany's most important trading partner, and Germany is acutely vulnerable to risks of contagion from disturbances in the euro area, such that a failure of the euro area could cause an unravelling of the single market, which is the foundation of Germany's economic success; moreover, this newly muscular Germany cannot do without Europe as a maximizer for its global strategic ambitions.[11] For all these reasons, and despite its global trading engagement, it will always have a strategic interest in remaining a member of the EU and the euro—and in investing heavily in the future of both.[12]

Yet the paradoxical aspects of German power are, if anything, starker in the European context than in any other arena of its external policy. On the one hand, Germany is truly a giant in Europe. Germany's gross domestic product (GDP) is the largest in the euro area, at 28 percent. It has a cast-iron AAA rating, its economy is the most competitive on the Continent, and in the context of the sovereign debt crisis, it has not only proven the most resilient, but become the largest lender in the euro area. This makes Germany the key actor, whose actions or inactions automatically have implications for the rest of Europe and without whom no serious decision is possible.[13] But that does not give Germany the kind of power that the United States has in NATO; no single state, however powerful, can retain that much strategic autonomy as a member state of the EU. Berlin does have huge influence in the EU, but its power to shape long-term outcomes in accordance with its preferences is limited. In the course of the crisis, it has had to adapt its policy preferences significantly to react to events and pressure from smaller and weaker EU member states. In that sense, it is like Jonathan Swift's hero Gulliver—a giant, but firmly tied down.

At the heart of Germany's EU strategy is the goal of integration through monetary union. Berlin has treated the euro area as a stability union, in which an independent, stability-oriented monetary policy is underpinned by sound fiscal and economic policies, including structural reforms designed to enhance member states' competitiveness. In the course of the crisis, the German government was able to shape the pace and the instruments of crisis management, as well as of subsequent governance reforms in the euro area. It handled the sovereign debt crisis as a fiscal crisis, rooted in irresponsible risk-taking by governments.

Consequently, when the crisis escalated and Germany became the main donor, its focus was on avoiding moral hazard, setting up preventive policy frameworks (reflected in the January 2012 Fiscal Compact), increasing competitiveness (the Euro Plus Compact of March 2011), as well as restoring trust in the Lisbon Treaty's no-bailout clause (the European Stability Mechanism treaty of February 2012). Yet in order not to have to accept the creation of an unlimited rescue mechanism, Germany ended up agreeing to let the European Central Bank take on the role of potential guarantor of last resort.[14]

Germany's insistence on the fiscal responsibility of governments, supply-side reforms, and rejection of mutual risk-sharing earned it massive international criticism in the early years of the crisis. But the firmness of the German government—to be more precise, of the Chancellery's Europe division, which on core issues of European policy has always held absolute sway over the foreign ministry—in asserting its position in European negotiations was rooted in a normative preference for regulated market liberalism that goes back to the German postwar economic miracle.[15] Even more importantly, it was seen within Germany as triumphantly validated by the 2003 "Agenda 2010" reforms, which are thought to have ended the country's economic invalid status, and made it resilient against external shocks.[16] It was greatly assisted by the fact that German diplomats in Brussels could make threatening references to the fact that the question of ultimate budgetary authority had become a balance of powers issue back home, where the Bundestag (federal parliament) and the Bundesverfassungsgericht (federal constitutional court) staked out powerful claims and fought hard to preserve their veto roles.

In the end, the governing coalition parties were able to rally support for the chancellor's policies domestically by appealing to Germany's tradition-ally pro-European and integrationist national consensus, as well as to a sense of moral responsibility for the future of the EU, including within the op-position camp.[17] Even the court, which was asked to review several cases challenging the government's European crisis management measures from 2010 onward, has generally chosen to protect the legislature's budgetary co-decision-making authority (or to remind it of its responsibility in this regard), but never to the point of undercutting the government's policy.[18]

Ultimately, however, Germany's resolute (many partners would call it in-transigent) stance was less than effective because it failed to calm the markets (critics would say it contributed to their nervousness). As a result, Berlin was forced several times to scramble toward compromises it had hitherto resisted, crossing its own "red lines" repeatedly in the process, for example on reform of the European Financial Stability Facility.[19] Matters were not helped by the government's fumbling and ambiguous messaging style.

Germany's European crisis management in the first three years of the sovereign debt crisis thus serves as a potent illustration of the simultane-ous strengths and weaknesses of Germany's complex system of domestic checks and balances, which both enhances and undermines its ability to project power externally. It is a remarkably effective mechanism for building and maintaining a national consensus, yet it clearly hampers the executive's ability to react flexibly and appropriately to sharp external shocks. To put it metaphorically, the system works for the ebb and flow of business as usual, and has survived some floods, but it struggles in a tsunami like the sovereign debt crisis that began in late 2009.

Since 2012, Germany's European crisis management appears to have em-barked on a course of self-correction. Berlin's policymakers seem to be rec-ognizing that their single-minded advocacy of fast-paced fiscal consolida-tion in Europe's crisis zones has been one-sided—and incomplete—fueled by growing evidence of social, economic, and political instability in Europe's most troubled member states, which has drawn a new north-south demar-cation line through the Union.[20] After a phase of inter-governmentalism (Merkel's "Union method"), Berlin appears to be rediscovering the value of integration, moving toward "a fiscal union with stronger integration and control of national policies, but also democratic legitimacy on the EU level— but all of this under German stability terms."[21] There is also a growing open- ness toward correcting imbalances by promoting more domestic demand, for example through investment in German domestic infrastructure, or a more permissive wage policy.[22]

Yet to preserve its leverage in Europe in the future Germany will have to work much harder at persuading other member states to accept its poli- cy proposals and at brokering compromises across intra-European divides. There can be no move forward in the EU without a functioning Franco- German partnership. However, France seems to be falling politically and economically on the other side of the north-south divide, so Germany will have to build a rapport with the group of pro-growth southerners, while preventing breakouts from fiscal discipline. But it is no longer possible for a Berlin-Paris axis to direct the future of Europe. Berlin will have to con- vince the smaller members of the euro area, as well as non-euro countries like the United Kingdom and Poland, which have mixed feelings about integration and growth policies but are nonetheless deeply concerned about growing political and security problems in Europe's southern and eastern neighborhoods.

The European project remains very much in flux and at risk, and so, there- fore, does Germany's Europe policy as well as its power in Europe, not to mention its overall power. As long as Europe is threatened by crisis, it will continue to engage a very large share of Germany's attention. But the fact that Germany is obviously willing to do whatever it takes to preserve the Eurozone, and the European Union itself, is proof that it sees European integration as its strategic destiny.

Germany and Its Strategic Relationships

Before 1989, Germany's principal strategic relationships—those with France and the United States—were either firmly anchored in a larger collective framework encompassing a number of other like-minded Western democra- cies (the EU, NATO) or, like the bond with Israel, rooted in an immutable commitment to responsibility.[23] The Soviet Union was a looming presence on the Continent, a threat-in-waiting, but not a partner except in the most technical sense of the term, and China was a faraway country with which Germany traded.

However, Germany's global operating environment has seen significant shifts since 1989. The fall of the Wall and the end of the USSR, the uncertain transition of the Western postwar order and its multilateral institutions, the rise of non-Western powers, and the new worldwide linkages brought about by the forces of globalization have seen Germany suddenly caught up in an uneasy balancing act between its traditional attachments, on the one hand, and the allure of trade with emerging non-Western powers, some of whom can provide high growth rates, above-average returns on investment, and privileged access to scarce resources, on the other. This tension between old and new interests, which has caused some speculation that Germany is recasting itself as a "geo-economic power" at the expense of its alliances, is amplified by the fact that Germany, too, has begun to think of itself as an emerging major power.[24] But, as has been noted earlier, the tension itself is unresolvable; the central question is how to bring it into a constructive equilibrium.

Perhaps the most startling aspect of Germany's three principal strategic partnerships today, with the United States, Russia, and China, is the fact that its bond with the only democracy of the three should be as troubled as it currently is.[25]

Germany's relationship with the United States has undergone a long evolution since the days of cozy (and often resentful) co-dependence in the Cold War and the bitter recriminations of the post 9/11 and Iraq War eras. President Obama and Chancellor Merkel are both far removed temperamentally from the hegemonic hubris (in the United States) and the soft power delusions (in Europe) of an earlier decade.[26] In one important sense, the contrast between the two leaders could not be more marked: Merkel is visibly skeptical of Obama's predilection for grand strategic visions and soaring rhetoric. But they appear to share a matter-of-fact understanding that much of modern strategy, regardless of how national goals are articulated, is in practice about managing the interdependence of very dissimilar powers. They have also established a friendly personal rapport. The two have recalibrated the bond between Washington and Berlin as a transactional relationship, a pragmatic mutual maximization of interest by two key Western democracies with a broad set of shared values.[27]

There have been harsh disagreements between Berlin and Washington on, above all, intervention in Libya, how to react to war in Syria, drone warfare, and global trade imbalances. Yet U.S. and German leaders also appear to see a great deal of consensus on significant issues: the Afghan drawdown, negotiations with Iran, and reinforcement of the relationship through the

Transatlantic Trade and Investment Partnership (TTIP), the latter made urgent by the global financial crisis, which exposed for the first time how deeply interdependent the transatlantic economic space has become. From the viewpoint of Berlin, the close and deep working relationship with America may no longer be existential in the way it was during the Cold War, but it remains essential for both sides.

The Ukraine conflict has introduced a new set of tensions into the relationship, one rife with historical ironies. The crisis is playing out in a geostrategic theater that American and German realists alike had been willing to acknowledge tacitly as a legitimate Russian sphere of (co-) influence—a calculus upended in late January 2014 by Ukraine's civil society asserting its European aspirations, pushing Washington to do a double take on its "pivot to Asia" and to question its "Russia reset." It is compelling Berlin to acknowledge that its Europe strategy and its eastern neighborhood policy were passive and lacked critical dimensions: those of geopolitics, transformation, civil society, and security. The events in Ukraine are forcing Merkel and Obama to return to a paradigm of security cooperation and territorial defense in Europe in an overall context of systemic competition with Russia—yet not with the pre-1989 global superpower, but a fundamentally weak power whose leadership appears to have turned its back on the modernization pact with the West.[28]

U.S.-German disagreements on how to handle Ukraine have been substantial, most notably on sanctions against Russia and on reassurance for Eastern European members of NATO, but they are neither fundamental nor exclusive to the relationship between Washington and Berlin. However, the bilateral bond and the trust it is based on are being gravely endangered by a series of revelations about U.S. National Security Agency (NSA) spying on German leaders and ordinary citizens. The anger this has produced, shared by elites and the general public across political camps, is capable of poisoning relations in many fields where there is ample overlap between U.S. and German interests as well as an urgent need for cooperation, such as the TTIP negotiations.[29] The German government's decision in July 2014 to eject the CIA's Berlin station chief and to begin "360-degree" domestic surveillance (including allies) offered a taste of what might lie ahead.

Meanwhile, no aspect of Germany's foreign policy is watched as closely and nervously by its neighbors and allies as its relationship with Russia, and with good reason. Russia only ranks in eleventh place on the list of Germany's bilateral trading partners, but it supplies a third of its oil and gas and, according to German business representatives, accounts for more than 200,000 German jobs in key industries.[30] Germany, for its part, is Russia's seventh-largest trade partner. The historical ties between the two countries are a dark tangle of reciprocal attraction, affinity, complicity, exploitation, and victimization, particularly in the twentieth century, with often terrible consequences for the lands (termed the "Bloodlands" by American historian Timothy Snyder) between them.

For nearly two decades after 1989, Berlin policymakers were convinced that Germany could not just profit handsomely from this relationship, but could also transform and tame it via a kind of *Ostpolitik* 2.0, called *Annäherung durch Verflechtung* by its proponents, or rapprochement through interdependence.[31] Germany fostered exchanges on culture, the rule of law, and regional issues, all in the hope that this might slowly reel Russia into the fold of a rule-based European order and turn it into a stakeholder in the global order, thereby leveraging Berlin's power in Europe as well as constituting the ultimate triumph of the new German soft power. In many ways, this was a projection onto Russia of the transformation Germany had undergone at the hands of the United States a half-century earlier.

Conversely, Germany was clearly Moscow's strategic prize in Europe: a source of luxury goods and industrial knowledge, but also a transmission belt for the modernization of the Russian economy and state, as well as a bridgehead and power maximizer in Europe and a potential neutralizer of American influence on the Continent.[32] The new Eastern European member states of the EU and NATO, meanwhile, were treated by Berlin with friendly condescension at best, and brushed off as irritants at worst.

This state of mutually delusional allure became history with the events of 2014 in Ukraine. It was the Russo-Georgian war of 2008, however, that had marked the beginning of the end for Germany's optimism with regard to Russia. From then onward, German officials looked with increasing skepticism on the prospects of cooperation with Russia—an assessment based not only on the personalities of its leaders, but also on the country's decaying infrastructure, its treatment of civil society activists and journalists, and, finally, its corruption, bad governance, and inability to wean itself off dependence on fossil fuel income. Still, it was generally believed that the regime's hold on power was stable and that this would enable a pragmatic and selective cooperation, including in the EU's eastern neighborhood.

That assumption was overturned by the Euromaidan protests in Ukraine, Moscow's coercion of Kiev to abandon the association agreement with the

EU, and the annexation of Crimea by Russia. German policy on Eastern Europe and Russia has since shifted significantly (if not always consistently or coherently, and despite a preference for negotiations and a dislike for sanctions or military options that appear to be hardwired into Germany's DNA). Berlin's posture now rests on three principles: political reassurance for eastern EU members, support for Ukraine's transition, and condemnation of Russia's actions. Notably, the mood in the center-left Social Democratic Party (SPD) and the business community—both traditionally friendly to Russia—has become far more critical of Moscow.[33]

Moreover, many observers in Berlin recognize that the Ukraine conflict, regardless of its outcome, is likely to be a tipping point—not just for Ukraine, but for the entire eastern neighborhood of Europe, and very possibly for Russia as well. Worse yet, Russian propaganda, influence peddling (including through the funding of right-wing extremist parties such as France's Front National), and bullying appear to be directed *at the European project itself,* touching an existential German strategic interest. But that would mean Germany and Europe are only at the beginning of what could become a generational challenge—one that could involve significant and enduring instability, and even conflict, in Europe. Given the vulnerability of many EU member states to Russian pressure, that is a daunting prospect.[34] Under the circumstances, the real risk is not so much misguided hope or an overly conciliatory approach in Berlin—but a paralysis and political fragmentation of Europe that Germany might be powerless to prevent.

Germany's third key strategic relationship, with China, is far less troubled. Beijing was Germany's second-largest export market in 2013 (after the EU and ahead of the United States). If Germany cherishes one "geo-economic" partnership above all others, it is this one, and with good reason, because China is its largest power source and multiplier after the EU.[35] As Russia's hold on Germany decreases, China's is growing. Judging from the assiduousness with which Beijing is courting Germany, its main partner in Europe, the interest is mutual.[36]

Nonetheless, the German-Chinese relationship is full of ambivalence. Its value as a trading partner notwithstanding, Germany's business community has had some sobering brushes with reality in China: with bureaucracy, corruption, and unfair competition, but also with a ruthless worldwide pursuit of industrial secrets, scarce resources, and strategic investment opportunities. German policymakers, meanwhile, see China as the ultimate potential *Gestaltungsmacht,* the one rising power in the world capable of challenging the primacy of the United States and reshaping the international order based on its sheer size, growth, and determination.

Yet China is also a shape-shifting power—presenting itself as a confident and tough authoritarian alternative to the Western model on some days and as a struggling and hesitant emerging power on others.[37] Germany's China-watchers are conscious of the tensions and internal risks accompanying China's self-transformation. The more farsighted policymakers in Berlin do know that they will have to consider the potential implications of China's aggressive stance in its neighborhood for the stability of the region—and its capacity to act as a spoiler for Germany's global interests. But the consideration that still trumps all others is that China is the largest business opportunity for Germany on the planet. Few in Berlin appear to share the American perception of China as a security threat—or, at least, not for Germany.[38]

As a result, Germany's China strategy has been selective and somewhat shortsighted. It has emphasized rule of law and governance issues, and Merkel, unlike her Social Democrat predecessor Gerhard Schröder, has met with the Dalai Lama despite strong objections from Beijing.[39] But Germany avoids taking a stand on regional security issues, and it has preferred to manage its relationship with China bilaterally, rather than in an EU framework, making it easier for Beijing to split the EU.[40] As one dispassionate observer noted recently, "China's leaders mostly take a utilitarian approach to their relationship with Germany," which suggests that Germany ought to think hard about how its current privileged role in the relationship might suffer under adverse economic conditions, or if China's authoritarian and aggressive tendencies become more pronounced.[41]

Germany and Security Policy

Nowhere is modern Germany's power paradox—full sovereignty, but increasingly limited autonomy—as markedly apparent as in the arena of security policy. It bears pointing out, however, that few aspects of the country's transition from limited to full sovereignty were as demanding as the transformation of its military. Alone among Western Cold War armed forces, the Bundeswehr was configured for one main mission, the defense of 1,700 kilometers of intra-German border for a maximum of three weeks until the onset of nuclear warfare, a chilling scenario that probably contributed at least as much to German pacifism as the reluctant and painful admission of the country's horrific guilt in the Holocaust and World War II. In 1990, the Kohl government had to set in motion not one, but two costly and politically sensitive military transformation processes: the dissolution of the GDR's (East Germany's) Nationale Volksarmee and the downsizing and redesign of the Bundeswehr.

Germany is the only major Western power which does not publish a national security strategy at regular intervals, an idiosyncrasy which is increasingly questioned by its own strategic community, but which appears to be firmly entrenched in the country's constitutional culture.[42] Still, its current defense documents (the 2006 White Book and the Defense Policy Guidelines of 2011) lay out a strategic analysis that is in line with its Western peers—a view largely shared by Germany's foreign and security policy elites (with the exception of those elements of the political spectrum which have found a home in the Left Party).[43] Why, then, do Germany's allies and partners have the persistent impression that it is unwilling to take on security responsibilities concomitant with its power? And why does Germany insist that this depiction is unfair?

Part of the explanation lies in the fact that there are two competing narratives of German security policy since 1990. Proponents of the "see how far we've come" version, like Patrick Keller, can point to the streamlining of Germany's bloated armed forces, to planned defense budget increases, to the abolition of conscription, to the end of the prohibition on women serving in the armed forces, to a landmark constitutional court decision in 1994 permitting "out-of-area" missions, to twenty years of operational experience in the Balkans as well as Africa and Afghanistan, and, most recently, to the coalition against the Islamic State (ISIL).[44] A former German defense minister is now heading a commission which is reviewing how Germany's parliamentary deployment authorization processes can be made more flexible.[45] And, in March 2015, the German defense ministry began planning a new white book, to be published in 2016.[46]

But the alternative account ("too little, too late") has much evidence to support it, too. Germany's eagerness to withdraw from Afghanistan, its reluctance to follow France's lead in sending stabilizing missions to Africa, its abstention on intervention in Libya, a long series of defense budget cuts, a small number of deployable forces and usable capabilities, and a general habit of hedging commitments with restrictions and caveats are all examples. Germany has failed to comply with NATO's 2 percent benchmark for defense expenditures relative to GDP, and it has hung back on providing military reassurance to Eastern European NATO members in the context of the Ukraine crisis.

One key cause for Berlin's dwindling capabilities has nothing to do with political will: they are the result of the inexorably rising costs of technology, which is making full-spectrum forces unsustainable, even for major powers. Berlin has proposed that Europe's large powers (including Germany) should act as "framework nations" in NATO, sharing their essential capabilities, and allowing smaller states to specialize; and German experts have made proposals to prevent European capabilities from losing critical mass.[47] Germany has also tried to keep down unit costs by promoting exports for its arms industry, but the fact remains that the European defense market is oversaturated and defense budgets continue to shrink. In the end, a Europe that can no longer rely on an unconditional American security guarantee faces a stark choice: disarm or Europeanize.

Still, German political culture remains uniquely reluctant to deploy hard power.[48] It emphasizes historical and personal responsibility, normative framing, and constitutional safeguards—a vital moral from its bloody past. But that same lesson has also been used to sidestep responsibility, or at least to push the threshold for action so high that it becomes nearly unreachable. Generations of German policymakers have framed decisions to use military force as permissible only if required of the nation by compelling moral, legal, or alliance imperatives—and have thereby locked themselves into a deterministic trap with a very rigid trigger. (In this model, the use of force in Bosnia, Kosovo, and Afghanistan was legitimate, because unavoidable, whereas Iraq and Libya were illegitimate wars of choice.) It helped that the enlargement of NATO and the EU surrounded Germany with friendly nations, producing a decade-long blissful security illusion and pushing out the problems of the periphery to its neighbors.

German policymakers are now finding it difficult to argue why contributing a notional quantity of soldiers to a small stabilizing mission in Central Africa (or failing to do so) has an impact on their country's interests or national security. Even more worryingly, they are also encountering resistance against the concept that in the context of the Ukraine crisis, effective military capabilities are key elements of reassurance, solidarity (for NATO allies), and deterrence (against Russia). But if they deplore the public's false sense of security, they have themselves to blame as well.

Challenges Ahead

Germany's reactions to the crises on Europe's eastern and southern peripheries suggest that its leaders are indeed going through what could be called a strategic moment. Berlin is taking the lead in the management of the Eurozone sovereign debt crisis, as well as in the standoff with Russia over Ukraine. German officials are also reviewing the country's foreign and security policy machinery in order to make it more purposeful: to allow the government to act, rather than to react, and to allow it to shape its surroundings, rather than be shaped by them. Still, policymakers face formidable challenges: deepening European integration in order to make the EU more resilient against the next crisis, while bridging a deep north-south divide, and working with the United States to defuse a looming crisis with Russia over the future of Europe's eastern neighborhood. They will have to explain more forcefully to a reluctant public that Germans stand before a fundamental choice: do they want to live in a globalized, liberal, and open Germany that engages with the world at a level of responsibility commensurate with its strength—or in a Greater Switzerland, furled up into itself, shoring up its prosperity and social cohesion against the challenges of the outside world and navigating it only to the extent necessary to replenish its resources?[49]

More simply, they will have to make the case that responsibility is the price for power and that the price for irresponsibility is the loss of power.

CHAPTER 4

INDIA

Modernization in a
Safe Neighborhood

SRINATH RAGHAVAN

I NDIA'S principal strategic ambition can be stated quite suc-
cinctly: to ensure a stable and conducive external environment
that will enable its internal economic and social transformation and in turn allow India to play a larger international role. This seemingly
straightforward objective, however, is driven and shaped by several factors:
domestic and economic, strategic and ideational, regional and global. And it
is subject to competing pulls and pressures on the assessment of priorities,
balancing of trade-offs, and acquisition of capabilities. Not surprisingly, the
question of who, if anyone, makes Indian strategy remains an intriguing and
contested one. It is equally unsurprising that the answer that has acquired
most resonance, especially in academic discussions, is that India lacks a "strategic culture"—that it is incapable of linking ends, ways, and means.[1] Contrary to these claims, this chapter argues that India has in practice identified
and pursued its key strategic aims with a reasonable degree of clarity.[2] This is
not to suggest that India has always adopted a *consistent* or a *coherent* strategy.
But in a democratic political system consistency and coherence are not necessarily the most important features in the making of strategy.[3]

The chapter focuses on two broad but interlinked aspects of India's strategy in the recent past. The first is the quest for a secure periphery, including
India's immediate and extended neighborhoods. The second is the attempt
to ensure an enabling global context for the pursuit of India's internal objectives as well as its desire to play a role in the international system commensurate with its growing economic and strategic weight. The chapter suggests

that in its external engagements India remains a regionally focused power— although its definition of what constitutes its region has significantly expanded—and that it aims at an incremental expansion of its larger international and global role and aspirations. In unpacking each of these aspects of the Indian strategy, I try to uncover the various material, security, and ideational drivers that underlie this emerging strategy. The sketch of strategy provided here inevitably leaves out large swathes of issues that keep Indian policymakers busy on a daily basis. But hopefully this simplified picture captures more precisely their core concerns and preoccupations.

India's engagement with the world did not begin with independence in 1947. Yet the emergence of independent India did mark an important moment of rupture from the past. The new Indian state set for itself—to a far greater extent than any predecessor—the task of transforming a society that was rife with gross inequalities and multiple cleavages and to improve dramatically the life chances of its inhabitants. What's more, these were undertaken against the backdrop of the introduction of democracy.[4] The scope and scale of this effort can be gauged from the fact that India attempted four large transformations: economic transformation of a large, poor, and predominantly agrarian economy; social transformation of a deeply hierarchic and tradition-bound society; democratic transformation of an inegalitarian polity; and the national transformation of an incredibly diverse people with a bewildering range of religions, ethnicities, and languages. More strikingly, these large transformations were undertaken simultaneously. In this respect, India was different from Western states wherein these transitions were staggered over time. It is in this context that India's external ambitions came to be yoked to its internal ones.

Over six decades, internal economic and social transformation continues to be the core objective of the Indian state. In current parlance, this is often expressed as the ambition to maintain high annual GDP growth rates of 8 percent and more, which will not only expand the overall size of the economy and opportunities for citizens but also enhance the state's ability to provide for those least able to benefit from economic growth. India's external strategic aims are fundamentally geared toward securing these internal objectives, although they are inflected by numerous other considerations.

Before we delve into the details of India's strategy, it may be useful to understand just why India's external ambitions are so intimately intertwined with its domestic aspirations. In its quest for internal transformation, the Indian state has, in the past six decades, experimented with at least three developmental models. The first, which lasted from the early 1950s to the mid-1960s, attempted a fairly typical set of import-substituting industrialization policies in a mixed economy and resulted in average GDP growth rates of around 4 percent. In the next phase, from the late 1960s to the late 1970s, there was a lurch to the left with strong state controls on private enterprise and a resulting slump in GDP growth rates to an average of 3 percent. And from the early 1980s onward there was a shift toward pro-business and pro-market policies, and a consequent rise to 6 percent GDP growth rates.[5]

Until the early 1990s, though, external trade formed a minor component of the Indian economy. External investment was mainly channeled through foreign aid programs. This changed dramatically in the wake of economic reforms and liberalization from 1991 onward. India's embrace of globalization—in trade, investment, and, to a lesser extent, finance—enabled it to achieve growth rates averaging 8 percent beginning in 2004 and to weather the global financial crisis of 2008. Throughout this period, India pulled unprecedented numbers of its population out of poverty—although the scale of the challenge remains daunting.[6] Since 2011, though, there has been a sharp downward turn in the growth of India's economy.

The experience of two decades of pro-globalization economic reforms and growth—set against the more modest longer-term performance as well as the disappointing recent downturn—has created a strong consensus in India on the need to get back to a higher growth trajectory. The challenge is not mainly of crafting the right economic policies, but of dealing with a range of political interests that have created a system of governmental subsidies that actually benefit relatively well-off groups. Perhaps the best indicator of this widespread desire for economic growth and reforms is the outcome of the general elections of May 2014. On this occasion, a party that promised strong leadership with a focus on growth was voted into office with a clear majority—an outcome that marked a sharp departure from the coalition governments of the past two decades.

Like its predecessor, the new government under Prime Minister Narendra Modi confronts a series of challenges and opportunities. With a young and growing workforce, India will achieve a "demographic dividend," provided it creates the requisite employment opportunities and revamps its education and skill-development systems. If it fails, the demographic dividend could well turn into a demographic disaster with serious consequences for India's stability. Further, India has the market scale, natural endowments, and entrepreneurial drive that could make it an economic powerhouse. But this is contingent on continuing structural reforms, deepening its links with the global economy, expanding its industrial base, increasing exports, and attracting investment. Finally, while aiming for convergence with more advanced economies, India cannot afford to replicate its patterns of resource-intensive growth and will have to adopt a more sustainable growth strategy. Mr. Modi's foreign policy has been explicitly geared toward these large economic ambitions. The centerpiece of his economic policy has been the "Make in India" program, which aims to turn India into a manufacturing powerhouse. The success of this effort is dependent both on drawing foreign direct investment in infrastructure and industry and on continued access to foreign markets for Indian goods and services. At the same time, the government has laid ambitious plans for ramping up India's capacity for generating renewable energy—another area where external collaboration is crucial. Under Mr. Modi, therefore, India's external strategy remains geared toward enabling its internal transformation. If anything, the government is pursuing these objectives with unprecedented vigor.

Grappling with Pakistan

Flowing from this is the first major strategic objective: ensuring a stable and peaceful periphery. This in turn is usually divided by Indian strategists into the country's immediate and extended neighborhoods.[7] "South Asia and the Indian Ocean region are our home and immediate neighborhood," noted India's national security advisor (NSA). "We have a stake in the peace, stability and prosperity of our neighbours, whether across the waters or on our land borders."[8] This focus on the immediate neighborhood stems not only from geography but security as well. Indeed, many of India's key security challenges are seen as emanating from its immediate periphery: the threat from Pakistan; instability in Nepal, Bangladesh, and Sri Lanka; and, of course, the rise of China.

From the time of decolonization and independence, Pakistan has posed persistent and, at times, acute challenges to India's security. Over the past decade and a half, India has adopted a two-pronged approach in dealing with Pakistan. New Delhi has tried simultaneously to work toward achieving a degree of normality in bilateral ties and to tackle present and potential threats posed by Pakistan. The former mainly entails diplomacy, political dialogue, and negotiations, while the latter relies on military strategy coupled with international diplomacy.

Two factors complicate the crafting of India's strategy toward Pakistan. First, the nature and scale of threats emanating from Pakistan reflect the latter's weaknesses, as well as its strengths. It is not clear, for instance, that the Pakistani state would be capable of stanching terrorist attacks against India even if it resolved to do so. Second, the structure of the Pakistani state, with its multiple centers of authority and influence—military, intelligence, bureaucracy, political parties—makes it difficult to deal with Pakistan, both diplomatically and strategically. One of the central conceptual dilemmas of Indian policymakers is whether to treat Pakistan as a unitary strategic entity or as a segmented one. In practice, the first assumption is easier to conceptualize and to sell within the government and beyond. The second may seem more nuanced, but is liable to be criticized as giving a free pass to Pakistan, particularly on the issue of terrorism.

New Delhi tends to veer between the twin extremes of full-fledged engagement and near-total disengagement. The first approach rests on the premise that in order to achieve a stable relationship with Pakistan, it is important that New Delhi agrees to talk with Pakistan not only on issues of concern to India, such as terrorism, but also on issues like Kashmir that Pakistan treats as its "core" concerns. An additional premise is that a "comprehensive dialogue," which brings into the fold second-order problems such as the disputes over the Siachen Glacier and river waters, will enable both sides to build confidence by tackling the "low-hanging fruit" and so prepare them to resolve the more thorny problems. The second approach is based on the assumption that India should offer dialogue only if Pakistan behaves well and cooperatively. Diplomacy, in other words, is not to be used as a normal tool of engagement, but as a reward to shape Pakistan's attitude toward India.

India's adoption of either of these strategies is contingent, among other things, on the nature of its political leadership, the structures of decision-making, and the state of domestic politics. Comprehensive engagement has usually been driven by impetus from the highest sources of policymaking. Two recent prime ministers, Atal Behari Vajpayee and Manmohan Singh, for instance, have perceived a personal interest in achieving important breakthroughs with Pakistan—not least because of concern about their legacies. The fact that they managed to continue diplomatic engagement with Pakistan, if through back channels, despite major attacks on Indian soil by Pakistani terrorist outfits is testimony to the importance of individual agency in shaping Indian strategy.

Foreign policy and strategy have always been the preserve of the prime minister. And over the past decade and a half, changes in the structures of decision-making have led to even greater concentration of power in the prime minister's office. In principle, the Cabinet Committee on Security is the key decision-making body on strategic issues. Yet, in practice, it is the prime minister's office with inputs from key ministries such as external affairs and defense that makes the call on all major strategic decisions. The prime minister, in turn, is directly assisted by his national security advisor who ensures coordination among various ministries and agencies of the government on security affairs. To be sure, the entrenchment of this system has reduced the salience of the ministries and agencies in policy formulation. At the same time, it has enabled the prime minister to stamp his own authority on strategic issues. These institutional structures have been important in allowing the personal predilections of past prime ministers to shape policy toward Pakistan.

Prime Minister Modi, too, has indicated a willingness to reach out to Pakistan in his initial months in office. Unlike his predecessors, he has the political mandate to shape his policies untrammeled by coalition partners. That said, even resolute prime ministers have to work in the context of a pluralistic political system. While foreign policy issues may have low electoral salience, the crafting and execution of policies are invariably influenced by political considerations and assessments of public opinion.[9] Add to this the fact that foreign policy has ceased to be a nonpartisan matter in Indian politics—the opposition parties tend to oppose policies that they themselves pursued while in office—establishing a political context that strongly shapes the making of strategy. After getting off to a good start with his Pakistani counterpart, Mr. Modi felt politically compelled to inject various conditions for continued engagement with Pakistan. It remains to be seen to what extent he will be able to surmount the political constraints faced by his predecessors.

No external issue has as much resonance in India as the relationship with Pakistan. This is as much due to deep-seated drivers such as historical memory and identity as to more immediate issues such as Pakistan's sponsorship of terrorism against India. The latter, in particular, has immensely complicated the pursuit of comprehensive engagement with Pakistan. Terrorist attacks render the government vulnerable to charges of weakness and appeasement. A plethora of private media institutions, especially 24/7 news networks, increases the political pressure on the government. It also strengthens the voice of those parts of the strategic establishment—especially intelligence agencies and the military—which tend to take a pessimistic view of Pakistan. In consequence, every major terrorist strike leads to a swing from diplomatic engagement to disengagement. The latter, however, proves unsustainable for anything beyond the short term and the strategic pendulum swings back toward engagement—so long as the top leadership remains wedded to the hope of a breakthrough in ties with Pakistan.

Militarily, India's strategy toward Pakistan has been shot through with dilemmas, too. At one level, Indian military strategy aims to maintain a numerical and technological superiority in the conventional realm. At another level, it has sought to acquire and operationalize a credible and survivable nuclear deterrent. In both of these, India has largely succeeded. But it is on the third, subconventional level that India has struggled to evolve a consistent strategy. For it is the possession of nuclear weapons that has emboldened Pakistan to launch subconventional, especially terrorist, attacks on India.[10]

Through the 1990s, India focused its strategic efforts on counterinsurgency and counterterrorism inside Kashmir. As the insurgency reached a boiling point, particularly with the increased involvement of Pakistani outfits, the Indians periodically toyed with the idea of striking the insurgent bases across the line of control in Pakistan-held Kashmir. Indeed, the desire to break out of the strategic cul-de-sac was one of the factors contributing to India's decision to go overtly nuclear in 1998. The Indians believed that the tests would clarify to Pakistan that its nuclear capability could no longer serve as a shield behind which it could wage a campaign of terrorism in Kashmir. India's nuclear arsenal would deter Pakistan from threatening the use of nuclear weapons, and in so doing it would enable India to bring to bear its conventional superiority in dealing with the subconventional threat. Indian strategists hoped that the availability and exercise of such options would convince Pakistan to desist from fostering terrorism in India.[11]

The Kargil conflict of 1999 and the crisis of 2001–2002 called into question these assumptions. On both occasions, Indian political leaders sought to exercise military options that minimized the risk of major escalation.[12] The upshot of these crises was to underline the limitations of a strategy based on the threat of punishment and to convince the Indian government to fall back on a political approach to handling the problem of Pakistan-abetted terrorism. The Indian military, however, began contemplating contingency options to impose costs on Pakistan in the event of another major terrorist attack. The military believed that it had to cut down the long mobilization period for its strike corps (up to three weeks) and develop capabilities to inflict damage on Pakistan without giving the latter the time to mobilize its own defensive formations. This strategy, dubbed by some as "Cold Start," principally aimed to beef up India's defensive formations with limited offensive capabilities for undertaking shallow thrusts into Pakistani territory.[13] But this begged the question of how India could control escalation by way of tit-for-tat responses from Pakistan.

Indeed, when a major terrorist attack occurred in Mumbai in November 2008, the Indian response was different from those of the past. Despite vocal and voluble calls from pundits and former officials, the government neither embarked on preparations for "limited military action" nor carried out "surgical strikes" on the terrorist infrastructure in Pakistan. Although options for punishment were considered, the government came to an assessment that the potential risks outweighed any benefits that might follow. The prime minister was apparently convinced that punitive strikes would only worsen the situation vis-à-vis Pakistan and that the government should not be rushed into action by domestic political pressures.

Realizing the inherent limits to India's ability to pursue a punishment-based strategy, New Delhi focused on deterrence by denial as the best alternative. The government initiated a series of steps to beef up India's internal security and intelligence systems to thwart and blunt efforts by terrorists. Indian officials also sought to stigmatize Pakistan's support for terrorism and bring to bear the pressure of the international community's disapproval of its actions. In conceptual terms, this can be understood as deterrence based on norms rather than interests.[14]

The present government continues to grapple with these challenges. Several key members, including the defense minister, have claimed that India will respond strongly to any provocation by Pakistan. The NSA is on the record as saying that the government's stance toward Pakistan has shifted from a defensive posture to a defensive-offensive posture. The latter, he has explained, means that India will, if necessary, take the fight to Pakistan. As the NSA colorfully puts it, "You can do one Mumbai and you may lose Balochistan."[15]

The rhetoric of such pronouncements aside, the strategic assumptions underpinning this stance need to be unpacked. The NSA claims that Pakistan cannot be permitted to use its nuclear shield to protect itself against India's responses. He hopes that nuclear weapons will only come into play if India adopts a purely offensive posture. At one level, this is wishful thinking based on a misapprehension of how escalation occurs during crises. At another level, though, it is clear that the NSA is expressing the government's willingness to use tit-for-tat "unconventional" responses vis-à-vis Pakistan. Not only is the efficacy of such methods deeply dubious, the international opprobrium and reputational costs that they risk are considerable.

It remains difficult to predict how India's strategy vis-à-vis Pakistan will evolve. New Delhi has resumed the dialogue process and has strengthened its strategic capabilities to deter Pakistan. But both these prongs of its strategy remain hostage to events. If another major terrorist attack is traced back to Pakistan, it is unclear if India will revert to the strategy of attempting punishment or whether it will rely on international efforts to shape Pakistan's behavior. Much will depend on whether the prime minister is able to lead, rather than follow, domestic opinion. What does seem certain is that the diplomatic track of engagement will remain hostage to security concerns.

Stabilizing the Neighborhood

Pakistan apart, India's relations with its other smaller neighbors such as Nepal, Bangladesh, and Sri Lanka have also been fraught—though the scale and intensity of these problems are less salient. The principal challenges, from the Indian standpoint, have been threefold. The first is to prevent political instability and violence in these countries from spilling over into India. The second is to ensure that insurgent groups operating in India do not find safe havens in neighboring countries. And the third is to limit the opportunities for neighbors to draw in external powers to balance against India in South Asia. Until the 1990s, India's broad strategy was to intervene—politically as well as militarily—if instability in the neighborhood reached potentially dangerous levels, to dissuade neighbors actively from supporting anti-India activities, and to forestall the involvement of external players in subcontinental affairs. Thus, at various points, India played an important role in political crises in Nepal and Sri Lanka; undertook military intervention in Bangladesh (then East Pakistan), Sri Lanka, and the Maldives; and strove to keep out external powers such as the United States and China.

Over the past two decades, however, India has been more reluctant to demonstrate strategic activism in its immediate periphery and has preferred to play a quieter role behind the scenes. This is partly because of its previous experiences which suggested that overt alignment with any political entity in the neighborhood would limit India's options in the long run and because it is no longer feasible to keep external powers, especially China, out of the subcontinent. But this shift also has occurred because India now has other instruments with which to shape its relationships with immediate neighbors. The key driver of Indian strategy now appears to be economics.

The impressive growth of the Indian economy since the early 1990s has underscored the possibility of using economic integration to ameliorate political and security problems with its neighbors. Addressing a regional summit in 2011, Prime Minister Manmohan Singh said that "complete normalization of trade relations will create huge opportunities for mutually beneficial trade within South Asia."[16] India, he added, had a "special responsibility" to foster regional economic integration owing to "the geography of our region and the size of our economy and market."[17] India's free trade agreements with Sri Lanka and Bhutan and the trade and transit agreement with Nepal have showcased the potential benefits of regional economic integration. Moves are afoot to greatly enhance trade and connectivity with Bangladesh, and even to revive trade with Pakistan. Once the largest recipient of foreign aid, India now has begun giving aid to its neighbors. Afghanistan, Bangladesh, Nepal, and Sri Lanka are beneficiaries of this turn in Indian foreign policy.

This shift in India's approach to its immediate periphery is an important one. New Delhi regards closer economic ties as a way of indirectly addressing problematic relationships. By allowing its neighbors to partake in its economic growth, India apparently hopes to draw the sting from these relationships, secure a modicum of stability, and clear the way for eventual resolution of difficult problems. This seems a more cautious approach than the standard liberal assumption equating free trade and economic integration with peace. Prime Minister Modi has continued with this approach. During his visits to various neighboring countries, he has outlined a vision for shared prosperity in the region. Yet India's ability to persist with this strategy and translate it into tangible outcomes remains moot.

For one thing, the idea that India should accept asymmetric economic burdens is contested by groups within the country: by political parties that do not see why India should go out of its way to help "obdurate" neighbors and by trade lobbies that stand to lose from economic integration. Further, India's neighborhood policy is considerably influenced by the states of India that border other countries. Although India is technically not a federation, states have considerable power devolved to them. This, in turn, enables them to press their views on a range of issues relating to neighboring countries such as illegal migration, sharing of river waters, and oceanic resources. Tamil Nadu and West Bengal, to take but two examples, play an important role in shaping New Delhi's policy toward Sri Lanka and Bangladesh, respectively. At various times, they have blocked, as well as enabled, India's engagement with these countries. Even a strong central government cannot easily set aside their concerns. Finally, India's record of delivery on economic initiatives and projects in neighboring countries has been, at best, uneven, and the contrast with China remains particularly striking.

Deterring, Engaging, and Containing China

The rise of China is the central strategic challenge for India. For the first time since 1947, India has to contend with a great power on its immediate frontiers. The rise of China presents three sets of challenges for India. First, there is the unsettled boundary that has in the past resulted in a war (in 1962) as well as several armed standoffs between the countries. Second, there is China's increasing footprint in India's immediate periphery. And third, there is China's rising profile globally, and especially in Asia. The emerging Indian strategy to deal with various aspects of the challenges posed by China is an amalgam of efforts at internal and external balancing coupled with a deepening economic and diplomatic engagement.

Until 1989, India's strategy toward China was principally aimed at forestalling another attack along the disputed boundary. Toward this end, India gradually built up its military capabilities and entered into a close strategic relationship with the former Soviet Union. On the diplomatic side, New Delhi engaged in desultory negotiations with Beijing on the boundary dispute. Prime Minister Rajiv Gandhi's visit to China in 1989 injected muchneeded fresh thinking into India's strategic assessments of China. Gandhi and Premier Deng Xiaoping agreed that the relationship ought to be expanded beyond the narrow focus on the boundary.[18] Over the subsequent decade, India concluded important agreements, ensuring that the boundary dispute did not result in military standoffs or crises. Bilateral trade, too, began to pick up during this period.

By the early 2000s, India's strategy toward China underwent important shifts. India's steady economic growth paralleled that of China and created the context for a tremendous expansion in trade and investment. Successive Indian governments have seen this as a useful tool in fostering economic interdependence and thereby raising the stakes in a peaceful relationship for China. Today, India-China trade stands at over $70 billion and is expected to increase rapidly in the years ahead. But the trade balance is sharply tilted in favor of China. India has had limited success in securing market access for its information technology (IT), pharmaceuticals, and agricultural products. As both China and India enter a period of slower growth, tensions over trade could increase. But this unprecedented level of interdependence continues to be seen by New Delhi as a force for stability.

Concurrently, India has also sought to strengthen its deterrent capabilities against China. The rapid expansion and modernization of the People's Liberation Army and the impressive development of logistical infrastructure in Tibet have forced India to reconfigure its own strategy. Over the past decade, India has developed and deployed a credible land-based nuclear deterrent against China, and a sea-based deterrent is expected to be deployed soon. At the conventional level, India has had to revise its military strategy and capabilities over the past decade.[19] The level of military infrastructure available to the Chinese in Tibet has forced Indian planners to shelve their old assessments about Chinese offensive capabilities and to rethink their defensive plans. Further, India has sought to improve its own border infrastructure (albeit rather more slowly), especially roads and airfields, and to raise a new army corps for operating in high-altitude areas.

From a longer-term perspective, perhaps the most significant shift has been the importance attached to the maritime dimension of India's strategy. This shift, too, is spurred by India's recognition that a purely continental strategy against China would fail to leverage significant strategic advantages open to India owing to its geographic presence in the Indian Ocean region. Nearly 80 percent of China's trade, including its oil imports, passes through the Indian Ocean, especially via "choke points" like the Malacca Straits.[20] India is well positioned to influence China's interest and strategic calculus in the Indian Ocean region in the event of a crisis along the land frontiers. The development of such capabilities, India hopes, will act as a deterrent against any Chinese attempt to change the status quo along the borders by the use of force. This lesson appears to have been confirmed by the three-week stand-off between Indian and Chinese forces in the Depasang area in April 2013. That said, India does not have the luxury to make a clear choice between a continental and a maritime strategy toward China. Yet, in budgetary terms, there are limits to the pursuit of both strategies. In practice, therefore, politics among the services may play an important role in translating strategic aims into military capabilities.

Alongside security preparations, India has sought to impart momentum to diplomatic negotiations over the disputed boundary. In 2003, both countries agreed to commence political negotiations led by "Special Representatives." Thirteen rounds of these negotiations have been held over the past decade. In the early years, important progress was made in these negotiations. In 2005, the two sides signed an agreement on political parameters and principles for the settlement of the boundary dispute. From the Indian standpoint, a crucial feature of this agreement was the acknowledgment that the interests of "settled populations" would be respected in a final settlement. New Delhi interpreted this to mean that there would be no territorial exchanges in populated areas. This understanding is crucial for any Indian government to sell an eventual agreement in its domestic political marketplace. China subsequently indicated that it did not agree with the Indian reading of this clause. During Mr. Modi's visit to China in May 2015, the two sides agreed that the settlement of the boundary dispute had to be accorded priority. Whether China will agree to return to principles agreed upon in 2005 remains to be seen. In any event, domestic politics will play a crucial role in any diplomatic attempt by New Delhi to settle this most thorny bilateral problem with China.

India's strategy toward China also has a regional dimension. Indeed, the competitive dimensions of the India-China relationship have been most evident along the South Asian periphery of India. The strengthening—in some cases, the cementing—of ties between India's neighbors and China is hardly surprising. Given their structural asymmetry vis-à-vis India, most of these countries have looked for countervailing influences. At different points in the last six decades, Pakistan, Sri Lanka, Nepal, and Bangladesh have sought and obtained varying degrees of assistance from external powers. The current Chinese footprint in South Asia is largely economic and infrastructural (particularly the construction of ports), though there are potential—in some cases, immediate—security implications as well. In the past, India has invested inordinate levels of diplomatic effort to stanch the flow of any external assistance that could impinge upon its security. New Delhi now realizes that it is operating in a competitive marketplace: instead of remonstrating about China's presence, it should focus on rejuvenating its ties with neighbors and increasing its influence in South Asia. This has been a key consideration in India's attempts—discussed earlier—to deepen regional trade and connectivity.

The most novel dimension of India's strategy is its attempt to balance against a China that is now a great Asian power—and potentially a global power as well. Here, the external dimension of India's strategy has become rather important. The "Look East" policy initiated by New Delhi in the mid-1990s has acquired momentum over the last five years.[21] China's increased assertiveness in Asia has led India to improve its strategic ties with a range of countries, including Vietnam, Singapore, South Korea, and Japan. In the past year, Mr. Modi has made a determined effort to enhance India's strategic ties with these countries, especially Japan and Vietnam. The development of such countervailing coalitions will, New Delhi hopes, convince China that it is not in a position to dominate the security architecture of East Asia.

The relationship with Japan has acquired considerable salience in recent years. Prime Minister Shinzo Abe has been a champion of strategic ties with India since his first tenure in office in 2006–2007. He is currently pursuing a clear strategy for jump-starting Japan's economy and beefing up its military muscle. Economic ties with India have assumed greater importance in this context. The Japanese are eager to diversify their foreign investments in countries other than China. India is already the largest recipient of Japanese overseas development aid and is eager to use this opportunity to attract more Japanese investment in infrastructure and industry. Tokyo is also keen to build security relations that will restrain China, not just in the East China Sea but further to the west as well. New Delhi, for its part, has worked to deepen cooperation on security and defense. Indeed, Japan is one of only two countries with whom India has had an annual strategic dialogue at the prime ministerial level. The relationship with Japan is seen as advancing India's economic and strategic interests as well as enlarging its footprint in Asia.

Indian leaders have repeatedly insisted that India stood for "an open, inclusive and transparent architecture of regional cooperation in the Asia-Pacific region."[22] And India has backed the East Asia Summit as the best forum for developing such an architecture in the region.

Yet India has considerable distance to go before it becomes a serious player in East Asia. Its economic ties with the region are just beginning to grow. China's trade with ASEAN, for example, is almost five times that of India's. India is largely unplugged from the integrated supply and production chains that are central to East Asian economies. Similarly, although India does have a relative advantage in the maritime domain, it is far from being a maritime power to reckon with. Ideas about India playing a larger role in the "Indo-Pacific" have to be set against India's capabilities.[23] It is not surprising that Indian policymakers have been circumspect about embracing ideas for a strategic role for India in East Asia.

Securing the Western Periphery

India's extended neighborhood in the west encompasses the region from Afghanistan to the Middle East. The region accounts for over 60 percent of India's crude imports, over $90 billion in trade, and comprises six million Indian expatriate workers who remit more than $35 billion every year. These factors make the Middle East central to India's core interests. In recent years, this region has also been in the throes of various crises and upheavals ranging from the U.S. invasions of Afghanistan and Iraq to the various manifestations of the "Arab Spring." Recent crises in the Middle East brought sharply into focus India's strategic interests in this region.

Afghanistan is the most proximate country in India's extended western neighborhood. India's interests in Afghanistan stem from a variety of factors: its strategic location between Central Asia and South Asia, the threats posed to India's security in the past from developments in Afghanistan, and the need to ensure that Afghanistan is not destabilized by its immediate neighbors, especially Pakistan. Since the overthrow of the Taliban regime in 2001, India has sought to carve out for itself a distinctive space in Afghanistan. The emphasis in Indian policy has been on cultivating strong political ties with Kabul and on reaching out to the people of Afghanistan. The principal—but not the sole—instrument deployed by India in pursuit of these objectives has been economic and developmental assistance. India has emerged as the largest nontraditional donor to Afghanistan and has already extended aid to the tune of $1.6 billion. Much of this aid has gone toward the reconstruction of infrastructure (especially roads and electricity), health, education, and community development projects. Successive opinion polls and surveys have shown that the Indian effort is viewed positively by an overwhelming majority of Afghanis. The former president, Hamid Karzai, remarked more than once that India provides "emotional strategic depth" to the Afghan people.

More recently, India has pledged an addition $500 million for developmental activities. The focus will be on increasing its contribution in the areas of health, education, transportation, agriculture, and small developmental projects. Further, India will also scale up its assistance in building the capacity of the Afghan state at various levels. Equally significant is the decision to embark on a "comprehensive economic partnership." These initiatives, together with New Delhi's willingness to participate in the Turkmenistan-Afghanistan-Pakistan-India (TAPI) pipeline project, underline the new instruments of statecraft being deployed by India.

On the political front, India has focused on building links with the elected government of Afghanistan. After 2001, New Delhi has sought to shed its image as solely a patron of the non-Pashtun groups that had opposed the Taliban (the so-called Northern Alliance). It has not only built close ties with the government of former president Karzai, but has urged the other non-Taliban groups to work with Mr. Karzai and his successor. It is no coincidence that many of India's developmental projects have been undertaken in Pashtun-dominated areas. Indeed, India has systematically sought to refurbish its standing amongst the Pashtuns as well as other ethnic groups in Afghanistan. Similarly, India has sought to steer clear of the Western coalition in Afghanistan and has focused on interacting directly with the ministries in Kabul and in the provinces.

India's relationship with Afghanistan has an explicitly strategic dimension as well. The two countries signed a strategic partnership agreement in 2011 that reaffirms India's commitment to the reconstruction and development of Afghanistan. But it goes beyond the existing relationship and stipulates closer economic and security ties. On the economic front, the agreement aims to facilitate the economic integration of Afghanistan with other South Asian countries. This goal complements New Delhi's efforts in recent years to foster better trade and connectivity in the subcontinent, and so enable neighbors to partake in its economic growth.

The agreement also provides for security cooperation. Afghanistan and India engage in a regular "Strategic Dialogue" led by their national security advisors, providing a systematic framework for consultation and coordination of policies. More importantly, India has agreed "to assist, as mutually determined, in the training, equipping and capacity building programmes for Afghan National Security Forces."[24] Despite this relationship, the new Afghan government under President Ashraf Ghani has sought to downgrade strategic ties with India. Mr. Ghani appears to have placed his bets on improved relations with Pakistan to attain a durable peace agreement with the Taliban. China, too, has assumed a more active role in facilitating talks between Afghanistan, Pakistan, and the Taliban. Whether or not this yields results, India has to ensure that its interests in Afghanistan are protected. Afghanistan may well emerge as a key strategic challenge for Indian foreign policy in the years ahead.

Other flashpoints in the Middle East will make it very difficult to resolve priorities or balance interests. This is already evident in the case of Syria. From the Indian standpoint, the continuing crisis in Syria is problematic for a variety of reasons. Given India's dependence on West Asia for its energy needs and the huge presence of Indian expatriate workers in the region, protracted instability is highly undesirable. More worryingly, the Syrian civil war is fast becoming the focal point for regional rivalry centered on Saudi Arabia and Iran, both of which remain important for Indian interests. Equally problematic is the sharpening of the sectarian Sunni versus Shia divide in the region. Given that India has the third-largest population of Muslims in the world and that there is a sizeable Shia community among Indian Muslims, this worsening sectarianism has domestic security implications. India, therefore, prefers a strategy that will avoid sharp choices between the Arab Persian Gulf states and Iran. New Delhi has so far managed to walk the tightrope successfully, but in the event of a major regional crisis this strategy will be hard to sustain.

Since the late 1970s Indian foreign policy toward Iran has been pragmatic and attuned to the pursuit of its interests in Southwest Asia. Successive Indian governments have straddled the differences between a Shiite Iran and a Pakistan increasingly becoming a haven for Sunni extremists. New Delhi and Tehran also have cooperated in stiffening the resistance to a Taliban regime in Afghanistan. Moreover, Iran remains a key source of energy imports for India. As with Afghanistan, its strategic location also lends it considerable importance, both in terms of India's interests in the Persian Gulf and its efforts to tap into the resources of Central Asia.

A key irritant in India's relationship with Iran has been the latter's nuclear program. New Delhi does not want another nuclear power in its neighborhood. India has voted against Iran in the International Atomic Energy Agency (IAEA) and has urged Tehran to comply with its obligations under the Treaty on the Non-Proliferation of Nuclear Weapons (NPT). The problem is not that a nuclear Iran would pose an existential danger to its Arab neighbors and Israel. The problem is that the acquisition of nuclear weapons might embolden Iran to use its proxies to advance its influence in the region. The fear of escalation to the nuclear level would constrict the options open to Iran's rivals. The resulting instability would undermine India's interests in the Middle East.

Saudi Arabia is now the largest supplier of oil to India, such that India is the fourth-largest importer of Saudi oil—after China, the United States, and Japan. The "Delhi Declaration," signed during the Saudi king's visit in 2006, called for a closer economic engagement and energy partnership. The latter will remain a critical component of the relationship in the years ahead. New

Delhi is also looking to attract Saudi companies and investment in the infrastructure sector. Equally important has been the presence of nearly two million Indians in Saudi Arabia. They constitute the largest community of expatriates in that country and play an important role in its domestic economy.

It is no coincidence that in recent years New Delhi has attempted to infuse a more strategic dimension to its relationship with Riyadh. Saudi Arabia has cooperated with India on counterterrorism and has helped to apprehend and extradite key terrorists wanted by India. The two countries have also begun discussions of defense-related issues. From Riyadh's standpoint, the backdrop to this is the concern generated by Iran's determination to persist with its nuclear enrichment activities. The Saudis fear that a nuclear Iran will overturn the precarious regional strategic balance. Yet they are also unnerved at the prospect of a military strike on Iran by the United States or Israel. Notwithstanding the differences in perception about Iranian goals and capabilities, concerns about Tehran's intentions have provided an opening for India to build its equities with Saudi Arabia.

At the same time, India has refused to go along with U.S.-orchestrated sanctions on Iran. Iran currently accounts for over 11 percent of India's oil imports, amounting to $12 billion a year. Faced with sharp sanctions, Iran has accepted a rupee payment mechanism for 45 percent of its oil exports to India. This agreement, of course, works rather well for New Delhi, providing a major opening for Indian exports. Iran is already the largest importer of rice from India, accounting for half of the 2.2 million tons exported by India last year. New Delhi hopes to use this opportunity to push ahead with exports in higher value sectors. India also aims to upgrade the Chahbahar port and its transportation links with Afghanistan and other Central Asian countries. Chahbahar has been used by India to send food aid to Afghanistan. Investing further in its development will considerably increase India's economic footprint in these parts.

Measuring Global Obligations

India's strategic outlook, as the foregoing discussion shows, has largely remained restricted to its region—though the definition of India's strategic neighborhood has expanded both to the east and west. While India does not harbor pretensions to a global strategic role, it does aim to ensure an enabling global context for its continued internal growth and to play an international role commensurate with its increasing economic and strategic heft.

In these attempts India's relationship with the United States bulks large. Notwithstanding recent hiccups, the United States remains India's most important strategic partner. From India's point of view, a close partnership with the United States is both desirable and indispensable in achieving its ambitious economic and social objectives. The partnership with the United States is further strengthened by shared democratic values—intangible but important in sustaining the image of the United States as a nonthreatening, benign, and friendly great power. The presence of a large Indian diaspora in the United States also serves as a valuable conduit for conveying India's strategic interests to the United States.

China is America's principal competitor, more in economic terms and less, for the time being, in military terms. In this context, India regards its relationship with the United States as a key determinant of its own ability to balance against China. Nevertheless, from New Delhi's perspective there are two competing trends in the evolving U.S. posture toward China. One seeks to reconcile the United States to the inevitability of Chinese ascendancy in the Asian theater and position it as an offshore balancer. The other trend of thinking seeks to contain China as a threat to U.S. dominance, with the Asia-Pacific theater regarded as critical to maintaining U.S. preeminence globally. American policy appears to oscillate between these two ends of the spectrum, currently being closer to the latter. For India, Sino-U.S. collusion is as much a threat as the prospect of their open confrontation. In consequence, New Delhi seems to hold that while the United States could, in certain circumstances, emerge as a formal ally, for the present, Indian interests may be better served by a strong and broad-based partnership with the United States while managing the dynamic mix of competition and interdependence in India-China relations.

Mr. Modi has been exceptionally clear in articulating India's interests and trying to leverage the relationship with the United States and China. Thus, during President Barack Obama's visit, India issued a separate joint statement on security in the Asia-Pacific and Indian Ocean. And on Mr. Modi's trip to China, a separate joint statement was issued on climate change in light of the upcoming conference in Paris. In both cases, a gap between rhetoric and reality may exist. Yet Mr. Modi is clearly attempting to push the envelope and advance India's interests without making binary choices in its engagement with these countries.

Equally important for India is the U.S. leadership of a plethora of international institutions and structures of global governance. India's approach to these institutions is driven by a desire to expand its own position and role in them. India is not a revisionist power: it seeks not to alter the system radically in accordance with a particular strategic vision but to uphold and enhance these institutions. This approach, in turn, is conditioned by the recognition that India has been a prime beneficiary of the open global economic as well as political order that currently prevails. Since India's own interests are affected by the functioning and decisions of these institutions, ranging from the UN Security Council to the World Bank and the International Monetary Fund (IMF), India seeks to play a larger role in agenda-setting and decision-making.

In pursuing this strategy, India faces a fundamental dilemma. Should it lend its weight to global institutions even if it means accepting adverse consequences for itself? This dilemma is particularly acute because unlike the rising powers of the past, India remains a poor country. In aggregate terms, its economic and political weight looks impressive and underpins its claims to playing a larger role in global institutions. But in terms of most per capita economic and social indicators, India remains very far from being a developed, let alone rich, country.[25]

This tension between India's core interests and the expectations of the role that it can play in international institutions is evident in areas such as trade and climate change, where India espouses a multilateral solution, but one that differs significantly from those proffered by the United States and other developed countries. For instance, the issue of public stockholding of food grains has been a major sticking point in recent World Trade Organization (WTO) negotiations. India insists on being given a permanent waiver, which it argues is necessary for its domestic food security. Facing opposition from the United States and other developed countries, the Indian government has refused to give a go-ahead to the Trade Facilitation package—a move that threatens to stall ongoing negotiations. In climate change discussions, India has—despite some twists and turns—clung to the principle of differentiated responsibility. According to this principle, the core issue is not high levels of emissions, but high levels of per capita emissions. Given the historical responsibility of the developed countries, as well as the fact that they continue to score high on this count, India claims they must accept larger obligations and more stringent targets to mitigate the impact of carbon emissions on the climate. By contrast, the advanced industrial countries insist that the bill should be split equally by everyone around the table.

Not surprisingly, India tends at times to be seen as obstructionist in international negotiations. These perceptions create difficulties for India when the United States and its partners move ahead to create other, smaller institutional groupings that reflect their interests better. For instance, U.S. efforts to bypass the WTO and promote the Trans-Pacific Partnership and the Trans-Atlantic Trade and Investment Partnership pose important problems for India, which has benefited immensely from an open global trading order. Similarly, U.S.-led efforts to promote new norms around the use of force, such as the Responsibility to Protect, have undercut India's efforts to balance its interests in sovereignty, as well as human rights.

Handling such trade-offs may well be the most important strategic challenge for India as it engages with international institutions and manages its rise on the global stage. There are two interrelated aspects to these problems. On the one hand, India has a strong record in some areas, such as humanitarian intervention and democracy promotion, and wants to shape normative debates. On the other hand, the Indian government has a thin base of in-house experts to deal with key issues like finance, intellectual property, and climate change. But since there is no dearth of experts outside the government, the task is to create a policy ecosystem wherein the Indian government can tap the best talents to support its international initiatives.

This undertaking is essential not just to protect India's narrow interests on any particular issue, but to evolve gradually over time a set of systematic ideas about global governance. India, like other emerging powers, is often asked what alternative conceptions of global order it brings to the table, implying that if it does not have such ideas, it should simply embrace the existing order and the changes to it proposed by the prevailing powers. These expectations are unfair. No great power has sprung fully formed. It took the United States quite a long time to formulate and embrace multilateral ideas about global order and jettison its isolationist traditions.[26]

For the present, India expends more time and energy on its regional interests, but going forward the engagement with wider international issues and institutions is bound to increase. Managing this transition from being a predominantly regional player to a global actor will be the main testing ground for India's strategy in the decades ahead.

CHAPTER 5

ISRAEL

Strategic Vision Adrift

ARIEL E. LEVITE

HISTORICALLY, Israel's strategic outlook has been mainly shaped by the deep ties of its people to the Land of Zion, the challenging circumstances surrounding its establishment, the continuing struggle to firm up its existence in the midst of a generally hostile environment, and its desire to live up to its self-proclaimed mission of becoming a safe and attractive homeland for the Jewish people. The founding fathers of the state in 1948, first and foremost among them David Ben Gurion, wove all of these elements together to produce a coherent strategy that successfully guided Israel's conduct for its first few decades after independence. All of the factors shaping Israel's strategy remain salient to this day, although they have assumed new meaning and call for novel responses.

Although the founding fathers are long gone, they inscribed Israel's vision of itself and of its environment into the 1948 Declaration of Independence. Though lacking formal legal status, the Declaration of Independence has been recognized by Israel's Supreme Court, as well as in several of the Knesset's Basic Laws, as enjoying a unique stature codifying Israel's founding principles. The Declaration of Independence envisaged Israel as an independent, sovereign, liberal, pluralistic, Jewish, democratic state, providing a homeland to the long-prosecuted Jews around the world but still integrating and treating fairly its non-Jewish inhabitants. It laid out a vision where the establishment of the state reinforced the historical Jewish role as a beacon of inspiration to humanity writ large, while grappling with harsh local realities of hostility and aggression from its regional neighbors. To the latter, it nevertheless extended an olive branch, while also offering to cooperate with the UN to settle the Arab-Israeli dispute. And the Declaration of Independence underscored both the vision of Israel as the nation-state of the Jewish people, its inextricable historical and religious ties to the Land of Israel, and its attachment to universal humanistic values.

The Declaration of Independence marked a phenomenal accomplishment by David Ben Gurion and his colleagues. They managed to articulate core aspirational attributes of the new state by artfully reconciling (in part through constructive ambiguity) some basic tensions that defied consensus even at the time of the state's creation. They anchored the newborn state in the biblical/historical definition of the "Land of Israel" and sought international recognition of its sovereignty over this territory (and Jerusalem as its capital), while refraining from confronting the discrepancy between territory that the state of Israel controlled at its creation and its historical borders. The founders articulated a desire for peaceful relations with Israel's neighbors, notwithstanding the ominous reality of those relations. They defined the bonds between the Jews in the diaspora and their "homeland" in the state of Israel. They artfully reconciled Israel's Jewishness in the religious sense with its Jewishness in a secular sense (using the term "Hebrew" in the Declaration of Independence) to shape its national identity. Finally, the founding fathers asserted a commitment to treat their Arab inhabitants as full-fledged citizens, enjoying equal social and political rights while still declaring Israel's core identity as a Jewish state.[1]

Since its founding, Israel has made remarkable strides in many areas. After millennia of persecution and the Holocaust, the Jews have built a state of their own and turned it into an unqualified success story. They have maintained the sovereignty of the state, defended and consolidated its borders, repeatedly fended off and defeated its adversaries, expanded its territory, established peaceful relations with two of its Arab neighbors, welcomed millions of Jews from abroad, and nurtured a flourishing economy based on commercial enterprise and technological innovation. Ostensibly, the country has enjoyed great strategic successes, and in many areas still does. Yet none of the fundamental tensions bedeviling the state at its inception have been resolved. Sixty-five years after its creation, Israel continues to wrestle with the aspirational goals and attributes put forward in its Declaration of Independence. In fact, many of the tensions and dilemmas—so artfully reconciled at its founding—have grown starker and now challenge the core identity of the state of Israel.

In other words, Israel's many successes in defending its sovereignty, protecting its borders, expanding its territory, attracting immigrants from abroad, and nurturing a dynamic economy have brought to the fore vexing dilemmas about the state's core identity and its destiny, matters that for a long time had been suppressed or marginalized. The people of Israel, certainly its elites, now debate the state's core identity—a Jewish state versus a multicultural one. They argue over the balance between secular and religious norms and institutions. They wrangle over the state's social welfare origins and its increasingly capitalist socioeconomic orientation. Hovering over all these matters are the disputes regarding peacemaking, settlements, and the delineation of Israel's sovereign territory and its democratic character. Naturally, Israel's relationship with the region, world Jewry, and the world writ large are inextricably linked to these debates.

Israeli society is so deeply polarized on these matters that no formal document has ever been composed to lay out Israel's strategy for dealing with them. Nonetheless, it is possible and illuminating to describe the contours of Israel's strategic thinking and to highlight issues and forces shaping the discourse and beleaguering the formation of a new coherent strategy.[2]

Sovereignty

Historically, Israel has wanted to exercise sovereignty over its entire national territory and whenever opportunities arose to improve on its 1948 borders. Israel's post-independence borders, emerging at the end of the 1948 war and subsequent skirmishes, lacked geostrategic, historic, or ethnic credibility. For the most part, the frontiers between Israel and its neighbors were nothing more than cease-fire or armistice lines. Consequently, Israel found itself fighting hard to protect its sovereignty over these borders while yearning for an opportunity to expand them. Israel's neighbors were neither eager to respect Israel's sovereignty nor were they willing to prevent encroachment from their side into Israel's territory. Israel's efforts to redress this situation occurred piecemeal and consumed several decades of struggle, and led to three wars (1948, 1967, and 1973). The challenges to Israeli sovereignty partially subsided only after the peace treaty with Egypt (1979), the peace treaty with Jordan (1994), and the formal demarcation of the Israeli-Lebanese border in 2000 (based on UN Security Council Resolution 425). But to this day, neither Palestinians nor the Syrians have accepted similar demarcation lines and a few small but contentious issues remain with Lebanon. Moreover, the international community has yet to recognize Jerusalem as Israel's capital, underscoring (in Israeli eyes) the continued vulnerability of Israel's formal sovereignty.

The challenge to Israeli sovereignty is not confined to the contested areas along its current frontiers. It stems from the difficulty of exercising sovereignty within the (presumably uncontested) June 4, 1967, borders of Israel, particularly in the areas of southern Israel, heavily populated by Bedouins, and along its eastern border with the Palestinian territory (known as the "Triangle"), mostly inhabited by Israeli Arabs. While these two challenges differ in content and history, they have some important features in common. In both cases, the delineation of the border, making inhabitants legally part of Israel, has been rather artificial, arbitrarily separating families and tribes on both sides of the border. Likewise, in both cases the overwhelming percentage of the population is non-Jewish and these "citizens" retain rather tenuous relationships with the institutions of the state.

Recent governments in Israel have become painfully aware of the growing sovereignty challenge presented by these communities, but Israeli attempts to deal with them have been met with only limited success. In fact, tensions have been growing in response to agitation (some of it religiously inspired) over Israeli governmental policies. In the Negev, recent Israeli governments have tried to promote Jewish settlements in vacant areas while ending the illegal confiscation of Bedouin lands and supporting sizable social and infrastructure programs. Along the Israeli-Egyptian border, the Israeli government also has tried to scale back illegal crossings and illegal trade by building a security fence to separate Bedouin tribes on both sides of the border. In the "Triangle" area, the government has employed a similar mix of "carrot and stick" tactics to try to win the loyalty of Arabs to the state of Israel. But some members of the government, such as former foreign minister Avigdor Lieberman, hope to seize the opportunity created by negotiations with the Palestinians to redraw the 1967 borders in the "Triangle." Lieberman would like to see a voluntary territorial swap as part of any peace settlement whereby the Arab villages of the "Triangle," regardless of their preference, would go to the Palestinian state in return for the Israeli annexation of the blocks of Jewish settlements in the West Bank.[3]

While cross-border threats to Israel's security (mostly in the form of rockets) abound, Israel's sovereignty is no longer as endangered by external enemies as it is threatened by demographic challenges inside Israel. Although it was able to finesse such challenges during its initial decades of existence, demographic trends as well as Jewish territorial expansion into the Jordan's West Bank (often referred to by Israelis as Judea and Samaria) has made them all the more pressing.

The Character of the State

The evolving threat perception and Israel's responses have catalyzed a wrenching internal debate among Israelis over three core attributes of Israel's national identity: its democratic character, its Jewish makeup, and its international legitimacy. The most fundamental controversy concerns the compatibility of annexing territory heavily populated by Palestinians with Israel's liberal and democratic values. This issue is uppermost in the minds of all the left-wing parties, as well as some of the centrist ones. Moreover, it bears on the culture of tolerance and the possibilities of coexistence within Israel between Jews and non-Jews, as well as between Orthodox and secular Jews. A second matter of debate relates to the obvious tensions that inhere in the prospective absorption of massive numbers of non-Jews in the occupied areas with the commitment to preserve Israel's identity as a Jewish homeland. And a third realm of controversy concerning Israel's identity relates to its capacity to sustain its international legitimacy in the face of growing perceptions of foreigners that Israeli intransigence and expansionism are the primary obstacles to peace and tranquility, at least in this part of the region. The latter concern presently preoccupies the country's cosmopolitan elites, especially in business, professional, and academic circles, who are increasingly anxious about the adverse consequences of the long-term impasse in the peace negotiations and related settlement activity.[4]

These segments of society fear economic sanctions, loss of business opportunities, and the erosion of world-class academic institutions inside Israel. Notwithstanding the gravity of these concerns—amplified by mainstream politicians, media spokespersons, and shrill warnings from friends and foes alike in the European Union and the United States—Israelis remain deadlocked on how to regain legitimacy abroad without compromising security (or renege on Israel's historical vision) at home.

Notwithstanding the importance of Israeli relations with the external world, the first two controversies highlight the real existential dilemmas faced by Israel. These controversies reincarnate the identity dilemmas apparent in the 1948 Declaration of Independence—namely, how should the "Jewishness" of the state manifest itself in religious practices, national policies, territorial settlements, or cultural products? If it is appropriate to inscribe "Jewishness" into state institutions and practices, does this "Jewishness" mean Orthodox Judaism? Although the conception of a "Jewish Homeland" remains central in the Israeli national narrative and in its dialogue with the Jewish diaspora worldwide, there is no consensus on its meaning or its implications for the relations between Israel and Jews abroad, between Israel and the rest of the world, and, most importantly, between Israel's Jewish and non-Jewish population, the latter already accounting for roughly a quarter of its citizens and growing. How can Israel be both a haven for Jews abroad and afford equal opportunity and freedom to its non-Jewish citizens? Although such fundamental issues were finessed in its founding document, Israel now increasingly needs a coherent strategy to address them.

Meanwhile, Israelis task themselves with a responsibility beyond the confines of their own territorial state. As in the past, Israelis see themselves looking after Jews of the diaspora (especially in the context of growing anti-Semitic trends and hate crimes against Jews, for example, in Europe) and providing them with a safe haven, should they need it. They want Jews abroad to sustain close ties with Israel, if not to immigrate to Israel outright. Many Israelis also expect diaspora Jews to continue to support the "Jewish State" politically as well as economically. But the deeper, long-term implications of these bonds for Israel's domestic and foreign policies remain elusive. Once again, a coherent strategy has not emerged to reconcile Israel's appeal to Jews (and increasingly, also sizable Israeli communities) living abroad, most of whom are not Orthodox, with either its contemporary policies or the religious character of many state practices. Here again, the language and arrangements that artfully finessed difficult issues at the founding of the state beg for a strategy that is difficult to design in view of ongoing domestic rivalries and controversies.

Nor it is clear how Israelis can reconcile their desire for a "Jewish homeland" with their affinity for liberal and democratic universal values. Most Jews (and non-Jews) inside Israel seem resigned to sustain the heterogeneous character of the state. The Jews generally favor granting limited (cultural) forms of autonomy to their Arab neighbors and yearn for mechanisms and formulas to integrate them into mainstream Israeli society without diluting its fundamentally Jewish character. The growing Arab minority generally wants to coexist within Israel, yet seeks greater opportunities to realize their rights as Israeli citizens. They want more resources from the state, more freedom to cultivate their Arab identity within the state, and more flexibility to sustain ties with their brethren across Israel's borders. How to reconcile such objectives with Jewish Israelis' sense of security requires a strategy that has yet to be designed.

Territory, Peacemaking, and Normalization with Israel's Neighbors

Not surprisingly, the debates over territory, peacemaking, and normalization of ties with Israel's neighbors continue to be among the most contentious issues inside Israel because they affect the most basic elements of Israeli sovereignty, security, and identity.[5] After decades of wars, Israel has been able to establish formal peaceful relations with both Egypt and Jordan, codifying its borders on both frontiers in the process. Yet the peace treaties have not paved the way for full normalization of relations with either state or with the Arab world, more broadly. Israel's permanent borders remain in flux, and not for lack of effort in trying to settle them. First and foremost, this is because of the failure to settle the Palestinian conflict, although lack of progress in talks with Syria (and, as a result, also with Lebanon) constitutes an added liability and constraint.

There seem to be at least four clusters of obstacles that stand in the way of a Palestinian- Israeli settlement, conveniently subsumed under the following headings: Jerusalem, refugees (and their "right of return"), borders (and territorial swaps), and security arrangements (inevitably meaning infringements on future Palestinian sovereignty). These issues have stymied all Palestinian peacemaking efforts to date. Tactical flexibility on solutions aside, core Israeli requirements in these four domains would not fundamentally change regardless of the government in power. Israeli-Palestinian negotiations are now further complicated by an ideologically and emotionally charged debate over Israel's insistence that Palestinians recognize Israel as the "Jewish homeland." While this demand by Prime Minister Benjamin Netanyahu and several other leading Israeli politicians is not universally supported within Israel, it nevertheless enjoys, in its crudest form, broad popularity because Israelis see it as the functional equivalent of their earlier demand that a Palestinian-Israeli settlement have finality ("an end to all claims"). The Israeli determination to seek finality in a political settlement with the Palestinians and to see language regarding a "Jewish homeland" as a prerequisite to an irreversible historical reconciliation with the Arabs is natural, given the risks that inhere for Israel in making the concessions it will have to make. This is why the steadfast refusal by Palestinian Authority (PA) president Mahmoud

Abbas, very much like his predecessor Yasser Arafat, to address the issue of a "Jewish homeland" seems especially ominous to many Israelis.[6] This issue, in some form, will not go away. Vital to Israel's existential sense of its survival, securing recognition of the state as a "Jewish homeland" will remain part of Israeli strategy. It will impel officials to extract further territorial concessions and security arrangements as a bulwark against future Arab irredentism.

The skirmishes over this issue, coupled with the efforts of President Abbas to form a national unity government with Hamas (presently controlling Gaza and adamantly opposed to reconciliation with Israel), reinforce the changes already under way in Israeli attitudes toward the Palestinians. Israelis support security collaboration with the Palestinian Authority; in fact, a robust majority favor peacemaking efforts. However, declining percentages of Israelis believe in the sincerity and credibility of the Palestinians as peace partners. Israelis are sharply divided over the merits of making painful concessions on behalf of peace. Many feel fundamentally conflicted over the viability and durability of the trade-offs that inhere in any such settlement.[7]

In the Netanyahu government up to the March 2015 elections, no faction enjoyed a decisive majority, usually resulting in formal deadlock. Yet the practical agenda was shaped by the far better organized right-wing factions and by two of Likud's right-wing coalition partners. Because of this right-wing influence, the sharply divided government was unable or unwilling to interrupt the momentum for settlement expansion in the West Bank. Budget allocations continued to massively favor the settlements over all other segments of society, and the de facto annexation of nearby land increasingly diminished the prospects for a two-state solution. Within the governing coalition, there were several strains of thought regarding the peacemaking process, none of which gave much hope for a negotiated settlement. One right-wing approach implicitly rejected altogether the original two-state solution. Although not explicitly articulated, this approach offered a long wait, presumably pinning its hopes on the eventual transformation of Jordan, whose population already is mostly Palestinian, into the Palestinian state.[8] That new state would also control some densely populated Palestinian parts of the West Bank, while Israel would annex the remainder. Another right-wing strain within the governing coalition professed continued commitment to the two-state solution, but de facto put peacemaking on the back burner. Instead, it focused on strengthening day-to-day security arrangements and on effectuating a peaceful coexistence while promoting a regional alliance to check radical Islamic forces.[9] Conversely, the center-left within the governing coalition sought to place a renewed emphasis on political separation from the Palestinians. Where these center-left politicians differed among themselves was that one faction still believed in prospects of a civil "divorce" through peacemaking with the PA, while another faction put little faith in the prospects for success of such an approach and instead envisaged unilateral Israeli steps toward a separation that would safeguard Israel's future.[10] None of these factions advanced a coherent strategy for dealing with the nearly two million Palestinians living in the Hamas-dominated Gaza strip, other than through some ill-defined link with their brethren in the West Bank.

In the final determination of Israel's borders, any strategy that seeks peaceful relations with Israel's immediate neighbors, as well as a broader regional normalization, will require peacemaking with Syria, as well as with Lebanon. Yet the latter are presently off the agenda, following disillusionment with previous efforts to make peace with both states (with Syria obviously holding Lebanon hostage). Moreover, the recent internal dynamics in both Syria and Lebanon make them far less viable, willing, and desirable peace partners. Historically, the security (especially military) elites favored efforts to negotiate peace with Syria (and Lebanon), but their enthusiasm has waned given the civil strife and factionalism in both countries.

Israel's territorial gains in 1967, inspired by fear and a hope to safeguard its security, have complicated peacemaking, accentuated divisions within Israel, and made coherent strategic planning far more difficult than it was at Israel's inception.

Security and Military Doctrine

As long as Israel's external adversaries threatened not only its welfare, but at certain times its very existence, Israel's security doctrine enjoyed widespread domestic support and constituted a relatively noncontroversial pillar of its strategy.[11] The military was called upon not only to frustrate repeated Arab attempts to encroach on Israel's territory and harm its population, but also through decisive Israeli victories against Arab armies to dissuade adversaries from ever trying again to harm Israel militarily. The expectation was that this strategy would eventually reconcile Arabs to Israel's continued existence.

Consequently, from its inception, the cornerstone of Israel's security doctrine has been attainment of the capacity for Israel to defend itself, by itself. Officials assigned some emphasis to finding external allies or partners who would stand by Israel or, at least, provide it with much needed assistance. But the fundamental belief was that Israel would remain on its own (at least until it impressed others with its capacity to defend itself independently), with only world Jewry as a dependable strategic ally. Moreover, given the relative asymmetry in the size of its territory, population, and resources compared to its Arab foes, Israeli security doctrine postulated the achievement of qualitative superiority to offset its numerical inferiority. In military terms, the qualitative edge meant a quest for a formidable conventional military capability (and a defense industrial base to build and sustain it). But Israelis also interpreted a qualitative edge to mean scientific excellence, eventually translating into the development of a nuclear option to insure political deterrence against existential threats. These pillars of Israeli security doctrine remain virtually unchanged, notwithstanding the growing fragmentation of the Arab world and its deteriorating economic conditions.

Qualitative edge and self-sufficiency aside, Israeli military doctrine rested on three pillars to address the primary threat presented by conventional Arab armies: deterrence, early warning (intelligence), and decisive victories. And while the strategy was defensive in nature, its implementation often was highly offensive. Seizing the initiative in every confrontation and moving swiftly into enemy territory was intended to offset Israel's lack of strategic depth and to safeguard population centers close to its frontiers. Initially, Israeli ground forces bore responsibility for implementing this doctrine. In the mid-1950s, the air force gradually assumed a critical strategic role.

Over the decades, Israel's external landscape and threat perception have changed markedly. Peace treaties first with Egypt (1979) and subsequently with Jordan (1994) and modest progress toward peacemaking with the Palestinians following the "Oslo Accords" (1993–1995) significantly eased the defense burden, introduced a measure of security cooperation with both states and in recent years also with the Palestinian Authority, and reinforced the role of Israeli deterrence against remaining foes. But even as traditional threats modulated, new ones arose. Terrorism first became an Israeli preoccupation in the 1950s. In recent years, this danger has morphed into diverse threats from multiple nonstate actors, some of whom have embraced suicide attacks and others who have developed and acquired capabilities to launch rockets and missiles into the very heart of Israel. More ominous yet is the danger of proliferating weapons of mass destruction, recently highlighted by Iran's quest for a nuclear capability. In other words, peace with some of its closest neighbors has not stopped the emergence of threats from further away. Iran's support of proxies like Hezbollah, the Islamic Jihad, and occasionally Hamas fuels the perception of threat inside Israel. And now there is also the looming danger emanating from attacks in cyberspace, for which geographical distance matters little.[12]

Israeli capabilities have evolved in the face of these threats. After a short period of "splendid isolation," close defense ties developed with France and Germany in the mid-1950s. As these relationships frayed, Israel nurtured an especially close relationship with the United States beginning in the 1960s. Washington provided Israel with extensive security assistance and diplomatic support. Israel shared information and technology and acquired essential technology and weaponry from the United States. Together, they developed state-of-the-art capabilities, not least important of which related to missile defense. This support and collaboration diluted Israel's capabilities to depend entirely on itself. But Israel's determination to possess the capabilities to act on its own in order to safeguard its decision-making autonomy did not wither away.

The intimacy of the relationship with the United States and Israel's dependence on U.S. support has given Washington considerable leverage over Israeli decision-making. In practice, it is most pronounced on issues of foreign policy and national security (ranging from diplomacy and peacemaking to Israeli arms sales and even to the exercise of Israel's right of self-defense). U.S. leverage is weakest on ideological and social issues that are now at the core of Israel's strategic dilemmas. On the latter, American culture serves as a role model for large segments of Israeli society, and, on the former, the U.S. government often seeks to shape specific governmental decisions. But influence is a two-way street between the United States and Israel, and Washington's sway over Israel is limited in those areas deemed by Israeli governments to be of vital or existential importance. In these areas, Israel is resolved to act alone and to defy the United States, if and when absolutely necessary. Consequently, despite repeated attempts to persuade Israeli policymakers to negotiate with Arab leaders and Palestinian representatives, U.S. officials have consistently failed to convince Israeli leaders of the merits of returning to the 1967 borders or of freezing the expansion of settlements. Presently, U.S. influence seems to be waning because of friction over Iranian nuclear negotiations and the Palestinian peace process. Israelis see the United States pivoting away from the Middle East, leaving them to argue among themselves over the meaning and application of the values and principles they inscribed in their own Declaration of Independence.

Nevertheless, the relationship with the United States will continue to occupy center stage in the Israeli strategic outlook. Similarly, all prominent U.S. national leaders are likely to reiterate their unshakable commitment to the relationship (and alliance) with Israel and reaffirm their pledge to safeguard Israeli security. While these views continue to be translated into concrete actions by both sides, personal distrust has crept into the relationship between President Barack Obama and Prime Minister Netanyahu. It reflects not merely personality and ideological differences between the two leaders, but also serious disagreements over major policy issues ranging from settlements and peacemaking to the nuclear negotiations with Iran. Some of the strains in the bilateral relationship created by this personality clash may well dissipate with the end of the Obama administration. Other policy differences may endure, and the long-term consequences of such divergence are difficult to assess.

The changing nature and mix of threats facing Israel has led to a dramatic transformation in military thinking. Accompanying the new stress on missile defense and the construction of fences along its borders, Israel has a diminished appetite (and necessity) for offensive ground military operations (into enemy territory). Its present predisposition is to design defensive responses to threats in lieu of massive offensive operations. Its preference is to employ surgical strikes, especially airpower, when offensive military responses are needed. Israel tends to confine its ground operations to ad hoc precision raids when retaliatory action makes temporary and modest territorial conquest necessary. These characteristics were clearly evident in the summer 2014 military operation in Gaza, "Protective Edge."

Overall, then, Israeli strategy now envisages the primacy of intelligence and paramilitary operations, confining the army, air force, and navy in most circumstances to defensive operations or to limited, selective, surgical—often covert—offensive initiatives.

The Institutions of the State

Israeli society is notoriously fractious. The democratic political culture of Israel, the multiparty system, the vibrant media, the virulent discourse, the combative interest groups, and the friction between religious and secular interests institutionalize instability. Elected governments rarely enjoy their full four-year mandate to set goals and implement policies, and commonly face deep, often irreconcilable fissures over major policy areas even among (and within) the parties making up the governing coalition. Prime ministers do consistently try to steer the direction of the government and shape public opinion. But such efforts usually enjoy only moderate success, even in areas affecting vital national security interests. Generally, the absence of consensus on key matters of the day among the political elites hinders the capacity of governments to agree on and subsequently rally support behind official policies, which in turn reinforces the deep divisions within the society over most salient policy issues, including the conduct of military operations in Gaza in 2014.

This state of affairs mobilizes and emboldens key interest groups to try to shape the national and governmental discourse in an effort to impose their policy preferences on a case-by-case basis. In recent years, the most important of these interest groups probably has been the Eretz Israel loyalists (comprising West Bank settlers and their numerous right-wing sympathizers), who consistently manage to exercise massive influence over Israel's territorial strategy. At the same time, the Orthodox political parties continue to exert considerable clout because of their indispensable role in forming the political coalitions that govern the state. They seek to shape electoral laws and influence legal issues that preserve their unique political leverage, their religious predilections, and their privileged access to budgetary allocations; indeed, this narrow agenda makes them ideal coalition partners.

Similarly, the larger trade unions, operating both independently and through their national federation (the Histadrut), continue to promote their traditional pro-labor agenda. And while far less influential than in past decades, when their business holdings and social services dominated significant sections of the economy, they continue to protect labor rights zealously at the expense of slowing and complicating government initiatives to liberalize imports, privatize services, and stimulate free market competition in key sectors such as ports and energy. But these unions increasingly tangle with an emboldened business elite who discreetly and successfully lobby to dilute the socialistic values and practices that inspired the founders of the state.

Faced with fractious debate over all major policy issues, a handful of key institutions have evolved to overcome the political gridlock, inject a sense of strategic direction, and provide some coherence and continuity to national policies. Foremost among them, given the preponderance of the security agenda, is the so-called "security establishment," comprising the Israeli Defense Forces (IDF), including the all-important sector of military intelligence (Aman), the civilian ministry of defense, the two civilian intelligence services, both internal (Shabak) and external (Mossad), and occasionally the Israeli Atomic Energy Commission. These military and intelligence institutions have superior capacity to undertake staff work, engage in long-range analysis, and make plans. These attributes sometimes allow military officers to gain a relative edge in discussions with their political masters and civilian colleagues. And, naturally, military leaders exert a profound influence on budgetary allocations within their respective organizations and on countless operational decisions.

Nonetheless, the widespread perception of the influence of the security establishment seems greatly inflated, in part, because it is anything but unified in its outlook and, in part, because the civilian political elite has grown increasingly adept at pushing back, diminishing the role of the security establishment and imposing its own priorities. In the absence of agreement on any strategy, the civilian political elite increasingly shapes the direction of the state through a series of incremental, often ad hoc decisions. In fact, while the supremacy of civilian authorities over the security establishment has never been in doubt, their influence has grown a lot in recent years because the existential threat Israel faced in its early years has eased.[13]

The growing divergence in the security outlook between the political leadership and the security establishment manifested itself publicly in the run-up to the March 2015 general elections. Prominent former heads of both the Shabak and the Mossad, as well as numerous top retired generals and other senior officials in the various policy and security arms, openly challenged Prime Minister Netanyahu and his policies both on the Iran issue and on Palestinian peacemaking. They actively campaigned against Netanyahu and in favor of the opposition bloc, expressing their conviction that the election results would have profound ramifications for Israel's security and welfare. Predictably, these critics were rebuked by Netanyahu, his Likud party, and other right-wing parties. The election results demonstrated that the campaign against Netanyahu hardly dented his leadership credentials and probably consolidated his dominance over the increasingly politicized security agenda.

Given the evolution of threat perception, a significant transformation has also occurred within the security establishment. While the IDF remains powerful and influential, the role of the civilian intelligence services as a whole, and the Shabak in particular, has grown. Shabak (the domestic intelligence agency) has become the predominant counterterrorism organ, with the military playing a critical, but supportive, role. This trend has accelerated as the threat from conventional Arab armies has receded and as the friction with Hamas and Islamic Jihad in Gaza has escalated. Similarly, the growing threat of terrorism against Israeli targets from further away and the preoccupation with nuclear proliferation, especially from Iran, has produced a similar reversal of roles between the Mossad and the IDF, with the Mossad assuming the primary responsibility for dealing with these threats.

Another state institution of key importance in shaping national strategy is the legal establishment, most prominently the Israeli Supreme Court, which also doubles as the High Court of Justice. Every citizen can appeal directly to it if he or she feels aggrieved by any government omission or commission. While its imprint is necessarily selective because of the scarcity of time it has to address issues, its apolitical character means that its impact is often enduring. Moreover, its latitude is wide because of the very absence of a constitution. The influence of the Supreme Court on issues of human rights, civil rights, and even national security affairs (deeply rooted in the spirit of the Declaration of Independence) is quite pronounced, precisely because of the ease of accessing the court by all parties feeling aggrieved by the state.[14]

Many governmental decisions in the national security domain (over conscription, the security fence in the West Bank, interrogation techniques, and punitive measures such as demolition of terrorists' houses) are now subject to legal challenges, thereby slowing and complicating the decision-making process. Moreover, the impact of the Supreme Court transcends those occasions when it renders a decision because the mere specter of the court weighing in on an issue acts as a deterrent against blatantly politically inspired policies. The growing influence of the court as the impartial arbiter of an ever-larger cross-section of national issues has triggered repeated efforts by the parties in power to politicize appointments to the Supreme Court and to limit its constitutional powers to overturn Knesset legislation, but with very modest success to date. However, these efforts have regained new momentum in the aftermath of the Likud victory in the 2015 elections.

Beyond the Supreme Court, several institutions wield considerable influence over Israeli strategy, most especially the Bank of Israel (BOI) and the Ministry of Finance (MOF). The BOI always has been predominant in charting Israel's monetary policy. Enjoying an independent legal stature, it has long sought to protect exchange rates and foreign currency reserves from security-related challenges. But with the dramatic improvement in Israel's economic standing since the mid-1980s, and especially under the charismatic leadership of its former governor, Stanley Fischer, the BOI championed a new expansive legal charter for itself (2010) and wandered into areas of domestic policy (ranging from housing to integrating Orthodox Jews and Israeli Arabs into the workforce). The BOI also championed Israel's 2010 formal accession to the Organization for Economic Co-operation and Development (OECD). This move was conceived to enhance Israel's economic prowess and to align the course of Israel's economic and social development with that of other Western economies.[15]

The MOF also has been very important. Its professional corporate culture has made it both exceptionally assertive and a real force to be reckoned with when political pressures mount over budget allocations. Its staff typically consists of young and highly educated individuals who do a stint at the MOF and then move on to lucrative positions in the private sector. They not only determine overall budget allocations, but they also micromanage decisions and expenditures. By second-guessing the various ministries on their choices and retaining the final say on financial outlays, they exert great influence on national priorities across virtually all policy areas. Although the security establishment has often thwarted the efforts of the MOF to oversee its expenditures and rein in its budget, in recent years even the military establishment has conceded some ground on budget oversight, especially as the "Guns versus Butter" debate has entered the center stage of Israeli political life.[16] The 2015 election results reinforced the tendency in the coalition-formation process to award the MOF to politicians inclined to favor social expenditures, thereby augmenting the powers of the MOF bureaucracy.

The influence of the MOF bureaucracy on state conduct has been mostly positive. It has nurtured fiscal discipline, tamed inflation, cut budgetary deficits, and thwarted many politically inspired schemes of dubious merit. But the intrusive influence and institutional myopia of the MOF has often put short-term budgetary efficiency and oversight considerations ahead of strategy and innovation. For example, the MOF has blocked some major social integration programs as well as large infrastructure projects whose payoffs would be visible only over the long term. Hence many fundamental issues remain unaddressed.

While legal and financial institutions help to navigate Israeli society through the politics of everyday life, the gridlock over fundamental values remain. For many years, Shimon Peres, president of Israel from 2007 to 2014, used his exceptional reputation and vast political experience to wield considerable soft power and to modulate political rancor. As the last surviving member of the founding generation of political leaders, he grasped the need to preserve a precarious balance among the clashing values embodied in the Declaration of Independence—and among the groups who have never ceased to contest the priorities among those values. Peres successfully influenced the national agenda and strategy on negotiating peace with the Palestinians, avoiding a military confrontation with Iran, supporting science and technology, developing closer ties with the United States as well as Europe, and bridge-building between various elements of Israeli society. Notwithstanding these accomplishments, he simply helped finesse the gridlock rather than resolve it. Peres's presidential successor, Reuven Rivlin, is gradually assuming a similar role, gathering stature and seeking to shape Israel's national and international agenda in a centrist, liberal, inclusive direction.[17]

World Jewry, in particular U.S.-based Jewish organizations, has taken a strong interest in the internal developments and external factors bearing on Israeli identity and security. These organizations have tried to cultivate ties with Israeli governments and influence their decisions on matters of great long-term significance, especially those pertaining to Jewish identity and practices. They have opposed the impulse of religious Jews inside Israel to identify the state with Orthodox rituals and practices. But the competition among these outside organizations and the absence of a common perspective among them on many critical matters, such as settlement policy, undermines their overall influence and leaves Israeli Jews free to continue their internal contestation.

Prosperity, Equality, and Social Welfare

The desire for greater prosperity as part of one's national strategy is commonplace. Israel needs a safe and secure environment for its economy to flourish and for its investment and trade to grow. In recent decades, it has assigned priority to nurturing its high-tech sector, which is dependent on its interconnections with leading research and development centers around the world. Israel also has placed a premium on value-added manufacturing such as generic drugs, on exotic agricultural goods, on tourism, and on special services—all of which are linked to international flows of people, commerce, and capital. Discoveries of significant gas reserves off its Mediterranean coast now also mean that Israel can modulate its anxieties about energy security and shift some investment to the development of its own gas and oil requirements. Although its enviable economic performance over the last couple of decades has produced unparalleled abundance, it also has precipitated serious domestic debates.

Israel has seen impressive growth, remarkable financial stability, and rising standards of living over the past decade while maintaining, and even expanding, its elaborate social welfare state apparatus. Yet it also has witnessed growing inequalities in wealth and income distribution, as well as a dramatic rise in the cost of housing, the latter disproportionately hurting young couples and Israel's poorer citizens. At the same time, people are increasingly aware of and upset about the disproportionate burdens shouldered by the secular elements of society in comparison to the growing ranks of the ultra-Orthodox. The latter neither serve in the military nor earn meaningful income, largely living off massive transfer payments from the coffers of the state. In response to these trends and inspired by the ferment of the Arab Spring, a social protest movement erupted in Israel. Many young people in particular took to the streets in the summer of 2012, heavily influencing the outcome of the Knesset elections in early 2013 but also elevating prominent socially oriented politicians in the recent 2015 elections.

The long-term impact of this outburst of social dissent remains to be seen. Yet it has already shifted the national agenda, inspiring debates about economic competition and social justice. The Knesset passed some new legislation designed to tackle small parts of the larger challenge. Legislators introduced a mandatory military conscription quota for the ultra-Orthodox and sought to curtail excessive concentrations of economic power. They also took some significant steps to make housing affordable to first-time buyers. But disaffected constituencies in society are increasingly unhappy about the consequences of the trend toward unbridled capitalism and they demand more reform, more equity, more opportunity, and more justice.

One particular aspect of the debate about conscripting the ultra-Orthodox involves the effort to train and encourage more of them to join the workforce after completing their military service. In this respect, it complements a concerted effort to create religiously sheltered educational and employment opportunities for Orthodox women. The goal is to enable religious women to become more effective breadwinners and to encourage them, however indirectly, to have fewer children—without having to compromise their religious beliefs.

These initiatives resemble the efforts of the government to promote employment and educational opportunities among the Bedouins in the Negev and to get them to lower their record-breaking birthrates. These measures are driven by a realization that Israel's long-term prosperity hinges on redressing social injustices, demanding equal burden-sharing, and affording economic opportunities to all its citizens. The ultra-Orthodox and the Israeli Arabs remain special targets of these legislative initiatives because their numbers are growing rapidly as a percentage of the total population and because their participation in the workforce is relatively low (especially among Arab women and in high-earning jobs). These matters were not high on the nation's agenda at the time of independence, but they now must constitute a more pronounced pillar of Israel's strategy, notwithstanding the political clout of the religious parties who remain determined to thwart or reverse the legislative initiatives of recent years.

The Bottom Line

Israel has come a long way over its sixty-five years of existence. It has managed to weave together Holocaust survivors, impoverished and persecuted Jewish immigrants, and early settlers into a nation. Facing acute external threats, it has succeeded in nurturing the distinctive talents of its Jewish citizens and attracting external support. Finessing for decades deeply rooted internal disagreements over its identity, Israel has built itself into a formidable economic and military power. It has become a prosperous and secure state, as well as a lively society that nurtures scientific excellence, technological innovation, and cultural creativity. Yet the model that has worked so well now shows signs of fraying under a far more complex, if less dangerous, environment.

Israel's economic vibrancy and military strength can no longer overshadow the serious fissures undermining its domestic cohesion. The political leadership has been muddling through for decades, unable to forge an effective consensus on matters of coexistence, territory, religion, and citizenship. Unresolved at the time of Israel's founding and ignored or postponed for decades, these vexing issues have now resurfaced to haunt Israel at maturity, compounded by recent demographic, social, and political developments. Overshadowing everything looms the challenges associated with the demands of Palestinian Arabs for a state of their own. Neither Israel's leaders nor its Jewish citizens can agree on what to do or where to go, and hence the ship of state drifts aimlessly in both calm and occasionally rough seas. Unlike the founders, current leaders have proven unable to design a strategy (or a narrative) that can transcend contemporary dilemmas, even as they navigate Israel toward a creeping annexation of the West Bank, a trend likely to continue in light of the 2015 elections. This trajectory tarnishes Israel's international standing, agitates relations with traditional partners and allies in Western Europe and the United States, and endangers its economic, scientific, and cultural opportunities. It also impairs opportunities to build relations with China on the one hand and with the Sunni-dominated Middle Eastern nations on the other.

The innate strengths and creative energies of the Israeli population have not gone away. Nor has the competence of its governing elites to fend off predators and deal with current threats. The people and their leaders have constructed a formidable infrastructure and security arsenal to keep Israel safe from immediate dangers. However, the incapacity to shape a coherent strategy to deal with fundamental challenges does not augur well for the future. Israel desperately needs national leaders capable of taking fateful decisions and forging a workable consensus around a coherent strategy, much as its founders did in 1948.[18] Their strategy worked then, but will no longer suffice to deal with either the acute challenges or the considerable opportunities that lie ahead.

CHAPTER 6

RUSSIA

Geopolitics and Identity

FYODOR LUKYANOV

R USSIA'S twenty-first-century foreign policy was inaugurated on the night of June 11–12, 1999, when a battalion
of Russian paratroopers, stationed as part of a peacekeeping force in Bosnia and Herzegovina, secretly moved into the Autonomous
Province of Kosovo and seized Pristina's Slatina airport. The airport was
planning to host the NATO warplanes that would deliver Western troops for
deployment in the region. The day before, the UN Security Council adopted
Resolution 1244, which provided for Kosovo's de facto secession from the
Federal Republic of Yugoslavia (although formally the FRY maintained its
jurisdiction over Kosovo). Russia's action caused panic in the world. General
Wesley Clark, NATO supreme commander, demanded the removal of the
Russians from the airport by force, but General Michael Jackson, the British commander of Kosovo Force (KFOR), refused, reportedly telling Clark,
"I'm not going to start the Third World War for you."[1] Several days later,
the Russian paratroopers left the airport themselves. Four years later, Russia
withdrew from Kosovo and Bosnia.

Yet the taking of the Pristina airport delighted many Russian observers
with its reckless bravery and unexpected military prowess. It also ushered in
a new era for post-Soviet Russia. Struggling from the economic turmoil and
bankruptcy of 1998, and facing the collapse of its political system, Russian
leaders wanted to show the world that Russia still had an independent role in
world affairs. These factors—the desire to act unilaterally, the willingness to

use military force to achieve its goals, and the search for prestige—continue to inform Russian strategy today.

NATO's Yugoslav campaign was a turning point in Russia's perception of the West and its own place in the world. For Russians, the war in Yugoslavia, and the NATO intervention there, confirmed the boundless appetite of the West. As the prominent Russian foreign policy analyst Sergei Karaganov argues, most likely there was no chance for Russia to establish a normal relationship with the West after the NATO bombings of Yugoslavia, which even terrified the majority of pro-Western representatives of the Russian establishment.[2] It was widely believed in Russia from the late 1990s on that the West sought to expand its influence and hegemony in Eastern and Southeastern Europe. These past experiences continue to inform Russian perceptions of the crises in Ukraine and Crimea. Russians believe that the West will not give up its expansionist plans and will keep moving its geopolitical borders to the east, pushing Russia farther and farther back, establishing hegemony even in nations like Ukraine that have historical, cultural, and religious ties to Russia.[3]

Russia today maintains a strategy that seeks to regain its lost prestige in world affairs. To that end, Russia uses traditional geopolitical posturing and tactics to restore its influence over its immediate borderlands. Russia aims to recover from the "double collapse" of 1991: the disappearance of its *cordon sanitaire* between the West and the Russian heartland and the loss of status in world affairs. This chapter will review the path to Russia's contemporary strategy and then argue that such a strategy of geopolitical pressure and unilateralism, as a response to Western expansion after the Cold War, is unsustainable.

Geopolitics and Unilateralism

There was nothing inevitable about Russia's turn to a policy of unilateralism and traditional geopolitics. Addressing the UN General Assembly in December 1988, Soviet General Secretary Mikhail Gorbachev said that global politics should be guided by "the priority of universal human values."[4] In the summer of 1989, Gorbachev urged the Parliamentary Assembly of the Council of Europe to build a "common European home."[5] These keynote speeches followed on the ideas he voiced in his book *Perestroika: New Thinking for Our Country and the World*, published in two editions in late 1987 and mid-1988.[6] When Gorbachev was formulating his "New Thinking," there was still a balance in the global arena and the world's two superpowers were equal actors in international affairs. *Perestroika* theorists saw their future interaction in the spirit of convergence, a fashionable idea at the time, in which the two countries would borrow the best and reject the worst from each system. But the rapid decline of the Soviet Union put an end to dreams of rapprochement between equals and mutual ideological enrichment.

From 1993, when the question of Russia's form of government was finally resolved, until 2003, Russia tried to join the "civilized world" by various means and in the face of changing circumstances. Russia initially operated from a position of weakness as a result of its chronic domestic crisis and its dependence on foreign financial injections; later, it began to assert its equality with other powers. During his first term as president (2000–2004), Vladimir Putin proposed that Russia, Europe, and America devise a new model of mutually advantageous coexistence—a deal that would finally turn the page on the Cold War. Russia suggested investment and technology exchanges with the European Union and a close partnership with the United States against the common threat of terrorism and radical Islam. Putin fully endorsed the U.S. strategy after 9/11 (the Russian president was the first to call George W. Bush that day), actively cooperating in staging the operation in Afghanistan, including support of stationing U.S. bases in Central Asia, as well as closing down the Russian military base at Camran (Vietnam) and the Russian spying facilities at Lurdes (Cuba). In his famous speech in the German Bundestag on September 25, 2001, Putin stated: "Under the impact of the laws governing the development of information society, Stalinist totalitarian ideology could no longer oppose the ideas of freedom and democracy. The spirit of these ideas was taking hold of the overwhelming majority of Russian citizens."[7] Russian officials then discussed an in-depth partnership with the European Union based on an "asset swap," exchanging part of Russian oil and gas fields for access to European distribution networks. In broader terms, the asset swap was seen as extending further, to include Russian energy and consumption markets for European technology.[8] There was even a rumor that Russia might be interested in joining NATO—never confirmed directly, but floated in many leaks.[9]

The Western response to these offers of cooperation did not match the expectations of the Kremlin. In June 2002, the United States unilaterally withdrew from the Anti-Ballistic Missile Treaty, a cornerstone of strategic stability during the Cold War and a guarantee of effective mutual deterrence. The United States announced ambitious plans to launch an extensive missile defense program, which was perceived by Russia as an attempt to undermine the Russian potential to retaliate in case of nuclear attack. Although the initial reaction of the Kremlin was reserved, this initiative adversely affected the relationship throughout the early 2000s, especially as it was aggravated by ever-deeper involvement by the United States and the EU in the former Soviet area. The "Rose Revolution" in Georgia in 2003, enthusiastically welcomed and supported by the U.S. administration, and especially the "Orange Revolution" in Ukraine one year later, were perceived as proof that the United States was pursuing an expansionist agenda. Putin felt that Russia's overtures of the 1990s had been decisively rebuffed.

The 2003 invasion of Iraq, conducted without the authorization of the United Nations, made Russian leaders conclude that the United States had little respect for international law. Putin, who had been following roughly a plan that favored integration and rapprochement with the West, now decisively tacked in a new direction. From 2003 onward, Moscow sought to go its own way in world affairs. Putin opposed the U.S. invasion of Iraq in 2003, alongside France and Germany. Five years later, Russia used the war in South Ossetia to draw a red line, beyond which it would not tolerate further NATO expansion. It demonstrated that it would defend this line by all means, up to the use of force. And in 2013, Russia flexed its muscle as the European Union tried to draw Ukraine into its sphere of influence. Russia withstood Western pressure and sought to hold Ukraine firmly in the Russian orbit.

The Ukrainian crisis of 2013–2014, and especially its Crimean phase, supplanted all previous efforts to effect a rapprochement with the West. The collapse of the Viktor Yanukovych regime in Kyiv on February 22, 2014, which followed a "compromise" made under pressure from European ministers, and the subsequent legal and political turmoil served as a trigger for Russia's decisive action. The West did not realize that to Russia the Ukrainian issue was not just a red line, but a double solid line. And when it seemed possible that Ukraine, with active participation from Europe and the United States, could turn into a country built on different principles (in this case it does not matter whether it would have been more liberal and Atlantic or, conversely, nationalist), there was no longer any room for agreement. Classical geopolitical thinking made it an absolute Russian interest to have Ukraine as a strategically friendly and controllable territory. For example, while addressing the Russian Parliament, Putin noted that Crimea was historically important for Russia, claiming that "this strategic territory should be part of a strong and stable sovereignty, which today can only be Russian."[10] The issue of the Black Sea Fleet—that is, naval power projection into the Mediterranean and

Indian Oceans—was crucial for the Russian perception of its own security and its role in the world.

Ukraine had always been regarded as an important bridgehead upon which the balance of power in Europe and the physical security of Russia depended. There could be no question of relinquishing control of this important borderland. NATO's expansion eastward aggravated Russian sensibilities. In 2012, Putin highlighted this anxiety, saying that he would not be concerned with NATO's expansion if "these plans were not conducted in close proximity to Russian borders, if they did not undermine [its] security and global stability in general."[11] But the West appeared to be infringing on Russia's backyard in Ukraine. The West, argues John Mearsheimer, was "threatening [Russia's] core strategic interests, a point Putin made emphatically and repeatedly."[12]

Putin made little secret of his views on the geopolitical importance of securing Russia's periphery. In his address to the Federal Assembly in 2005, Putin famously said "the collapse of the Soviet Union was a major geopolitical disaster of the [twentieth] century," noting that Russia was now looking to "ensure the security of [its] borders" while continuing "its civilizing mission on the Eurasian continent."[13] Putin, a structural realist, saw developments in the world as an interconnected system of balances. From this point of view, the disappearance of the Russian empire and the Soviet Union, which had for centuries structured the vast expanses of Eurasia, was a highly destabilizing event portending long-term upheavals. Disliking chaos, Putin grasped that in a globalized world internal and external problems were intertwined.[14] People of his generation who had experienced *perestroika* and the Soviet Union's breakup at the height of their careers sensed how short the distance was from the best of intentions stated by Mikhail Gorbachev to a complete collapse.

It might be said that there has emerged in Russia a desire to replay the outcome of the Cold War. Many Russians still believe that the Soviet Union did not lose the Cold War; it surrendered and left the battlefield. This surrender was a result of naiveté, as Moscow was enthralled by the illusion of "universal human values" (though more and more conspiracy theorists believe it was the result of betrayal).[15] Because of the outcome of the Cold War, Russia was no longer viewed as an equal by the West and was forced to make humiliating concessions. This erosion of Russian power is what Putin yearns to redress.

Suspecting Western treachery, Russians looked for devious moves and prepared to respond immediately. At first, Russian strategists thought Europe and America would take deliberate action against Russia, but later they came to expect only ill-conceived and irrational behavior that, in their view, destabilized the world. In an important article, published in February 2012, a week before the presidential election, Putin emphasized that "the Americans have become obsessed with the idea of becoming absolutely invulnerable. This utopian concept is unfeasible both technologically and geopolitically, but it is the root of the problem."[16]

Subsequently, the substance of Russia's foreign policy became increasingly clear. Putin's main goal was to protect Russian security and enhance Russia's international status and its capacity to influence global affairs. He insisted that "global security can only be achieved through cooperation with Russia rather than by attempts to push it into the background, weaken its geopolitical position, or compromise its defenses."[17] He made it clear that he intended to engender a balance between international engagement and "an independent foreign policy."[18]

But this turn to confrontation revealed the exhaustion of the previous model of Russian social, political, and economic development. Instead of focusing on patient economic engagement, integrating itself into global economic and trade networks, and using interdependence to strengthen its position relative to other great powers, Russia reverted to traditional geopolitics and the use of force. The Crimean events in 2014 illustrated that Putin sought to create social cohesion not through economic growth and prosperity, but by ideologically exploiting Russian sensibilities and anxieties. "We Do Not Surrender Our People!" was the slogan used in the rapid campaign to incorporate Crimea into Russia.

In Russian strategic culture there is a deep-rooted belief that the primary way Russia can achieve its geopolitical interests is through military force. If it tried to act diplomatically and economically, Russians believe that other countries would thwart Russian ambitions. "Russia has only two allies—the army and the navy"; this is a frequently expressed aphorism in Russian foreign policy debates. (The quotation is from Emperor Alexander III, the czar who laid the groundwork for the *entente cordiale* with France and then Britain, but this irony is disregarded by Russian public opinion.) In his remarks to the Russian Security Council on July 22, 2014, Putin emphasized the unilateral approach. "Thank God," he said, that "Russia is not a member of any alliances, and this is to a large extent a guarantee of our sovereignty."[19] By saying that, he virtually repudiated the alliances that Russia was trying to build, like the Collective Security Treaty Organization and Eurasian Economic Union, but he was sincere.

Indeed, there has been a tension in one significant aspect of Putin's strategy to recover power and influence. In addition to his military and geopolitical moves in Ukraine, he has also been pursuing Eurasian integration through the creation of a Eurasian Economic Union with Belarus and Kazakhstan. The Eurasian project has been much discussed since 2011, when Putin published a keynote article in the newspaper *Izvestia* almost immediately after he announced his plans to run for president again.[20]

The Eurasian Economic Community was established in 2000 to help realize the goals of integration and to underscore the commonality of strategic interests between Russia, Belarus, and Kazakhstan. It eventually led to the creation of the Customs Union and the Common Economic Space. Inspired by the Commonwealth of Independent States, Russia's emphasis on integration with its post-Soviet neighbors highlighted a focus on regional politics in Russian foreign strategy. Putin believed that post-Soviet politics should focus on "integration [as] a comprehensible, sustainable, and long-term project."[21] These integration projects, Putin noted, should set the stage for the eventual formation of a Eurasian Union, which he envisioned as "a powerful supranational association capable of becoming one of the poles in the modern world and serving as an efficient bridge between Europe and the dynamic Asia-Pacific region."[22] In fact, Putin has said that a top Russian "priority for the entire 21st century" must be a turn toward Asia.[23]

This talk of cooperation and integration, however, masks the geopolitical ambition of restoring Russian influence over the old Soviet imperium. Occasionally Putin makes plain such intentions. For example, in March 2014, when speaking about the secession referendum in Crimea, Putin evoked what has become the standard narrative of Russian victimhood. He claimed that the dissolution of the Soviet Union, and the resulting inclusion of Crimea as part of a sovereign Ukraine, proved that Russia "was not simply robbed, it was plundered."[24] This self-perception of Russia as an aggrieved nation undermines ideas of a cooperative and collaborative union of former Soviet republics and instead stresses Russia's right to hegemony. Even the Customs Union project, which adopts the language of economic integration drawn from the European Union, obscures Russia's actual geopolitical ambitions.

Whatever the motivations, Eurasian integration has become part of the national discourse on a new identity. From the beginning, Ukraine was seen as an indispensable part of any integration project in Eurasia. Indeed, the struggle for Ukrainian membership in the Customs Union was one of the key reasons for the geopolitical storm that swept the region in 2014.

Ukrainian events then resurrected calls for restoring the boundaries of Russia—not by economic integration, but by rendering "historical justice"—that is, by returning territories that were considered indigenously Russian and that had been unjustly severed from historic Russia.[25] Clearly, Putin deploys both ethnic as well as economic arguments to justify a broad strategy of recovering influence and power in Europe and in Eurasia.

Ideology, Nationalism, and Strategy

Scholars of national strategy naturally must account for the place of ideology in a state's pursuit of its interests, but in Russia's case, it is not clear how to assess the role of ideology. Putin seemed initially to reject ideology. "I am against restoring a state, official ideology in Russia in any form," Putin said in July 2000 in his first presidential address to the Federal Assembly.[26] In place of ideology, Putin has proposed the traditional values of Russians: patriotism, statism, and social solidarity.[27] Putin claimed that "the new Russian idea will be born as an alloy, as an organic compound of universal human values and traditional Russian values that have stood the test of time."[28] Since then, Putin had showed little interest in "universal human values." He prefers a basic pragmatism with respect to foreign policy and strategy.

Russian policy in the Middle East illustrates Putin's pragmatism. For three years, Russia's stance on the Syrian civil war was based on considerations of "pragmatism," "economic efficiency," and "the priority of national tasks" and avoided adopting an inflexible position. Many observers branded this position as immoral and unsuccessful, yet it had the advantage of being consistent and predictable against the backdrop of the flip-flopping of Western powers. This factor has not made other countries love Russia more, yet it has won it respect and attention, even among ill-wishers. Paradoxically, such successes, brought about by a nonideological foreign policy, created a demand for ideology. U.S. miscalculations in the Middle East left a vacuum. Local actors expected that Russia, as in Soviet times, would return to the region as a systemic alternative—not only militarily and politically, but also ideologically. The confrontation with the West in the post-Soviet space has contributed to the impulse to express strategy in ideological terms.

There has been a recent tendency to depart from a purely pragmatic foreign policy and embrace a certain ideological conservatism, which implies upholding one's set of values, possibly even at the expense of short-term interests. Over time, it may pay off by facilitating a firm bond between allies based on common values. To become a real center of influence in world affairs, a state needs to possess a strong ideological position. As a matter of fact, Putin counts on this: "We know that there are more and more people in the world who support our position in defense of traditional values, which have for millennia served as the spiritual and moral basis of civilization."[29] He believes that many people in China and India share his insistence on the defense of sovereignty, and he insists that the Russian Far East and the Pacific region are priorities for the twenty-first century. No one in Russia is against this, since the future of Russia as a great power depends on whether or not it is able to project its influence in those regions. However, in that part of the world people value, above all, pragmatism and economic efficiency, and only afterward do they pay attention to "what color the cat is," as Deng Xiaoping used to say. Putin grasps that too much focus on ideology could be counterproductive. So he modulates his ideological discourse even while he supports traditional values and trumpets the safeguarding of Russia's national sovereignty.

In fact, Putin vacillates between his ideological predilections, romantic-nationalist impulses, and imperial ambitions. The fall of the Yanukovych regime in Ukraine inspired discussion about which model of state-building to choose—imperial or national—and placed Russian leaders in the most difficult position they had been in since Putin gained power in August 1999. The possibility that Ukraine, under a new government, might finally turn toward the Euro-Atlantic alliance caused Moscow to intervene suddenly in Crimea, with the rapid seizure of the peninsula and its placement under military control, followed by a referendum and its immediate incorporation into Russia. The developments in Crimea were sparked by two motivations. One of them was strategic, connected with the need to possess a bridgehead for basing the Black Sea Fleet and projecting force. The other inspiration was national/cultural—Crimea was a territory which was populated predominantly by ethnic Russians. Only by historical accident had it found itself incorporated into Ukraine and now faced with violent action from the new authorities in Kyiv. Thus, two motives—imperial/strategic and national/ethnic—reinforced one another. Proponents of intervention hailed the Crimean decision with much enthusiasm—some as a step toward the restoration of Russia's great power status and the expansion of its strategic reach and others as an action to protect ethnic Russians.

To judge from Putin's previous record, his real motivation was strategic, since he was never inclined to play with ethnic nationalism. In fact, he used to emphasize the threat that ethnic nationalism posed to society. But since the intervention in Crimea was highly controversial from the point of view of international law and marked Russia's departure from legal norms, he had to turn to another kind of argumentation—namely, a stress upon uniting "lost" Russian peoples.

However, in the next phase of the Ukraine crisis, the two motives diverged. The civil war in eastern Ukraine quickly acquired a national-cultural tint in the public mind: ethnic Russians in the region claimed to be defending their dignity and rights against the Ukrainian nationalist regime. And since the protection of compatriots was officially declared a priority of the Russian state—this was the focus of Putin's historic Crimean address—there arose expectations, both in the east of Ukraine and in Russia, that Moscow would act as resolutely as it did in Crimea. But this illuminated a flaw in Putin's strategy: instead of pursuing a purely pragmatic, geopolitical strategy based on securing the borderlands, he unleashed the demons of ethnic nationalism and internecine war.

Moscow's behavior in eastern Ukraine remains a game of brinkmanship, common in major crises, in which the opponent's limits are tested.[30] If it is possible to advance without much risk, this will be done. If it is not, it is better to retreat and fix the problems. This is a great gamble in the spirit of realpolitik very dear to the Russian strategic mind. However, fighters in the east of Ukraine, and those in Russia who sympathized with them, were waiting for something different from the Kremlin—behavior in the spirit of national romanticism because, after all, they were fellow Russians. Of course, some people saw a geopolitical motivation here: the "surrender" of Novorossiya ("New Russia" as the eastern part of current Ukraine was called since the eighteenth century when it was obtained by the Russian empire) would result in Russia losing credibility and would enable NATO missiles to move even closer to Moscow. Yet nationalist idealism was more important here.

Russian leaders are faced with a difficult choice. Obviously, Putin's responsibility is to prevent his country from becoming involved in a conflict that would undermine its security. However, the emergence of the nationalist factor—not in abstract terms, but as a threat to fellow Russians, to which the president must react—challenges his personal credibility because he has uttered many strong words. For a long time, he focused on restoring the governability of the Russian state, which had become almost unmanageable in the 1990s. He achieved a great deal, restoring social stability and economic growth, thereby inspiring pride and confidence. But the events in

eastern Ukraine endanger the progress he has made. Russians who are fighting there have very different views, ranging from supporters of the "white"
idea (Tsarist Russia as opposed not only to the current one, but also to the
Soviet Union), to fighters against oligarchy, to socialists and leftist anarchists.
Yet they are united by a desire for justice, which they interpret in their own
way, mainly in nationalist terms—the protection of fellow Russians at any
cost. Ethnic pride and national identity may clash with Russia's own security
interests if prudence does not prevail.

Putin has not yet chosen between the temptations of an imperial model,
based on loose consolidation and control premised on Russian hegemony,
and a nationalistic state based around homogeneous nationality and ethnic-
ity, clearly defined borders, ethnic and moral categories, and national values
framed as the defiant answer to Western complaints against the Russian nation and people. Either path, empire or nation-state, contains risks not just
for Russia, but for the rest of Eurasia and the world.

Russia's Current Dilemmas

Russia finds itself on the eve of the next phase in its political history—both
domestically and internationally. For the past twenty years, Russia has struggled and failed to define a new path of national development or foreign policy. Trying to depart from the Soviet legacy, Russia instead made a circle and
returned to the same point from which it began its movement. The Russian
elite, as well as a big part of society, judging by the enthusiasm caused by the
incorporation of Crimea, has not overcome the trauma inflicted by the Soviet Union's breakup. The annexation of Crimea can be viewed in two ways:
as psychological compensation for overcoming the humiliations at the end
of the Cold War or as the beginning of a purposeful strategy to gather lands
of the "core," which Russia thinks belongs to it by right. Whatever the motives, the internal dynamics unleashed by events in Ukraine might constrain
Putin's policy options and create expectations of a nationalist consolidation
that Putin may come to regret.

Beyond the crisis in Crimea and Ukraine, Russia faces interlocking challenges that will define its strategy. Russia remains dissatisfied with its position on the world stage and has sought to take advantage of the failure of
the West to establish a stable post–Cold War order. Western domination
has not been achieved in full measure, and the growth of the East and the
emancipation of countries that previously had not played important roles in

the international arena provide many opportunities for a complex game that Russia can exploit. This contest may play out chiefly in Asia, toward which Russia may reorient itself. The development of Siberia and the Russian Far East is now viewed as a large national modernization project offering great opportunities for wealth, power, and influence. Yet this need to "pivot to the East" pulls Russia away from its cultural identity and historical links with Europe. Russia will have to find a way to combine its European heritage with the development of its Asian ties.

In addition to seeking new avenues for economic development, Russia is attempting to build a new national identity on the ashes of its Soviet experience. But this poses profound problems. Will this identity be based on a diverse and pluralistic model, favored in the West? Or will Russia attempt to craft an integral nationalism, drawing on the perception of long-standing grievances and antagonisms toward the West and toward other ethnic nationalities in Eurasia? The stakes are high here, for it is common to launch foreign adventures as a tool to build national unity, despite the risks that such entanglements like those in Crimea and Ukraine often create.

Perhaps Russia's main dilemma today is how to ensure its own sovereignty and independence in an interdependent world—even if that effort comes at the expense of neighbors like Ukraine. The desire to achieve complete sovereignty and get rid of dependence on external forces has motivated many of Putin's moves since the beginning of his presidency. Moscow seeks maximum self-sufficiency, but objectively this is hardly possible in a globalized world.

Vladimir Putin's multiple presidencies have coincided with Russia's journey from a period of profound crisis and domestic weakness to a reassertion of Russian power on the world stage. Putin has successfully restored the functionality of the Russian state and has developed a foreign policy enjoying wide public support. The Kremlin's strategy has been based on the assumption that Russia should be socially stable and economically strong in order to play a bigger international role. Worried about the proliferating activities of the West in what he regards as Russia's sphere of influence, Putin has drawn on his realpolitik beliefs, thinking that the balance of forces is a prerequisite for stability in bilateral relationships as well as in the overall international system.

Putin is now considered by many (some with admiration, some with disgust) as one of the most powerful leaders in the world, a cool and calculated chess player with a grand vision. In fact, he has never been a big strategist, but a skillful tactician who has reacted to evolving circumstances based on an instinctive sense of realpolitik. When he switched course in 2014 and moved toward a national strategy based on appeals to an archaic nationalist-romantic ideology, Putin created a fundamental contradiction between this nationalist ideology and his quest for Russian national renewal through modernization, integration, and stability. Until this tension is resolved, Russia may face many more crises of the kind that burst forth in Ukraine in 2014.

CHAPTER 7

TURKEY

Populism and Geography

YAPRAK GÜRSOY

URING the Cold War years, Turkish strategy was defensive, status-quo oriented, and relied on the use of military instruments. In the late 1990s, and especially after the Justice and Development Party (Adalet ve Kalkınma Partisi) came to power in 2002, Turkish strategy changed; it began to seek regional power status with a potential to influence international politics beyond its neighborhood.[1] Although this goal did not evolve much over subsequent years, Turkish tactics did continue to change. Between 2002 and 2011, Turkish officials often employed economic and diplomatic instruments to achieve their goals; after 2011, they used them more sparingly and increasingly embraced populist rhetoric to portray Turkey as the leader of the oppressed Sunni Muslims of the Middle East and elsewhere. In President Recep Tayyip Erdoğan's perceptions of international politics, Western powers treated Sunni Muslims unfairly and overlooked the atrocities of coercive Middle Eastern regimes.[2] Although Erdoğan talked as if he would not hesitate to use military capabilities to protect his religious brethren, Turkey would never start an outright war with any of its neighbors, or with Western powers, over such matters. Nonetheless, Erdoğan's populist approach juxtaposed Sunnis against "the other," and this rhetorical posturing was a major departure from the pre-2011 conduct of Turkish strategy and diplomacy.

This chapter examines the recent evolution of Turkish strategy by looking at three factors: the international, the national, and the individual. Two developments abroad necessitated a reassessment of Turkey's tactics. The first was the halting of the negotiations regarding Turkish membership in the European Union; the second was the onset of the Arab uprisings in late 2010. At the domestic level of analysis, Turkish politics entered a new phase. The elite coalition that first supported the Justice and Development Party (JDP) in its rise to power crumbled, and yet the party managed to maintain its primacy. Its leader, Erdoğan, responded to his domestic critics by linking them to foreign powers and their regional collaborators. Using foreign policy for domestic political purposes, the prime minister harnessed populist, anti-Western sentiment to secure his domination of Turkish politics, thereby highlighting the importance of the individual.

This chapter is organized into six sections. The first provides a brief overview of Cold War Turkish strategy, focusing on the decision-makers and their goals and tactics. The second section outlines the evolution of Turkey's strategic ambitions in the 1990s and highlights the circumstances conditioning Turkey's quest for regional power. The third part analyzes the tactics that were used between 2002 and 2011 to achieve this goal. The following section examines how these soft power instruments comported with the interests of the domestic political coalition that formed around the JDP. The fifth segment illuminates the international causes of the tactical shifts in 2011 and explains why it became impossible to use economic and diplomatic instruments to realize Turkey's strategic ambitions. The chapter concludes with an analysis of domestic power struggles, an examination of Erdoğan's efforts to preserve his political base by linking his domestic foes to external enemies, and a consideration of whether these tactics can be successful in achieving Turkey's goals.

Turkish Strategy during the Cold War

One of the primary goals of Turkish strategy during the Cold War years was to defend against the Soviet threat. Turkish leaders viewed military power as the most important instrument to guard against the USSR and other regional foes. They regarded NATO and the Western alliance as indispensable to their success. Officials in Ankara viewed Turkey as a critical geopolitical asset bridging Europe, Asia, and Africa.[3] In their view, the interests of Turkey and the West were interdependent; an unstable Turkey would weaken efforts to contain the Soviet Union and unsettle surrounding regions.

The secular republican character of the Turkish state after the collapse of the Ottoman Empire led to a defensive worldview. The republican military leaders who fought the war of independence against the Allied forces after World War I and who established the new state, embraced Westernization as the nation's most important objective and guarded its domestic system. For many years, along with the bureaucrats of the Ministry of Foreign Affairs, they shaped Turkish strategy.[4] Turkey's secular elites perceived Islamic Middle Eastern countries as threats and preferred to disengage from them.[5] Seeing enemies to the north and the south, Turkish officials wanted to use military capabilities to deter their foes, not to alter the status quo. Embracing the motto—"peace at home, peace in the world"—of their founding father, Mustafa Kemal Atatürk, they acted in ways that did not challenge the status quo in the international system or with their neighbors. Perhaps the only country against whom they pondered the use of military power was their NATO ally, Greece. Disputes over the Aegean Sea and Cyprus periodically brought the two allies to the brink of war and were mediated at times by U.S. diplomatic interventions.

During the Cold War years, realpolitik concerns of security dominated Turkish politics.[6] Military leaders emphasized territorial integrity and national unity. They viewed leftists, religious fundamentalists, and the Kurdish minority with great mistrust. Seizing power in 1960, and again in 1980, military officers coupled foreign and domestic threats, linking the Turkish left to the USSR, and conflating the threat from Middle Eastern neighbors, political Islamists, and Kurdish separatists. They also distrusted their Western allies, occasionally suspecting that they supported the Kurdish separatists and wanted to keep Turkey weak and dependent. Throughout these years, Turkey's strategic dilemma was that its leaders yearned to be accepted into the modern civilization of the West yet also desired autonomy and wanted to prove the country's worth.

The Transformation of Strategic Ambitions in the Post–Cold War Era

In the late 1990s, Turkey's strategic ambitions evolved from a defensive status-quo orientation. There were three main reasons for this transformation. First, the end of the Cold War brought about new challenges and opportunities. Turkey had emphasized its geopolitical position as an asset in order to secure a place in the Western camp. Now that the threat from the Soviet Union was over, Turkey's proximity to the "danger zone" could not be the only reason for its alliance with the United States and European powers. If

Turkey wanted to become part of the West, it had to show its worth through a different strategy.[7]

The end of the Cold War had also brought about an opportunity to increase Turkey's independence from the West. The dissolution of the Soviet Union allowed Turkey to seek new partnerships with the Turkic republics of Central Asia and the Muslim populations in the Balkans. Turkey could now stress not only its geopolitical position, but also its cultural and historical qualities. A republican, secular, and democratic Turkey, with a majority Muslim population and Ottoman past, could still serve as a bridge between the Middle East, Central Asia, and the West.[8] Turkey's value to the West would persist, but Ankara could now pursue its own interests independent of its Western allies.

Turkey's strategic ambitions also changed because of regional politics. In 1999, the leader of the Kurdistan Workers' Party (PKK), Abdullah Öcalan, was captured after Turkey threatened war with Syria, where he was based. Syria deported Öcalan, who sought shelter in different countries, including Russia, Italy, and Greece. He was finally apprehended in Nairobi, Kenya, as he left the Greek embassy. The provisional resolution of the conflict with the Kurds increased Turkish self-confidence while also eliminating perceptions of a Syrian threat and eradicating suspicions of Western support to the terrorist organization. Greek involvement also paved the way for a rapprochement between the two Aegean countries.

The third factor that led to a transformation in strategic ambitions was the decision of the European Union (EU) in 1999 to grant candidate status to Turkey, partially due to the Greek decision to lift its veto. Turkey had had a long and disappointing journey with the evolving EU. In 1963, Turkey signed the Ankara Agreement with the European Economic Community, which planned full integration. Turkey applied for full membership in 1987, but was rejected for its insufficient democratic credentials. Although a customs union agreement was signed in 1995, the EU excluded Turkey in 1997 when it accepted the former Eastern Bloc countries and Cyprus as candidates for membership. The reversal of this decision two years later marked a key transitional moment.[9] As the contemporary prime minister Bülent Ecevit remarked, this decision "was not only a significant achievement for Turkey," but was also an event that interested the entire region and the world. Stressing the geopolitical position of Turkey, Ecevit added that "Turkey is [now] a key country in the most sensitive region of the world."[10]

Altogether, 1999 constituted a turning point in Turkish strategy. No longer viewing neighbors and global powers with fear and suspicion, Turkish officials possessed more self-confidence. After 1997, Minister of Foreign Affairs İsmail Cem advocated a more active policy that highlighted Turkey's European and Asian identities as well as its cultural and historical assets. Turkey, he believed, could be more independent and assertive. It could become a "world state, meaning a state that does not envy others, but is envied." Explaining Turkey's strategic vision, Cem claimed that instead of being on the periphery of Europe, Turkey was "the biggest economy, the most deep-rooted democracy and the strongest armed force in the wider region." Given its qualities, Turkey's aim was to become the "central country of the evolving Eurasian reality" and utilize the political "opportunities that surfaced with the end of the Cold War."[11]

The JDP Embrace of Soft Power

If the goal of becoming a regional power was set in the late 1990s, the instruments that would be used to achieve this ambition were laid out more clearly after the moderately Islamist JDP won the elections in 2002. Ahmet Davutoğlu, who served in the Turkish government first as an advisor to Erdoğan, then after 2009 as the minister of foreign affairs, and currently as the prime minister, identified four interrelated tactics.[12] First, rather than viewing Turkey encircled by enemies, he drew a new image envisioning the possibility of cooperative relations across borders. Turkey, therefore, pursued "zero problems with neighbors," even with previous adversaries such as Russia, Armenia, and Greece. Friendly relations with neighbors would alter the status quo of existing hostility.

Second, Turkey used economic and diplomatic instruments in its relations with other countries. Erdoğan and Davutoğlu strengthened economic ties with Middle Eastern neighbors, especially Syria and Iraq, and launched new diplomatic initiatives of a bilateral and multilateral nature. The use of multilateral channels was underlined in the policy of "rhythmic diplomacy," which meant active participation in international organizations.

Third, Turkey assumed the role of mediator and tried to serve as a model and leader in the Middle East, Balkans, Caucasus, and Central Asia. The three roles complemented one another: Turkey was a leader because it mediated between hostile nations, such as Israel, Palestine, and Syria, and also because it could maintain contact with antagonistic groups, such as Shiites or Sunnis, in Iraq and Lebanon.[13] Turkey was a model because it was an exemplar of an Islamic country with a democratic regime. "Turkey's most important soft power," Davutoğlu argued, was "its democracy" and its ability to reconcile security with freedom and human rights.[14]

The JDP's fourth tactic was to continue Turkey's cordial relations with the West. In the auspicious atmosphere of the 1999 EU decision, the party was openly pro-EU and advocated reforms in domestic politics that would secure eventual Turkish membership in the union. Erdoğan and Davutoğlu also remained staunchly committed to NATO, allaying concerns that the JDP had an Islamist agenda or was contemplating an "axis shift" to align more closely with Middle East neighbors. JDP leaders viewed Turkey's historical, cultural, and geographic position as central to different regions and continents, which made it possible to be anchored in both the Western and Islamic civilizations simultaneously. It was this blend of Western and Islamic identity that actually made the other tactics feasible. Turkey was a credible leader, or model, because of its connections with both civilizations. Similarly, Turkey's simultaneous membership in diverse international organizations, such as the Organization of Islamic Cooperation and NATO (as well as possibly the EU), allowed for the use of multilateral channels.

Domestic Politics and the Use of Soft Power

The tactics of the JDP government reflected new power configurations in Turkish domestic politics. The JDP was formed after the military—in collaboration with secular political parties, several civil society organizations, and sections of the media—forced the two-party coalition government that included the Islamist Welfare Party (WP) out of power. The leader of the WP, Prime Minister Necmettin Erbakan, had intimidated secular elites by his religious rhetoric and independence in foreign policy, such as his visits to Libya and Iran. In 1998, the WP was closed down by the secular judiciary and three years later its offshoot was banned. The party then split into two factions, and the moderate, younger generation formed the JDP. Erdoğan had been the WP mayor of Istanbul between 1994 and 1998 but was imprisoned due to a speech he delivered in December 1997. He served four months and was prohibited from holding political positions. He then founded the JDP in 2001. A year after the party won the 2002 elections, he became the prime minister when the new parliament lifted the ban on his political participation.[15]

Apart from successfully receiving votes from urban lower classes, the JDP was also endorsed by a coalition of forces, some of which formerly supported the WP. The small- and medium-scale entrepreneurs of Anatolia were one

such group. They had opposed the privileged positions of the bigger industrialists and traders, who were mostly located in Istanbul and who possessed
a more secular political outlook. The smaller businessmen of Anatolia were
more conservative and religious.[16] These "Anatolian tigers" had increased
their power substantially during the era of pro-market economic policies
of the 1980s. In 1990, they formed the Independent Industrialists and Businessmen Association (MÜSİAD). Although some MÜSİAD members were
harassed and persecuted by military and secular leaders in the late 1990s,
these pro-Islamist businessmen continued to increase their economic power
and backed the JDP.[17] Shortly after the party came to power, several regional
business associations established the Turkish Confederation of Businessmen
and Industrialists (TUSKON). Businessmen affiliated with TUSKON frequently joined government officials on their foreign visits.

A second group supporting the JDP's political rise was the religious
brotherhoods, especially the movement led by Fethullah Gülen. A moderate
and modern preacher as well as an opinion leader, Gülen mobilized millions
of followers inside and outside of Turkey. The movement funded schools all
over the world and established links with media, business, and civil society
organizations. Gülen was a resident of Turkey, but in 2000 he was accused
of attempting covertly to bring down the state, leading him to remain per-
manently in the United States, where he already resided because of health
problems.[18] Although Erdoğan was not linked to Gülen's movement, its media and business wings did support the JDP in its early years. In return, the
JDP permitted Gülen's followers to increase their influence in state organs,
especially in the judiciary and police.

Liberals also backed the JDP in the early 2000s—academics, newspaper columnists, younger generation businessmen, civil society activists, and
policy experts loosely united in terms of their democratic ideals. Although
they represented a small minority in Turkish politics and society, their secular outlook and aspirations for more democracy and freedom for everyone
(including pious individuals) put them in a unique position. The JDP initially garnered their support by its pro-EU rhetoric and reforms. Democratic
constitutional amendments and laws enacted by the JDP during its first two
terms in office inspired hope that religious politics could be reconciled with
a secular state.[19]

A common disdain for the military's involvement in politics fostered unity
among these diverse groups and encouraged them to coalesce around the
JDP. The temporary defeat of the PKK had already decreased the significance

of the military in providing internal security, and the reform packages passed by the JDP to fulfill the political criteria for EU membership also helped to gradually dismantle the dominance of the military in Turkish politics. Zealous state prosecutors, who may have been Gülen supporters, opened two separate cases in 2008 and 2010 against current and retired members of the armed forces. The former military officers were charged with planning coups against the JDP government. The government then prosecuted hundreds of military leaders, including former commanders and a chief of the general staff, sentencing them to terms in prison.[20]

The influence of the armed forces in strategic decision-making receded as their members faced court charges and prison sentences. The civilian bureaucracy in the foreign ministry and elsewhere also lost influence as Erdoğan and Davutoğlu assumed control over all critical decisions. While Davutoğlu acted as the theoretical and intellectual architect of Turkish strategy, Erdoğan clearly had the final say.[21]

The constituencies that had thrown their support behind the JDP benefited from the party's growing power and played a key role in extending Turkey's soft power. The JDP allowed the Gülen movement to expand in various parts of the world. Liberals were encouraged to pursue their quest for closer ties to the EU. Businessmen were supported in their efforts to expand trade and investment with Turkey's neighbors. Turkish industrial and construction firms pursued new export outlets, especially in the Middle East and Africa. Segments of the business community who were associated with the JDP advanced faster than their competitors. These businessmen, however, were not the drivers of Turkish strategy; nonetheless, they promoted the ambitions of the JDP by increasing Turkey's soft power in the region.[22]

Aid organizations, civil society groups, and NGOs also increased their visibility after the JDP came to power and helped to extend Turkey's soft power. The Turkish Cooperation and Coordination Agency (TIKA) operated as the Turkish equivalent of USAID. It garnered a budget approaching $1 billion, establishing offices in thirty different countries and distributing assistance to one hundred states.[23] Civil society organizations, including Islamic organizations, such as the Association of Solidarity for Human Rights and the Oppressed (Mazlum-Der) and the Humanitarian Relief Foundation (IHH), became active in the Balkans and Africa and also distributed aid, especially among Muslims.[24] These groups had no direct links to the government, but like their counterparts in the business community, they advanced the JDP's agenda abroad through a strategy of soft power.

International Complications

Soft power proved less efficacious than its advocates had hoped in advancing Turkey's regional power and allowing Turkey to serve as a bridge between Western powers and the Islamic states of the Middle East. In 2003, the Turkish parliament rejected the use of Turkish territory by American forces during the Iraqi war, and relations with the United States quickly deteriorated. Turkey's ties to Iran and Syria also agitated Washington, as did Erdoğan's criticism of Israel after its offensive actions against Palestine in 2004.[25] In 2009, the public row at the World Economic Forum between Erdoğan and Israeli president Shimon Peres over Israeli operations in Gaza signaled a precipitous worsening of Turkish-Israeli relations. When Israel attacked the aid flotilla to Gaza, sponsored by the IHH, the following year, nine Turks were killed. Turkish and Israeli officials venomously blamed one another, and Turkey's relations with the United States soured as well.

EU actions further thwarted Turkish aspirations. In 2006, the EU halted Turkey's accession process by freezing eight out of the thirty-five negotiation chapters because of Turkey's failure to apply the provisions of the Additional Protocol to the Ankara Agreement to Cyprus, one of the EU's new members. The next year, France blocked negotiations on four additional chapters and in 2009 Cyprus added six more to the list. These decisions aggravated the deep-seated belief in Ankara that the Europeans were treating Turkey unfairly. The EU had favored Cyprus over Turkey, and it had minimized the JDP's efforts to carry out legal reforms in accordance with EU requirements. No other candidates for EU membership had encountered hurdles similar to those faced by Turkey. Turks could only conclude that they were being excluded because of their predominantly Muslim population. Rebuffed, JDP officials accused Western governments of insincerity and began constructing Muslims as martyrs of Western prejudice and bigotry. The EU setback negated Turkey's desire to augment its regional influence by serving as a bridge between the democratic West and the Islamic world.

Although the JDP won a resounding victory in the June 2011 elections, other regional developments shattered Ankara's ability to use its soft power to achieve regional status and international influence. Having "zero problems with neighbors" became impossible as neighbors faced growing internal turmoil and civil strife. Economic and diplomatic ties suffered. With the advent of protests in Arab countries, Turkey was forced to make excruciatingly difficult choices between supporting the rebels or the regimes with whom it had previously cooperated.[26] Ankara found it hard to play a role as mediator in a region buffeted by ferment and radicalization. In general, Turkey sided with the protesters, such as the Muslim Brotherhood in Egypt, and alienated Egyptian military leaders who seized power and who reminded JDP leaders of the military secularists whom they had struggled against for years inside Turkey.[27] In doing so, Turkey further jeopardized its relations with Western and other regional powers. And even when it cooperated with NATO in taking military measures—for example, against Gadaffi in Libya—Turkey undermined its previous championing of soft power.

The most important challenge to Turkey's policies came in Syria. At the start of the insurgency in March 2011, Turkey initially tried to mediate. Erdoğan appealed to Syrian president Bashar Al-Assad, whom he had once referred to as "my brother," and asked for reforms and a gradual transition. However, the attacks in Hama by Syrian forces and the subsequent futile visit of Davutoğlu to Damascus in the summer of 2011 alienated Turkish leaders. Turkey then sided with the insurgents, who established the Syrian National Council in Istanbul, and Ankara eased border controls allowing critical supplies to be transported to the rebels. Faced with a dire threat to his regime, Assad then permitted Kurdish forces in Syria to gain ground, engendering fears in Ankara about further unrest among the Kurds in Turkey. In May 2013, Turkish government officials held Syrian intelligence responsible for carrying out a terrorist attack in the Turkish province of Reyhanlı, killing more than fifty people. Ankara then hardened its policies even further, collaborating with, and possibly supplying arms to, the insurgents.[28] Ensnared in Syria's civil war and engulfed by its repercussions for Iraq, Turkey's hopes to use soft power to serve as a regional mediator and power broker were dashed.

The Syrian crisis in particular and the Middle Eastern uprisings in general jeopardized Turkey's relations with its other neighbors—namely, Russia and Iran. Turkey had cooperated with both countries on trade, energy, and tourism facilitated by visa-free travel. Yet differences simmered below the surface. Moscow was an ally of the Damascus regime, arousing anger in Ankara. At the same time, Iran wanted to increase its influence over the Shiite population in the region, challenging Turkey's support of Sunnis. Meanwhile, Turkey's cooperation with NATO's missile defense system and the arrival of Patriot surface-to-air missiles prompted resentment in both Tehran and Moscow. Overall, Ankara's quest to be a bridge between Iran and Russia on the one hand and the West on the other hand failed.[29]

Nor could Turkey exercise much of its vaunted soft power in Iraq. As elsewhere in the Middle East, the intensifying strife inside Iraq made the conduct of diplomacy exceedingly difficult for Turkey. Overcoming its initial hesitation, Ankara established a flourishing trade with Kurdish Iraq and began importing oil from that region.[30] However, the central government in Baghdad looked upon Turkish ties with Iraqi Kurds as a threat to the unity of the country. Washington agreed with Baghdad and warned against arrangements that would bypass the Iraqi government.[31] In return, Ankara criticized Shia officials in Baghdad for their authoritarianism and supported moderate Sunnis. Turkey, for example, granted asylum to Tariq al-Hashimi, the leader of the Islamic Party, against whom Iraqi courts issued a death sentence.[32]

Turkey's hopes for "zero problems with neighbors," for serving as a mediator of disputes in the Middle East, and for constituting a bridge between East and West were thwarted by a series of regional and international events which officials in Ankara could not control. As the value of its soft power waned—in the summer of 2014 Turkey did not have ambassadors in Israel, Syria, or Egypt—temptations to use military power increased, as was apparent in Syria. But Erdoğan much preferred to seek regional power status by employing a populist rhetoric, by appealing to disillusioned Middle Eastern publics, and by claiming to be a representative of the downtrodden. This populist posturing had an audience at home and was useful to mobilize his internal constituencies against domestic foes.

Domestic Politics and Populist Posturing

While the rebuff from the EU and the turmoil in the Middle East emasculated Ankara's soft power, domestic political dynamics made populism a useful tool for audiences at home and abroad. After the June 2011 elections, the JDP's alliance with its previous partners ruptured. The liberals, already disillusioned by faltering talks with the EU, were infuriated by Erdoğan's response to protests against a plan to reconstruct the city center of Istanbul. When he dispersed protesters and ignored critics, liberals concluded that the government would never carry out democratic reforms and they condemned Erdoğan's growing authoritarianism.[33] In return, the president claimed that the protests were instigated by Turkey's foreign enemies, including the United States and Israel, in collusion with domestic foes, such as the Republican People's Party (the party that had founded the republic and is currently the largest opposition in parliament). Erdoğan also accused the "interest lob-by"—specifically, businessmen who were profiting from the ongoing crises and the resulting increases in interest rates.

After 2011, the JDP's relations with its other constituency, the Gülen movement, shattered. Initially, the JDP and the Gülen movement were unit-ed in their disdain of the military establishment. However, as time passed, it became clear that Erdoğan and Gülen were on opposite sides of key issues, especially after the Israelis attacked the flotilla carrying aid to Gaza. In May 2010, Gülen argued that "failure to seek accord with Israel before attempting to deliver aid" was a mistake.[34] Erdoğan, meanwhile, condemned Israel's ac-tions and said they must be punished.[35]

Afterward, the rift between the JDP and the Gülen movement intensified. In the winter of 2013, the JDP attempted to close down schools linked to the Gülen movement that were preparing students for university entrance ex-ams. In response, alleged Gülen prosecutors began a corruption investigation leading to the arrest of a construction tycoon, an Iranian-Azeri businessman, the sons of three government ministers, and the general manager of a state bank.[36] Subsequently, prosecutors stopped a truck supposedly carrying arms to the Syrian rebels. They wanted to search the truck, but the Turkish Na-tional Intelligence Agency (MİT) did not allow it.[37] The raid on the truck and the corruption charges were perceived as efforts by Gülen movement prosecutors to undermine the government.

After the corruption investigation, government ministers were changed, and since then, there have been attempts to cleanse the police and judi-ciary of suspected Gülen supporters. Erdoğan began to dominate Turkish politics by sidelining other decision-makers and increasingly relying on ad-visors such as the chief of the MİT.[38] Erdoğan also embraced populism as he sought to campaign for the presidency. Like other populists, he divided society into antagonistic groups, the "pure people" and the "corrupt elite," and presented himself as a leader embodying the general will of the people.[39] He blamed "the elites" or "the establishment" for the ills of society and argued that imminent dangers required decisive action.[40] He assailed rich business-men and the Republican People's Party for orchestrating the summer 2013 street protests. He claimed that Gülen supporters were the "parallel state," giving the impression that they were also part of the establishment. Accord-ing to Erdoğan, these groups were trying to prevent the advancement "of the people," described variously as the nation, the general will, the Sunnis, the electoral majority, or a combination of these groups.

Like populist leaders in Latin America, Erdoğan positioned himself against U.S. imperialism and denounced the unjust actions of the West. In his view, the 2013 protests and the corruption inquiry were orchestrated by the collusion of the United States with his domestic foes. Allegedly, these internal enemies and external adversaries wanted to prevent Turkey from carrying out democratic reforms or solving its Kurdish problem—or more broadly from becoming stronger or taking independent action in the region.[41] Moreover, according to Erdoğan, the plots were not just against him and his supporters, but against popularly elected Sunni politicians throughout the region. Oppressed people in Egypt, Syria, Palestine, and elsewhere were all victims of Western power and American hubris. Erdoğan embraced the mission to thwart America's collaborators inside Turkey and was prepared to confront them throughout the region and elsewhere. He sought the benedictions and prayers of "the Turkish nation" and presented himself as the champion of "the aggrieved Palestinians," "Somalians in poverty," "oppressed [children] in Syria," and "the waifs and strays" of the Islamic world.[42] He embodied the struggle between good and evil, the powerful and the weak, and the West and Islam.[43]

In a regional and international context, where old instruments and tactics did not work and where Turkey's soft power had eroded, populism became a vehicle to gain influence among the Sunnis of the region. Although Erdoğan gained some support among the Arab people, his populism did not achieve any concrete gains for Turkish foreign policy.[44] Nonetheless, Erdoğan used his populist rhetoric to tarnish his domestic foes and identify them as the pawns of foreign powers. In a country where xenophobic tendencies run high and where foreign and domestic enemies are historically linked, Erdoğan's populist politics inspired the loyalty of his party supporters, discredited his critics, and identified him as the authentic and organic leader of Turkey.

※ ※ ※

As the JDP's initial coalition shattered and as Davutoğlu's soft power tactics foundered as a result of the EU's rebuff and Middle East ferment, Erdoğan embraced a form of populist politics that shaped Turkey's overall strategy and foreign policy. While his critics assailed his mistakes in the neighborhood and his worsening ties with traditional allies, Erdoğan reframed Turkish strategy with a form of populism that was designed to unite his supporters at home and to project Turkish influence abroad. In this way, he sought to sustain Turkey's ambition to gain regional power and international influence. Erdoğan's populist rhetoric might work at home to mobilize his supporters but will probably not yield successful results in a neighborhood undergoing extraordinary turbulence and strife. Nor is Erdoğan likely to allow his populist discourse to disrupt Turkey's long-standing relationship with NATO. Overall, then, Erdoğan will find it hard to reconcile Turkey's historical goal of defending against external enemies with its ambition to become a regional power. In reality, Turkey's conflicting Muslim, Western, democratic, and Ottoman identities do not sit easily alongside one another. Consequently, Erdoğan's populist strategy is likely to remain only at the discursive level, adding layers of complexity to the historically troubled relationship between Turkey and the West on the one hand and between Turkey and neighboring countries on the other.

CHAPTER 8

UNITED STATES

Grappling with Rising Powers

JAMES B. STEINBERG

A COUNTRY'S national security strategy does not exist in a vacuum. Indeed, the essence of strategy is a road map for pursuing national interest in context. The external environment conditions and constrains what goals a nation chooses to pursue, as well as the means that will be available and necessary to achieve those goals. There are many different elements that make up the external environment. Some are relatively fixed: geography, climate, and natural resources, for example. But others change over time: demography, technology, and, perhaps most important, the goals and objectives of other nations (and increasingly today, nonstate actors). For this reason, it should be obvious that a good strategy must take into account the strategies pursued by others. This should go without saying, but for a variety of reasons in the United States in recent years, there has been a deficit of attention to this critical issue.

Of course, that wasn't always the case—at key points in our history, American political leaders and thinkers have been keenly focused on the strategies of others states. In the early years, when our relatively weak new nation had to navigate among the great powers to assure our survival and economic growth, American strategy depended heavily on the insights provided by our remarkable diplomats—Franklin, Jefferson, Adams, and Jay—about the intentions of European nations. During the Cold War, our leaders turned again to diplomats and analysts for an understanding of Soviet strategy—hence the enormous influence of Kennan's Long Telegram and the "X" article on the "Sources of Soviet Conduct."[1] The global contest with the Soviet Union required the United States to pay attention not just to our main adversary— but to the other players on the chessboard—from our allies to the complex machinations of the nonaligned. We didn't always get it right, but from East Asia to Africa to Latin America, legions of Foreign Service officers, intelligence analysts, and scholars devoted time and resources to divining the plans of others, even in relatively obscure corners of the earth, from the jungles of Southeast Asia to the Horn of Africa.

At other times in U.S. history we were less attuned—geographic isolation and growing power often led to a belief that Washington could unilaterally secure American interests without deep engagement with, or understanding of, the goals and strategies of others. This was true for much of the nineteenth century and again between the two world wars. Americans have come to see that the failure to understand and to shape the choices of others through U.S. engagement has proved costly.[2]

The end of the Cold War ushered in another moment when it appeared that the United States could safely ignore the strategies of others. The enemy was gone, the strategic rationale for alliances evaporated, U.S. power was unmatched, and American values were ascendant. The end of history promised the prospect of good relations *tous azimuts.* The few remaining spoiler states were weak and would soon be swept away by the great democratic transition brought about not by coercion, but by the invisible hand of economic interdependence and modern information technology. For some observers, the "end of history" meant the end of strategy, as the emergence of a democratic liberal order would naturally align the interests of the "rest" with those of the United States, with no peer competitor or counterbalancing coalition to challenge U.S.-dominated international order.[3]

The reality proved more complicated. The end of the Cold War meant that America's allies were less dependent on the United States for security—and therefore freer to pursue their own national strategies, even at the risk of offending their erstwhile patron. Even fellow democracies could no longer automatically be counted on to side with the United States. The dramatic transformation of the economic landscape boosted the capacity of emerging economies to play an influential role not just in the economic realm, but in political and security affairs. The unipolar moment—if there ever was one— appeared to be just a brief transition from bipolarity to a complex and more multidimensional world in which more states have the capacity to influence international events, are less beholden to the United States, and cannot easily be divided into friend or foe.

This is the context in which the United States finds itself today and the lens through which Americans must understand and adapt to the strategies being pursued by other countries—especially those emerging economic, political, and, in some cases, military powers—a constellation including Cold War allies, Cold War adversaries, and neutrals. For some analysts, the need to focus on the strategies of others stems from the relative, or even absolute, decline of American power.[4] For others, interdependence and the emergence of common threats creates opportunities for new partnerships, while others see new strategic threats to the United States from revisionist powers.[5] In any case, the rise of new powers presents U.S. strategy with two fundamental and complementary challenges: first, how to reduce the risk that one, or more, will threaten important U.S. interests and second, how to increase the chance that these new powers will work cooperatively with the United States to achieve common interests.

These are widely accepted objectives, shared by left and right, realists, international liberals, and so on—but even if the goals are broadly agreed, the debate over the best way to achieve them is hotly debated. The choices range from a global preeminence based on broad engagement and overwhelming power to offshore balancing to a growing reliance on international institutions and international law—or even to acquiescence in co-leadership or spheres of influence for emerging powers. Which of these strategies (or hybrids) emerges depends not only on theories of international relations, but also on understanding the choices and strategies of others—with the awareness that their choices, in turn, will be shaped by the choices the United States makes.

Both historians and international relations theorists are keenly aware of the perils of periods when power balances are shifting. At the time of the centennial of the conflagration of World War I, the risks should be vividly recalled.[6] Fear of rising powers, and strategies to counter them, have produced conflict since the times of the Peloponnesian Wars.[7] Yet history also suggests that while the risks are real, the outcome is contingent—conflict is not inevitable, but a product of choices.[8]

To achieve American goals, it is imperative for U.S. officials to understand what drives the strategies of these new powers. But it is equally important to recognize that their strategies are not entirely exogenous to the choices that Washington makes. While many internal factors will shape the goals and means of China, India, Russia, Brazil, Turkey, Germany, and Israel, their strategies will be powerfully shaped by others—especially the United States, as the dominant actor on the international scene. Washington may lack the means to order the world unilaterally, but it most certainly can shape it.

In this complex international environment, there are two overwhelming imperatives for U.S. strategy. The first is to avoid the emergence of an adversary or coalition of countries which have both the means and desire to threaten vital U.S. national interests—as the Soviet Union and its allies were perceived to have done during the Cold War. The second is to find ways to maximize the international cooperation needed to address the growing number of problems—from sustaining economic growth to combating terrorism, nuclear proliferation, climate change, and threats to public health—that cannot be solved by one country acting alone. The choice of strategy to meet these two goals, and to address the tensions inherent between them, must begin with an understanding of the likely strategies of other key actors—who have the potential to be either adversaries or partners.

What Do They Want?

In developing a strategy to deal with emerging powers, the starting point is to begin with an understanding of their objectives and the degree to which their goals are compatible with or antagonistic to U.S. objectives. But this question is more easily asked than answered, for several reasons. To begin with, the strategies of the emerging powers are shaped by distinct forces evolving from each one's unique history, political culture, geography, and the like. Second, even within individual countries, there are divergent views on the goals they should pursue and how they should pursue them.[9] Finally, their views evolve over time and are shaped by both internal and external trends.

Despite these uncertainties and the wide variation among the countries discussed in this book, a few broad observations emerge. Perhaps the single most important conclusion of the authors included in this volume is that none of the emerging powers is fundamentally "revisionist," and none has the near-term ambition to replace the United States as the global dominant power or to supplant the liberal U.S.-led order with a different ideology.[10] Each sees important interests served by the current international order, particularly in the economic realm, and each values the benefits of free-riding on U.S.-provided global public goods.[11] For those countries still focused on economic development (especially China and India), the Pax Americana provides a conducive environment for achieving this preeminent goal, at least in the near term.

At the same time, none is fully satisfied with the status quo. They believe, for a variety of reasons, that they would be better off if U.S. power were more constrained.[12] For the non- and partial democracies, particularly China and Russia, unconstrained U.S. power coupled with America's universalist values are a threat to their political systems and the ruling authorities' hold on power. But even for those who share America's values (Germany, for example), unconstrained power contributes to U.S. unilateralism and disregard of their perspectives—from questions of how to sustain global economic growth to climate change and privacy.[13] Indeed, in virtually all of the countries analyzed in this volume, achieving a degree of distance from, and even resistance to, the United States is an important domestic political mobilization tool.

Third, while there is broad consensus among the emerging powers that there is a need for revision to the international order, differences in the goals and strategies of the emerging powers are as significant as their common interest in altering the status quo. Equally important, there is no natural convergence of interests among the rising powers—no common ideology or economic imperative that binds them together as a bloc. Differences in values, in economic interests, and even in security concerns mitigate strongly against emerging powers coming together and balancing against the United States, as illustrated by the continuing tensions and rivalry between India and China or the complex interactions between China and Russia. Rather, relations between the emerging powers themselves are a pragmatic calculation of national interests, shifting from issue to issue. The chapters in this book suggest that the concepts like the BRICS are an artifice—and that relations among the emerging powers will themselves be a blend of cooperation and conflict.[14]

Finally, there are important differences among the rising powers in what they hope and fear from U.S. strategy. For some—notably China and Russia, but also for Brazil and to some degree Turkey—the greatest fear is from what they perceive as an aggressively assertive America. But for others, notably Germany and Israel, the concern is over the prospect of U.S. withdrawal and/or retrenchment.[15] For these latter countries, questions about the reliability of U.S. commitments and engagement—in terms of both capability and intentions—are at the forefront.

What Does This Mean for U.S. Strategy?

These observations frame the context for U.S. grand strategy. Taken together, they suggest that the emergence of new powers presents a blend of risk and opportunity for achieving U.S. interests—a world of systemically significant actors which neither fully share, nor fundamentally oppose, U.S. interests. Going forward, the challenge is to shape a broad framework that takes into account the emergence of a more "multipolar" world of regional and potentially global state actors, complemented by specific policies tailored to the challenges and opportunities presented by individual "emerging" powers.

Some observers have suggested that the United States build its strategy around maintaining its current level of unchallenged preeminence—to sustain as much as possible "unipolarity" as the best way to secure global peace and stability in the face of rising powers.[16] But the essays in this book suggest that a single-minded focus on preeminence is unnecessary and potentially counterproductive. Unnecessary because the rise of others can, but does not inherently threaten U.S. interests, and may actually contribute to achieving them; counterproductive because such an effort could increase the insecurity of rising powers by raising doubts about U.S. intentions, thereby triggering arms races.[17] Such a strategy would, at best, be enormously costly for the United States and, at worst, lead others to band together against the United States to thwart the pursuit of American objectives. As the previous discussion suggests, there is no natural convergence of interests among the emerging powers, but an ill-considered strategy focused primarily on dominance by the United States could help to forge such a convergence.

Somewhat more promising is a strategy of "off-shore balancing"—working with others to assure that none of the rising powers are able to dominate others either regionally or globally.[18] Balancing strategies have been prominent in other periods of multipolarity—notably by Great Britain through much of the nineteenth century. While such an approach can be useful in moderating threats, it complicates the building of trust, as the reliability and durability of commitments is always in doubt, thus making it difficult to sustain cooperation.

The problem of credibility can be mitigated by building long-term alliances, but alliances pose difficulties of their own. To the extent that balancing is based on long-term alliances, it runs the risk of stimulating bipolar tensions between those in and those outside the alliance system—a benefit when there is a clear enemy, but problematic when the United States has an interest in cooperation with rising powers who are outside traditional U.S. alliances. As the essays in this volume show, many of the rising powers, including, for example, India and Brazil, share U.S. interests in assuring stable regional and global balances, but are reluctant to enter into even informal alliance arrangements with the United States. At best, such a strategy is fragile and requires effort and skill to maintain. At worst, the United States risks getting caught in regional rivalries, a problem that long complicated U.S.-India relations (because of the U.S. "alliance" with Pakistan) and which poses a particular problem in East Asia, given the growing tensions between China and Japan.

Alternatively, the United States could pursue a strategy of greater accommodation with key rising powers—or even "condominium"—at one extreme, conceding a regional "sphere of influence" to key states where the United States would subordinate its interests to those of the new regional hegemon (recognizing at least tacitly the right of regional powers to establish their own "Monroe Doctrines") or, at a minimum, seeking to accommodate what the other defines as its "vital" or "core" national interests.[19]

Given the nature of the problems facing the United States, a fourth strategy, based on a growing emphasis on building international institutions and the rule of international law, has considerable appeal. Embedding emerging countries in enhanced international institutions serves several important purposes: it responds to their clear desire both to enhance their own influence in international affairs and constrain unilateral actions by the United States, while opening the door to facilitating cooperation on common challenges. For many of the countries surveyed in this volume, upgrading their formal roles in key institutions like the UN Security Council and the International Monetary Fund (IMF) is seen as a key objective. To the extent the United States is viewed as supportive of, and even facilitating that goal, the greater trust the United States builds in its long-term intentions toward those rising powers. But this benefit comes with a cost—the real constraints it imposes on U.S. freedom of action, as well as the difficulty of mobilizing effective action through multilateral mechanisms.[20]

Perhaps not surprisingly then, no "pure" strategy ideally suits U.S. interests. A hybrid strategy drawing on the strengths of each of these broad approaches better meets the unique challenges of today's international environment. Thus, while the United States cannot, and should not, define its strategic objective as overwhelming military dominance, there are compelling reasons to make the investments that sustain unique U.S. economic, technological, and military advantages, both to reassure friends and deter adversaries.

Similarly, while a pure balancing approach neither serves U.S. interests nor its values, long-term alliances with countries that share American values can form an important framework for sustained cooperation between the United States and emerging powers. But care must be taken to complement those alliances with constructive engagement with those outside the alliance. This task will be especially important with rising powers like China and Russia who, for reasons of both values and interests, are not likely to become U.S. "allies."

Finally, enhancing the role of international institutions, and the voice of the emerging powers within them, can help reinforce the sense of ownership of rising powers and moderate their revisionist tendencies. The United States has nonetheless to be cautious about over-empowering these countries within institutions, lest they use those institutions to harm vital U.S. interests or undermine other forms of international cooperation.[21] A judicious blend of formal, inclusive institutions like the UN and IMF, coupled with informal institutions both of like-minded states (for example, the Organization for Economic Co-operation and Development) or capable states (G20, Major Economies Forum for climate change), offer opportunities to enhance the influence of emerging powers, while developing new institutional capacities to address shared problems.

What Might This Hybrid Look Like in Practice?

On the security front, the United States still has a compelling interest in maintaining a significant qualitative and quantitative edge over potential rivals, both globally and regionally, as well as a sustained military presence in regions of importance to the United States, notably East Asia, the Middle East, and Europe. Stability is enhanced if the United States makes clear that the emerging powers cannot achieve their objectives through coercion or use of force.[22] At the same time, the United States needs to give more emphasis to reassuring emerging powers that the United States does not seek to use this superior military capacity to threaten the security or legitimate interests of others. Reassurance can take many forms in the bilateral relations between the United States and emerging powers. Security dialogues, transparency, and confidence-building measures (joint exercises, hot lines, and even formal agreements, like the U.S.-Russia New Start) can reduce the risk of arms races and build trust.[23] Reassurance can also be achieved through increased reliance on regional and global multilateral arrangements, which have the advantage of broadening the range of actors involved and thus reducing the risk that bilateral discussions will be seen in zero-sum terms. Efforts like the use of the ASEAN Regional Forum in East Asia to craft a Code of Conduct for the South China Sea allows the United States to advance its interests (in this case freedom of navigation and peaceful resolution of disputes) with greater legitimacy (since it has the support of the countries of ASEAN). Such efforts undercut arguments by China that the U.S. goal is merely to weaken or contain it. Similar fora include the Asia Defense Ministers Meeting (ADMM), the Arctic Council's efforts to craft policies for the increasingly open Arctic Ocean, and the Western Hemisphere Defense Ministerials.[24]

Alliances continue to play an important role in U.S. strategy. For alliance members, including emerging powers like Germany and Turkey (as well as others, like Australia, Japan, and South Korea), the alliance mechanism is one avenue for them to achieve an enhanced voice in international affairs and coordinate with the United States. It also avoids the increased instability that would arise should they feel the need to assure their security unilaterally in the face of other emerging powers—a problem most acute in East Asia and Europe. But in the post–Cold War environment, the challenge is to maintain the stability-enhancing feature of the alliance without antagonizing those outside the alliance, or causing them to band together in counteralliances. Groupings like the BRICS, the Community of Latin American and Caribbean States (CELAC), the Shanghai Cooperation Organization, and the new "Asia Security Concept" championed by Chinese President Xi Jinping through the Conference on Interaction and Confidence Building in Asia (CICA), all foreshadow the danger that emerging powers will seek to create structures that deliberately exclude the United States.[25] This means that the United States needs to focus heavily on infusing substance in bilateral security relations with nonallied emerging powers (through, for example, the U.S.-China Strategic Stability Dialogue or the U.S.-India Strategic Dialogue, inaugurated in 2009). It must also support the development of inclusive multilateral security arrangements, such as the Organization for Security and Co-operation in Europe (OSCE), the East Asia Summit (EAS), and a reformed Organization of American States (OAS).

The Security Council continues to be a focal point for discussions about how the United States should respond to newly emerging powers. Although the United States has expressed support, in principle, for Security Council reform, achieving that goal has proved difficult. The United States has an interest in opposing changes that undermine the already limited efficacy of the council, yet many of the emerging countries will not accept cosmetic reforms that do not offer them a meaningful role or voice. The Obama administration has expressed support for India's inclusion on the council, albeit without a veto.

One promising avenue is a transitional period of reform, extending permanent membership to emerging countries (particularly India and Brazil) without a veto but with a fixed period (say, ten years) after which the issue could be revisited and experience with their membership on the Security Council evaluated.

Economic policy has a central role to play in U.S. efforts to manage the rise of new powers. While economic interdependence is not a guarantee of peaceful relations, it can act as a constraint on provocative behavior that could lead to instability and threaten growth, as well as contributing to a sense of common interest. But the effort to promote integration through economic liberalization is challenged by the fact that many of the rising powers reject, either implicitly or explicitly, the liberal economic principles at the heart of U.S. strategy. Mercantilist and protectionist policies in China, Russia, India, and Brazil are sources of conflict rather than cooperation between the United States and these rising powers. The signature trade negotiations of Obama's second term—the Trans Pacific Partnership (TTP) and the Transatlantic Trade and Investment Partnership (TTIP)—do not include any of them. At the same time global negotiations (the Doha Round) have come to a stalemate.

This is not to say that the United States should abandon TPP and TTIP—they can provide an incentive for other countries to move their policies toward the high standards envisioned in these agreements, especially as they come to see the limits of what can be achieved through state-centric and protectionist policies. But the United States needs to fashion a clearer path to include these rising states in regional and global trade negotiations. Some accommodation will be necessary for practices that the United States frowns on, as was the case when China joined the World Trade Organization (WTO) and the United States accepted an extended period of transition. Inclusive regional free trade agreements, like the proposed Free Trade Area of the Americas and the Free Trade Area of Asia, are important means of helping to avoid the creation of regional trading blocs that pit emerging powers against the United States. Similarly, rather than rejecting outright participation in new regional economic institutions like the proposed Asian Infrastructure Development Bank and encouraging U.S. partners to boycott the institution (out of fear that it would undermine global norms embedded in organizations like the IMF and the World Bank), the United States should seek to be an active participant with a meaningful voice in shaping the goals and methods of the new entities. Such an approach would allow the United

States to focus on legitimate substantive concerns, while allaying allegations that it is only supportive of institutions that it creates and dominates.

In dealing with nontraditional threats such as terrorism, international crime and drugs, and global public health, the United States has an opportunity to build constructive relations with emerging powers. Innovative arrangements, such as the Financial Action Task Force for money laundering and the Global Counterterrorism Forum (co-chaired by the United States and Turkey and including among its members China, India, and Russia), offer a means of including these powers in crafting common policies and strategies.[26] On issues where the interests of emerging powers and the United States can diverge, such as climate change, mechanisms such as the Major Economies Forum can provide both a voice for emerging countries and a forum for action to complement the more unwieldy global organizations like the UN Framework Convention on Climate Change (UNFCCC).

Although this chapter has focused on state-to-state relations in the development of U.S. strategy toward emerging powers, it is increasingly apparent in the twenty-first century that nonstate actors will play a growing role in shaping the international environment. This is true not only in democratic countries, where the electorate has a formal role in determining policy, but also in semi- and even nondemocratic states like China, where civil society organizations and the Internet play a significant role in shaping the decisions of governments.

The increased roles of civil society and the media represent both a challenge and an opportunity for the United States. It is a challenge because the news media is the filter through which foreign publics come to understand the goals and objectives of U.S. policy, where it is often portrayed in terms very different from what U.S. policymakers intend. Sometimes these media-driven views are supported and encouraged by their home governments, but in other cases they simply cater to public sentiment suspicious of U.S. dominance. Even if the United States adopts policies that are designed to give an increasing role to emerging countries and seeks to accommodate their interests, the value of these efforts will be limited if they are undermined by hostile portrayals in the media.

But where there is challenge, there is opportunity. The new social media offer the United States a chance to reach around governments to build support. As with Radio Free Europe and Radio Liberty during the Cold War, the new media can facilitate direct engagement with the publics in emerging countries who share U.S. values and goals, whether on human rights, the environment, or economic opportunity.

In dealing with both the challenge of hostile media and the opportunity presented by new media, the United States will need to place increased emphasis on public diplomacy as part of its strategy toward emerging powers—both by directly engaging publics in these countries and by creative use of the media, especially social media.

Tailored Strategies

These basic principles form a framework for U.S. strategy but, as the essays in this book make clear, a one-size-fits-all approach to emerging powers fails to take into account the wide divergences among them. Thus, a U.S. strategy must be tailored to account for these differences.

U.S. strategy toward the emerging democratic powers should be shaped by our shared set of values, while recognizing that shared values do not mean that our interests will converge on all issues and at all times. The United States has an incentive to promote a growing role for these countries in the international system. In part, this is a value statement in its own right—a respect for the decisions of democratically elected governments and an inducement for other countries to follow the democratic path. In part, it is a pragmatic judgment that over the long run democracies are more likely to see eye to eye on a broad range of issues—from war and peace to economic prosperity to human rights. Moreover, rather than depending on overwhelming clout to coerce or induce "bandwagoning" by unenthusiastic partners, respecting the voices of other democracies may make them more willing to find common ground with the United States.

To be sure, there will be times when an enhanced voice for these countries will come at a cost to the United States. The Turkey/Brazil proposal for a nuclear deal with Iran in 2010 is an example of how views can diverge. Moreover, a willingness to "stand up" to the United States may confer significant political advantages for emerging powers—for example, Turkey's refusal to support the intervention in Iraq in 2003 and its limited support for the U.S. campaign against the self-proclaimed Islamic State in Iraq and Syria (ISIS) in 2014, President Rouseff's cancellation of a state visit to Washington following the revelations of U.S. secret surveillance, and Germany's opposition to U.S. data privacy policies.[27] But the United States has often had differences with its democratic allies, such as with France under Charles de Gaulle and, more recently, with Germany over the authorization of force in Libya. Yet these examples also suggest that the benefits of tolerating divergence can be substantial.

The essays in this volume highlight the importance that Brazil, India, and Turkey attach to a greater voice in international organs. The United States has made an important gesture in this regard by indicating its support for India's and Japan's membership on the UN Security Council. Taking the next step with Brazil is particularly compelling given its central importance in this hemisphere, though the United States will need to find a way to assure that enhancing Brazil's voice will not be seen as indifference to the views of other important hemispheric partners, particularly Mexico.

The United States has also sought to enhance the voice of emerging democratic powers through the creation of informal international institutions based on common values, including the Community of Democracies and the Open Government Partnership (OGP). OGP is a particularly creative response. By including Brazil, South Africa, and Indonesia on the Steering Committee at the outset, the United States empowered these emerging nations in setting the agenda for the group and emphasized their commonalities with the United States—implicitly in contrast with the other BRICS (China, India, and Russia), who were not participants.[28]

For traditional allies, such as Germany and Japan, continued U.S. commitment in the face of rising regional powers remains central. While neither would welcome or benefit from deteriorating relations between the United States and the emerging regional powers (Russia and China), both need reassurance that U.S. strategy will not subordinate their interests to building cooperation with these powers. The recent revision of the U.S.-Japan defense guidelines represents a positive step in this direction, along with the reiteration of the U.S. commitment under Article V of the U.S.-Japan Security Treaty, as it applies to the Senkaku Islands. Similarly close coordination between the United States and Germany (along with other members of the EU) in connection with Russia's intervention in Ukraine in 2014 has helped build confidence in how the United States supports allies in dealing with an assertive Russia.

In the case of Israel, the challenge for U.S. strategy is in some ways the mirror image of dealing with the other democratic emerging powers. The United States and Israel share a broad range of common interests, and the United States would welcome a more active and influential role by Israel on regional and global issues. The barriers to Israel playing this role come not from Washington, but from others who oppose Israel's policies, particularly with respect to Palestinian issues, and who seek to marginalize Israel as a way of inducing change in those policies. The United States has wisely resisted this strategy, even though in some cases (such as with the settlement policy) the United States strongly disagrees with Israel's approach. Maintaining a cooperative relationship with Israel has served, and continues to serve, multiple purposes as a part of U.S. strategy. It demonstrates respect for Israel's democratic values, deters efforts to challenge Israel's security, and demonstrates to other U.S. allies and friends the reliability of the U.S. commitment, despite the emergence of policy differences from time to time. This is an important perspective to keep in mind as the United States seeks to resolve the challenge of Iran's nuclear program while making clear to Israel that Washington understands and is prepared to take into account Israel's security concerns (along with those of other U.S. partners, particularly the Gulf States, Egypt, and Turkey).

U.S. strategy in the face of an increasingly powerful and more assertive China is the most complex of the cases posed by the essays in this volume. Of all the emerging powers, China most clearly is positioned to develop the capacity and the motivation to challenge U.S. dominance regionally, if not globally. Despite Chinese leaders' repeated assurances of their commitment to a "peaceful rise" and to a cooperative relationship with other powers, particularly the United States, there is growing anxiety that China's real long-term intentions are highly revisionist—nothing short of a desire to replace the Pax Americana with a Pax Sinica.

The United States has a profound interest in cultivating a positive relationship with China. Given their mutual economic interdependence, conflict would only harm both parties. On many of the great world challenges, from environment to terrorism to global public health, U.S. and Chinese interests are more aligned than in conflict and neither can address these problems effectively alone.

Yet there are enormous risks that the relationship will become more adversarial, and even evolve toward direct conflict. In part, this is a product of real differences in goals and values, reflected in forms of government and in approaches to human rights, both at home and abroad. But the danger of conflict is fueled by the dynamics of the "security dilemma"—each side pursuing what it believes are legitimate defensive security capabilities, yet at the same time inducing fear that those capacities will be used to thwart or harm the other's interests.

Both the United States and China have rhetorically acknowledged the structural challenge posed by this relationship—and have embraced the idea of "building a new model of major power relationship."[29] Yet, despite this awareness, the relationship remains tense. Areas of divergence—from maritime disputes to cyber-espionage and trade—increasingly trump areas of cooperation.

Michael O'Hanlon and I have written at length on how the United States and China should seek to manage this dilemma.[30] At its core, this strategy suggests that the United States should be prepared to take action to demonstrate its willingness to support China's emergence as an increasingly influential regional and international actor, and should respect its right to develop legitimate defensive capabilities, so long as China takes reciprocal steps to indicate its intent to respect the legitimate interests of its neighbors and the United States.

This has largely been the approach taken by the United States since normalization with China in the 1970s. Although the initial rapprochement was driven primarily by considerations of balancing during the Cold War, since the 1990s the strategy has tried to capture the benefits of cooperation with an increasingly capable China, while deterring aggressive Chinese actions against U.S. interests, allies, and friends on both the economic and political fronts. Washington has welcomed a wider regional and global role for China in international institutions—supporting a seat for the PRC on the Security Council in the 1970s and its inclusion in formal and informal global economic institutions like the IMF and the G20, as well as the Major Economies Forum on climate change.

But the strategy requires the United States to walk a delicate line between reassuring China and maintaining the credibility of U.S. alliances in East Asia—the challenge inherent in the Obama administration's "rebalance" to Asia. Many Chinese leaders and analysts see the rebalance and the perpetuation of alliances as ill-disguised efforts to contain China. Yet the alternatives—either a condominium with China or a retreat from the region—would create deep anxieties among China's neighbors, causing them either to bandwagon with the regional hegemon or to seek security and independence through their own military buildups. Neither result serves U.S. interests. Sustaining the strategy of engagement through presence and alliances should remain at the core of U.S. strategy to deal with China's rise.

Despite the hope in the 1990s that Russia would emerge from the end of the Cold War as a democratic partner of the United States and the West, the reality has been disappointing. Under Putin, Russia appears increasingly reluctant to participate in the international status quo led by the United States and its allies. As with China, the tensions between the United States and Russia are a product of many factors—divergent economic and political interests as well as values. But a central element derives from the very nature of the U.S.-led order itself—a belief by many Russians that the United States seeks to weaken and marginalize Russia's regional and international role. This explains in part the importance of the conflicts in Georgia and Ukraine—seen by some Russian strategists as clear indications of U.S. efforts to reduce Russia's sphere of influence by incorporating parts of the former USSR into Western institutions (NATO and the EU). This has led Russia to adopt militarily aggressive actions in both those countries as well as to seek to build alternative regional structures (Eurasian Economic Union, Shanghai Cooperation Organization) that give Russia a prominent, and in some cases, preeminent voice.

In the years following the end of the Cold War, the United States sought to temper the growing tensions in the relationship by offering to find an appropriate role for Russia in the regional and global architecture, through the institutionalization of the OSCE as a pan-European security organization or the NATO-Russia Council, as well as the possibility of future Russian membership in NATO itself. After these efforts at rapprochement faltered following the ascension of Putin, the Obama "reset" was an attempt to find a path toward more cooperative relations with Russia on common objectives, while recognizing that important differences would likely remain. This path included bringing Russia into the WTO, negotiating the New Start nuclear arms control agreement, facilitating United States and NATO involvement in Afghanistan, and working together to secure and dismantle Syria's chemical weapons.

The Russian intervention in Ukraine has rekindled the strategic dilemma that the United States faced at the end of the Cold War. In some ways, it mirrors the problem that the United States faces with China: how to accommodate a growing regional role for Russia, even if that approach might jeopardize relations with friends and allies in the region. In the 1990s, some strategists argued against expanding NATO because they feared this would stimulate Russian hostility toward the West.[31] They proposed that the United States should subordinate the security interests of Central and East European countries and not incorporate them into NATO, in order to sustain good relations with the dominant regional power, Russia. On the other side, proponents of NATO expansion argued that giving Russia a veto over others' membership in the international institution would be inconsistent with U.S. values, would encourage increasingly ambitious Russian demands, and would perpetuate regional tensions.

Events have served to underscore that these trade-offs are real. They also show the linkage between how the United States manages the rise of individual emerging powers with the wider problem of the shifting balance. It is no accident that the U.S. approach to the Russian incursion in Ukraine has generated so much interest in Asia. If the United States is willing to accommodate Russian predominance in Central Europe by ruling out Ukrainian membership in NATO or the EU, this will be seen—rightly or not—as foreshadowing how the United States might react to increasing Chinese pressure to end arms sales to Taiwan or to China's claims for disputed islands, like the Senkakus in the East China Sea and others in the South China Sea.

This is not to say that Russia's actions should spur the United States to adopt an updated containment strategy. From nuclear arms control to terrorism to energy security, the United States has far more shared interests with Russia than during the Cold War. An "all-or-nothing" approach would be counterproductive. The underlying premise of the "reset"—to deal with each issue on its merits and limit cross-issue linkage—serves the interests of both the United States and Russia.

※ ※ ※

It has become commonplace to argue that the emergence of new regional powers has complicated the task of U.S. strategy. On one level, this is true, since a one-size-fits-all approach is ill-suited to the diversity of the strategies of the emerging powers now shaping international affairs. Yet this very diversity offers the opportunity for the United States to craft an imaginative and flexible approach that offers a much more hopeful prospect than the perilous strategic challenges we faced during the Cold War. The hybrid approach suggested in this chapter focuses on a willingness by the United States to support without prior conditions a growing international role for emerging democratic powers (including India, Brazil, and South Africa). With regard to the less democratic and nondemocratic emerging powers, the United States should take a more contingent approach. It should display a willingness to support a broader role for these powers as they offer reassurance that they do not seek to use their enhanced status to undermine the fundamental interests of the United States, its allies, and like-minded states. At the same time, the United States must demonstrate the will and capability ("resolve") to resist revisionist goals that threaten American interests. By understanding the possibilities as well as the dangers posed by rising powers, U.S. leaders can help shape a peaceful and prosperous future for the next generation.

CONCLUSION

The World They Will Make

JEFFREY W. LEGRO

$\mathbb{S}$ CHOLARS and policymakers alike debate the future of world politics.[1] They differ on whether it will be peaceful or war-prone, whether the United States will remain preeminent or be replaced by another major power, whether international order is weakening or strengthening, and whether sovereignty and the nation-state are maintaining their centrality or are eroding. There has been no resolution to these arguments. Judging from the literature we may have spent too much time looking in the wrong places.

The debate to date has been dominated by global concepts, broad historical trends, and the dynamics of major powers. Some scholars want to analyze the distribution of power to understand the future—whether the world will be multipolar or bipolar or whether a prevailing hegemon will decline or a new one will arise. Other analysts dwell on the increasing economic, environmental, and social interdependence of the world and the shape of global capitalism. Yet as important as these global factors are, they do not determine what different countries actually resolve to do. International order is rooted in the policies and actions of the main actors in the global arena—states. That is why scholars have examined in depth the most powerful countries.[2] Much less attention has been paid to the strategies of an unusual configuration of rising countries, a group of not traditional great powers, but "shapers" in terms of their emerging impact.[3]

The central aim of the essays in this volume is to address the nature and sources of shaper strategies. Judging from the literature on strategy based on the behavior of great powers, we would expect these shaping states to follow a regular pattern. They would have clear central authority and act coherently to connect means to ends. They would focus on the threats and opportunities they see and make rational choices that would maximize their security. The sources of strategy in this view would be primarily in their geopolitical environment.

But that is not what we find. Instead, these states struggle to define themselves and react coherently to their world. Strategies seem to be shaped as much by domestic politics as they are by traditional external strategic conditions. Leaders are certainly concerned with objective security challenges, but internal economic opportunities and challenges, shaped by the global economy and the role of other states, often take priority. Ideology, national identity, and the perception of history play a central role in the evolution of strategy. And state responses are sometimes absent or implemented incoherently by disparate governmental entities.

These ascending countries—collectively and interactively—will define twenty-first-century world politics. That their strategies have been formed in a way not expected by conventional wisdom raises a pressing follow-on question: What kind of world will they create?

The answer to this question does not begin with global concepts or the plans of the traditional "great powers." Instead, starting with the strategies of shaping countries themselves, five broad traits of future order (or disorder) come into view. First and foremost, *world politics will be distinguished by unusual uncertainty* as a result of the dynamics within shaper states and in the international environment. A second trend is that *collective goods will be underprovided* as global needs increase and shaper states focus on the often daunting tasks of internal economic development and political consolidation. Third, *countries will focus on regions* versus broader world order. Most shaping powers do not have the reach to shape international order, but they uniformly aspire to leadership if not domination of their respective regions. Fourth, *the personalities and preferences of leaders will play an increasingly important role.* Despite the fragmentation of authority, leadership traits and personal diplomacy loom large in the international relations of the twenty-first century. Even as states are stymied, "leaders" are gaining more influence on the world stage. Finally, given the analysis above, one might expect significant international conflict, but *the outlook for war and peace will be mixed.* On the one hand, with partial exceptions, no state has overambitious plans for expansion and the threat of terrorism has often united these states; on the other, the strong interest in regional dominance will fuel intense security dilemmas that could generate significant armed clashes and the potential for broader escalation.

Most significant is the combination of these trends. Taken together, they may create a world that is especially fluid in terms of the alliances and partnerships that might be struck. Given the ambiguities of unresolved national identities and state difficulties in marshaling authority, it will not be easy to strike durable deals. Similarly, in the absence of significant—or even catastrophic—shared threats brought on by terrorism, climate change, economic setbacks, or potential pandemics, states will tend to shirk global challenges, especially if collaborative action threatens to impede economic growth or equality. The impact of individual leader preferences means it will be more difficult to extrapolate national policy from standard bureaucratic procedure and national tradition. At times leaders will surprise us with new proposals that might produce unexpected cooperation or, conversely though less likely, shock us with ominous actions that could threaten the peace, particularly in contests over regional dominance.

The key point is that these countries will shape international order; they are the shapers. At this point they do not seek to overturn the existing global order, but all of them want more of a say in international institutions and rule-making. But how this develops will not rest solely on their actions alone. Equally important will be the response of the extant developed countries, especially the United States. Whether pessimism or optimism is warranted will depend much on the quality of strategic thinking both among the shapers and in the United States and how they interact.

The five dynamics outlined above—as well as the importance of the U.S. response—merit elaboration because each reveals itself in distinct ways in particular countries and regions.

Shaper Effects

National strategies of shaping countries reflect and contribute to a world of uncertainty. This uncertainty results from several causes: the weakening of the identity and authority of states, changing power trajectories and doubts about the United States as the leading global power, the strategic ambiguity of national policies, and the erosion of existing institutions and alliances that are becoming increasingly "transactional." Though these developments affect all countries to varying degrees, they are more pronounced in shaper states.

Fragmented Identity and Authority

A major source of global uncertainty is the weakening of either a central identity or the authority of the state in many of these countries. In the wake of dynamic growth and change, governments have had a hard time unifying their societies around a shared identity. In addition, the locus of decision-making across issues has become more diffuse in a number of countries. As a result, states have struggled to understand allies and adversaries, and cutting deals has become more challenging. These dynamics are seen in debates over identity, the distribution of decision-making to multiple nodes, and the rising saliency of domestic politics in foreign policy.

Many of the shaping countries are undergoing identity debates that involve fundamental questions over what type of countries they are and what goals they should seek. Israel is tied in knots over what type of Jewish state and democracy it is, with implications for Middle East peace and the quality of its relationships with other states in the region. Turkey is enmeshed in a struggle between its European and Asian identities. China remains a communist state but it is not clear what the word "communist" actually means or what other adjective might replace it. Brazil continues to ponder divergent statist and neoliberal trajectories, as well as debate whether it seeks to be part of the nonwhite south or join the Great Power elite who oversee the international political economy. India similarly struggles with its legacy of anti-imperialism and identity as a leading "nonaligned" power that favors independent action. Yet India also has significant incentives to join various forms of entangling economic agreements pertaining to trade and investment and to sign security deals regarding nuclear power. Russia, searching for a unifying formula, has veered toward a nationalist neo-imperial conservatism fueled by revisionist resentment, but its economic development requires accommodation with other states, including those threatened by its forays in the Crimea and Ukraine.

Fractured identities are being matched by dispersed authority structures.[4] Consider the seeming archetype of unified authority, the Communist Party of China. Headed by a president and small Politburo, the central government is thought to be all-powerful. But actual authority is quite distributed in China, particularly among China's far-flung regions and in certain functional areas like military affairs or energy policy.[5] Similarly, India often seems less like a sovereign country and more akin to a loose federal union of independent states that vary widely in their cultures and preferences. National policymaking, including foreign policy, has been a challenge, especially out-side the realm of national security.[6] In Israel, power is distributed among political, judicial, financial, security, and religious officials, with stakeholders in other countries (especially the United States) also playing a critical role. And in Germany, there is no formal national security interagency strategy process. As a result, Germany has been less adroit in designing a strategic trajectory than in making tactical decisions.

As William Hitchcock notes in the introduction, identity politics and the diffusion of authority are two dimensions of the rise of domestic politics in national decision-making. Global dynamics are involved as well. States to-day face increasing pressures to open up and connect with other parts of the world, primarily to make economic gains through commercial and financial exchange. But as they do, their citizens feel more empowered, authority dis-perses, and nonstate actors gain more influence in a world of low-cost com-munications and travel. These developments raise new challenges for lead-ers attempting to solidify national opinion and control. Perhaps that is why China, India, and Russia among others have initiated laws to control foreign nongovernmental actors.[7] Fyodor Lukyanov writes about his country: "Per-haps Russia's main dilemma today is how to ensure its own sovereignty and independence in an interdependent world" (p. 122, this volume). Many shap-ing countries are struggling to define themselves and garner authority amidst intrusive globalization, thus adding more unpredictability to world affairs.

Shifting Power

A key source of uncertainty and potential change in international politics is the evolving power trajectories of major and would-be major powers. Power tran-sitions have traditionally been associated with turmoil and even war through-out history.[8] Some scholars posit that a clear power hierarchy leads to a more stable international order, one where the dominant power provides "collective goods."[9] The United States is often portrayed as a "hegemon" that helped lead an unprecedented development of international institutions and rules after World War II. Since the end of the Cold War, the United States has arguably been the main provider of collective goods such as protecting the freedom of the seas, managing global financial flows, enforcing the nuclear nonprolifera-tion treaty, and leading the fight against transnational terrorism.[10]

Now, however, there is considerable debate over whether the U.S. posi-tion is eroding as a result of the rise of China. Moreover, the emergence of a number of countries—Brazil, India, Turkey, Israel, and a revanchist Russia— constitute a formidable group of powers with whom Washington must negotiate. At the same time, long-standing allies, like Germany and Japan, who have habitually sided with the United States, now debate assuming more activist and independent roles in the international arena.

While it seems that no country will replace its dominant position anytime soon, the fading willingness of the United States to incentivize others has raised uncertainty about the perpetuation and enforcement of international rules. In addition, in different regions around the globe the prevailing balance of power seems endangered and the United States cannot be everywhere. Regional dynamics based on shifting global trends may take on a life of their own, as illuminated by China's struggle to dominate its surrounding seas and Russia's quest to control its western borderlands.

Countries do not know exactly what to think about such shifts. As Matias Spektor explains, there is an active debate in Brazil (one that has its parallel everywhere) on the future distribution of power in the international arena. Will the United States continue as the "unipole" in the global system or will it become just one of several major powers? In Spektor's account two successive presidents of Brazil—Fernando Henrique Cardoso and Luiz Inacio Lula da Silva—offered two divergent views: the former saw U.S. hegemony as enduring and thought Brazil should "duck" from U.S. attention. Lula, meanwhile, believed that U.S. power was in decline and he tended to distance himself (even as relations grew closer).

And, of course, there are power transition dynamics within regions that also introduce new and unpredictable dynamics. Consider, for example, the enhanced tensions between China and Japan, India and China, Turkey and Israel, Russia and Germany, or Brazil's overall standing in Latin America. Power trajectories that have shifted significantly in recent years have unsettled patterns of behavior, making the way forward more unpredictable.

Ambiguous Policies

A number of the emerging countries act in ways that make their intentions unclear. Such ambiguity adds to a climate of strategic uncertainty, as illustrated by Russia's policy on its borders. Where does Putin's ambition begin and end? On the one hand, Russia is trying to modernize its economy; on the other, it aims to gain political, if not physical, hegemony over its periphery, precipitating clashes with Georgia and Ukraine. Russian aspirations in the rest of Ukraine and Eastern Europe seem unclear. It has sent mixed signals that have provoked much discussion and contingency planning in a number of countries.[11]

China has proclaimed its policy of "Peaceful Rise" for many years. It aspires to focus on economic development and cooperation with other countries. Beijing leaders say they do not want to dominate others or deploy military force to achieve their aims. Yet in clashes with other countries in the seas east and south of China and on the Indian border, Chinese military forces are assertive in defending Beijing's claims. Overall, China is augmenting its military capabilities. This expansion may be natural for a country with a vibrant economy and many neighbors on its borders. Nonetheless, the juxtaposition of the rhetoric of peace with the reality of military growth and the show of force engenders ambiguity about the future.

And in Brazil we have seen the significant divide in sentiment expressed about the current international order. While some argue that the system works for Brazil and only needs mild reform, others believe it only serves the "West" and should be changed. Which position most likely reflects Brazil's aspirations? The difficulty of answering the question has implications for a number of relationships, not the least with its neighbor to the north, the United States.

Mature emerging powers such as Germany and Japan also project strategic uncertainty. Debates exist in both countries on whether they should radically adapt their traditional postwar policies as "trading" states that tend to follow the lead of others, avoiding overt remilitarization and rejecting deployments of military power. Germany, for example, has been shaped by a "culture of self-restraint," yet is now being pushed and invited into a more active stance by circumstances and by a United States unwilling to bear the same burden of alliance defense that it used to shoulder. Which way will Germany go? Answers are not clear. Constanze Stelzenmüller describes a country that uses ambiguity to navigate the dilemmas and crosscutting pressures, but in doing so it raises the level of uncertainty both for allies and potential adversaries.

Weakened Institutions and Alliances

Global institutions that have provided rules of the road and helped coordinate response to international challenges seem moribund in the face of existing challenges. The UN Security Council has a permanent membership (five countries) that does not reflect contemporary realities (France and

Britain are members; Germany, Japan, Brazil, and India are not) and the International Monetary Fund and World Bank have similarly done little to redistribute power to emerging countries.[12] The World Trade Organization has not been able to move beyond the Doha Round. Climate conferences have made little progress despite scientific consensus on the scope of the problem. And the World Health Organization appeared impotent in the face of a massive Ebola outbreak.[13]

Some of the core institutions and alliances that have undergirded world politics for the past seventy years are either static or are changing in ways that exacerbate uncertainty. "The UN, the EU, and NATO provide far less normative and institutional definition for German policies than they once did," writes Constanze Stelzenmüller, who argues that "the European project itself is at risk." At one point, the U.S.-German relationship, according to Stelzenmüller, was deemed "existential"—fundamental to the very identity of each partner. Now, however, the ties between the two are increasingly "transactional"; they are about getting business done, not catalyzing norms, rules, and regimes of wider significance (pp. 55, 56, this volume). U.S. surveillance practices, Germany's tight-fisted response to the global financial crisis, and discord over actions in other countries have added to the erosion of trust and made more difficult the maintenance of rules, regimes, and alliances. Germany itself is often caught between established powers and rising powers, siding with Brazil (and against the United States) on Internet governance and viewing China as less of a security threat than does Washington.

Relationships in the Middle East are also changing. Growing resentment toward Israel's policies in the West Bank and Gaza have frayed strong ties with the United States and further eroded Israel's relations with European countries. Similarly, Turkey's ties to the United States, and especially to Europe, have shifted. After the rebuff from the European Union, Turkey has revived its Islamic identity and its future in the EU (which has always been shaky because of the EU's hesitance to accept Turkey as a full member). And the Israel-Turkey relationship has suffered in recent years, although there is still much exchange and traffic between these two regional powers.

New norms and alliance patterns have not compensated for the loss of the old. The United States and India have formed a new strategic partnership that involves the development of India's nuclear energy industry even while India remains armed with nuclear weapons—a deal ostensibly prohibited by the nonproliferation regime. Still, the interactions between the two have been contentious at times, and no broad program of collaboration has yet emerged.

In general, there is significant resentment in many shaping powers about the justice of the international order since World War II, even as it has taken new forms since the end of the Cold War. Brazilian textbooks portray it as a system in which powerful countries impose their will and control international institutions for their own purposes. There is deep suspicion toward all colonial powers. Russians are resentful over the settlements at the end of the Cold War. Turkey is bitter over its rebuff by the European Union. China still nurtures grievances over their treatment by the "barbarians" from the West. India remains wrapped in a mantle of anti-imperialism and despises outside encroachment.

China, Men Honghua argues, should build new bilateral alliances to bolster its position in the world. Perhaps some small countries will link up with China, but most of its larger neighbors are more likely to band against China. Elsewhere, China has struck a number of deals in Africa and is now that continent's largest trading partner.[14] Among the "BRICS" (Brazil, Russia, India, China, and South Africa) countries, there is a nascent pact, but collaboration among those very different states has not been easy. Russia and China have renewed efforts to establish tighter bonds, perhaps encouraged by its shared standing as nondemocratic shaping powers.[15] What remains unclear is whether such new deals can overcome the many factors that have historically undermined relations between these two shapers who share a significant boundary. China has also tried to lead other efforts that challenge existing institutions. For example, it has been the main contributor to a BRICS New Development Bank and an Asian Infrastructure Development Bank, both of which would be alternative sources of financing to the World Bank and the Asian Development Bank.[16]

The uncertainty caused by the rise of new powers will distinguish the strategic environment ahead and will shape the behavior of the shapers themselves.[17] To the extent that shaping nations experience rapid change in their own power trajectories, or have unsettled identities, or face fragmented authority, or must contend with partners with uncertain policies, or must contend with a weakened hegemon, they will have a difficult time setting long-lasting agendas and negotiating meaningful deals. They can be expected to hedge the risks of uncertainty by avoiding large investments in any one relationship, by seeking added measures of assurance against major threats, and by attempting to build alternative institutions or insurance schemes.

The Provision of Global Goods

Arguably, global goods have always been underprovided. What has changed is the rise in the magnitude of global problems as the world has become more interconnected. The United States may still be the most dominant country and may still want to lead collective action, but it will find it difficult to catalyze the scale of cooperation needed to address pressing world problems without fellow cooperators. A defining trait of shaping powers, whether they are relatively new, such as China or India, or developed, like Germany or Japan, is that they are singularly focused on their own economic development. As a result, they are loath to get enmeshed in global challenges, especially geopolitical ones, which drain resources from economic ambitions. States will be challenged in harnessing their fragmented and less unified societies to make sacrifices for global problems. To be sure, they seek to influence international order, for example, by becoming permanent members of the UN Security Council. But, generally, they do not want to be responsible for the order and security of the global commons. Developing counties will inevitably focus on a fairer distribution of authority and wealth in the global system, while richer countries will not fill the void if others are not doing "their fair share."

In 1985, political scientist Richard Rosecrance wrote a book titled *The Rise of the Trading State*.[18] He showed how Germany and Japan were setting new standards for success in an international system where "territorial states" could no longer prosper. Conquest had become too costly, and profits could be pursued more efficiently through economic initiatives. Moreover, publics everywhere wanted governments to focus on economic results, not security alone.

After World War II, Germany and Japan were prohibited from remilitarizing and they focused on constructing vibrant national economies. They tended to keep a low profile when collective action was needed, often with the encouragement of the United States and other countries that feared the revival of Germany's and Japan's independent power. Whether or not their critics were fair, they were perceived as "free-riders," taking advantage of the rules and regimes provided by others, while contributing less than they could. Germany and Japan prospered by keeping their heads down and avoiding too prominent a role in international institutions, rule-making, and collective security provision.

Many of the countries discussed in this volume are pursuing strategies focused on economic development while avoiding external entanglements to the extent that they can. The governments of Brazil, India, and China want to advance the prospects and well-being of their societies. They face significant challenges trying to ameliorate living standards, eradicate poverty, and spark overall development. But public expectations are high. Leaders are therefore wary of U.S. and Western requests that they direct their attention and resources to challenges like climate change, terrorism, nuclear proliferation, trade, and conflicts beyond their neighborhoods.

Shaping countries do not want to incur the bills for international order, especially if they endanger domestic development. Brazil, for example, refuses supranationalism and opposes much of the U.S. agenda. But Spektor emphasizes that Brazilians do not want to be "shirkers" or "spoilers"; they prefer to be "duckers," to avoid entanglements in events in which they have no direct stakes. However, they do want greater status and authority.

China trumpets its focus on "peaceful rise" or "peaceful development." Communist Party authority has been built on economic results, not on contributing to the international system. Men Honghua points out that China wants to be a "responsible stakeholder." China has contributed to maintaining financial stability in past crises, supporting UN peacekeeping forces, and resolving health and development challenges in Africa. Yet Chinese officials often deflect responsibility for dealing with other matters, such as climate change, because of the priority they assign to domestic economic development.

Indian leaders adhere to a doctrine of "nonalignment" and champion an independent foreign policy, hoping to avoid getting pulled into costly situations. As Srinath Raghavan explains, "India faces a fundamental dilemma. Should it lend its weight to global institutions even if it means accepting adverse consequences for itself? This dilemma is particularly acute because unlike the rising powers of the past, India remains a poor country" (p. 89, this volume). Indian officials want most of all to improve the living conditions of their own people, and this priority inevitably leads to positions that clash with those of established powers on issues such as trade, intellectual property, and climate change.

Developing countries are also hesitant to fund international public goods when they consider it more just for wealthier powers to incur burdens proportionate to their means. Why should very poor nations pay international bills when rich superpowers could do so with so much less harm to their citizens? Some developing countries feel that the major powers purposely attempt to spread the costs of international order to slow down the rise of new powers. Poorer countries object to the shares they are asked to pay to address global warming when the rich and powerful countries generate far more carbon on a per capita basis, precisely because of their extravagant life styles.

The net effect of the strategies of emerging and established countries is to insure that collective goods will be undersupplied given their focus on domestic economic development. Former providers of such goods—for example, the United States and arguably the European Union—will be more hesitant to shoulder those burdens should their relative wealth and power decline. Especially given the dispersal of authority within states, it seems likely that critical collective needs will go unmet and the international economy, the environment, and the institutions safeguarding global security will suffer.

The Region as Strategic Focus

To suggest that shaping powers may not contribute to international order does not mean they are uninterested in matters beyond their borders. Indeed, most show considerable concern with influencing or dominating their neighborhoods. Global order may be too expensive or unwieldy to mold, but the emerging countries see regional order as worth the investment: the immediacy and importance of their surrounding geography makes the difference.[19]

China has consistently foresworn any interest in replacing or joining the United States as a global leader. That, however, is not the case with respect to Asia. China has consistently attempted to establish its own dominance in the region and to marginalize the role of the United States whenever possible. China, for example, attempted to exclude the United States from the Chinese trade pact with ASEAN, from a northeast Asia regional grouping with South Korea and Japan, and from its dealings with the BRICS group.[20] As Men Honghua points out in his essay in this volume, China seeks a regionalism that serves the interests of many countries but China has consistently seen itself as the leader in its own region.

Like China, India aspires to be the leader in its neighborhood. As Raghavan points out, India is a regionally focused power, though defining its region as extending from the Middle East to Asia. India has claimed a "special responsibility" in spurring regional economic integration due to its size and geography (p. 89, this volume). Prime Minister Narendra Modi invited all the heads of neighboring South Asian countries to his inauguration, including

Pakistan, a gesture some saw as a renewed Indian effort at local control. The fact that India shares a long contested border with China keeps it focused on its neighborhood—and challenged in asserting its influence. Turkey is also regionally focused, striving to become the leader of moderate Islamic countries throughout the Mediterranean. As Yaprak Gürsoy argues, Turkey wants to be a regional hegemon with aspirations for global influence. President Recep Tayyit Erdoğan aims to become the leader of all Sunni people as well as to position Turkey as a bridge between the West and the Islamic world. This strategy insures tensions with Iran and breeds trouble with Arab nations like Syria and Egypt, as well as with Israel.

Germany has become the leader in Europe and an ardent proponent of the European Union. Some commentators believe that the EU is a perfect vehicle for advancing German aspirations while deflecting criticism for seeking to control the future of Europe. Germany, of course, played a key role in addressing the recent economic crisis. However, as Stelzenmüller points out, Germany does not want to be perceived as the hegemon in the EU. Yet in the economic crisis, and then again in the Ukrainian crisis, Germany has been forced to take action. Over time, it has seemed increasingly willing to do so, often with a push from the United States. However, German reluctance to act outside Europe leaves the region as its main arena.

Brazil presents a more complex picture in terms of regional aspirations. It dominates South America as a result of its economic size and plentiful resources, but it has not historically pursued a regional order with itself at the center. In recent years, under Presidents Cardoso, Lula, and Rousseff, that has changed somewhat and regionalism receives more attention. Observers nonetheless view that commitment as uneven. Brazil has remained open to regional organizations like Mercosur, the Union of South American States (Unasur), and the South American Defense Council (CSD), and it has acted to insure that other Latin American countries do not control them or, in the case of Mexico, even enter them.[21] But within these organizations Brazil displays few supranational aspirations.

If emerging countries focus on regional control, order, and domination, several consequences follow. First, overarching global competition may be less severe as states focus on their local neighbors. Second, regional orders will become increasingly well-defined and different sets of regional rules may take shape as regions follow different trajectories. Third, regional leadership may be a stepping-stone to a larger global role. Finally, as we will see below, where regional shapers overlap or exist in the same region, friction may develop as they compete to set the agenda, influence friends and foes, and control the rules and rights of way.

The Return of the Ruler

Foreign policy often bears the imprint of whoever is leading the country. What is striking is that foreign policy in these shaping countries appears to be especially driven by the preferences and personalities of the leaders in charge. As human beings, we are inherently attracted to the notion that individuals are the movers of history; we find leaders endlessly fascinating. We discount the impact of the social, political, and biological circumstances that drive their choices. So there is danger in dwelling too much on the power of personality. But it may be that in an era when national unity is challenged and power is more dispersed, individual leaders gain more traction as a rallying point and their roles become more significant. The list of names speaks for itself: Xi Jinping, Modi, Putin, Netanyahu, Erdoğan, and Merkel. Personal diplomacy may be casting a much more significant shadow in the evolution of world politics.

The country studies in this volume often highlight the pivotal role particular leaders are playing—an influence that may well outlive the stewardship of the particular person. Consider, for example, Turkey's Erdoğan, who has repositioned Turkey between the Islamic Middle East and the European Union. He has been the main force in defining Turkey as a leader among moderate Muslim countries in the Middle East as well as positioning Turkey as a Sunni-oriented state. Gürsoy argues that another leader would have shaped a different identity for Turkey and we might infer that the core identity of the nation might change if Erdoğan left office.

Today, when we think of Russia, we think of Putin. And with Putin's evolution, so, too, has the country changed. Lukyanov argues that in the beginning Putin was a "realist," focused mainly on Russia's security and economic interests in light of the interests and power of other countries. Yet, starting in 2013–2014, Putin put a greater emphasis on conservative values. Although such feelings are broadly shared, Putin's personal beliefs about the unreliability and incompetency of the United States have shaped Russian attitudes and influenced its behavior.

Even more established older shaper countries like Germany seem heavily influenced by personalities. German policy, as Stelzenmüller points out, has fluctuated according to Merkel's predilections. Although her style has been that of an incrementalist, she will significantly influence which way Germany turns in the battle among its identities.

In other countries, the force of personality and individual preferences is readily apparent. Netanyahu has driven Israel's approach to Iran, one that has had a significant impact on relations with the United States as well. In Brazil, the switch from Cardoso to Lula, and now Lula's left-wing successor Dilma Rousseff, has impacted how Brazil discusses and approaches the international system. In China, Xi Jinping seems more inclined than his predecessors to confront regional states.[22] While India's policies had not been seen as personality driven under Prime Minister Manmohan Singh, the election of Narendra Modi raises the likelihood that his "cult of personality" may play a larger role in India.

There is a tension in the emphasis on the importance of the central leader's personality in the face of the claim that state authority is becoming more dispersed within the shaping powers. That tension is partially resolved in two ways. In shaper nations, centralized institutional authority is fragmenting yet gravitating toward individual leaders. Moreover, in order to get things done in societies where power is more fragmented, leaders may rely more on personalistic approaches, attempting to cut through the bureaucratic and regional barriers that would otherwise impede new initiatives. Although these trends may hold everywhere, they seem particularly relevant in countries that are experiencing a rapid rise in relative power and also evolving new institutions.

It is notable that the authors above do not see political systems—for example, democracy versus autocracy—as especially salient in the making of strategy or its effects. No doubt that distinction is part and parcel of the domestic politics discussed, yet there is no neat line between Russia and China and the other, democratic, countries in the previous chapters. What deserves more attention, however, is how the growth of individual authority might impede, advance, or collapse the development of democracy in places like Turkey, China, Russia, and India.

Shaping by Peace or War?

Will these emerging countries be more peaceful or warlike than others in history? There are grounds for optimism, but there are also warning signs that longer trends are problematic.

Optimism resides in three phenomena. First, countries making progress on their own economic development and domestic political consolidation are unlikely to spend much time on external military ventures. While most of these countries will not be only "trading" states, economic development will be a central concern for some time in India, Brazil, China, and Turkey. Moreover, since successful development in a globalized world requires cooperation with others, aggressive national strategies will likely impinge on growth prospects. Finally, many of the countries share an interest in combating radical terrorism: the need to coordinate on that threat may help to trump factors that otherwise might spawn armed clashes. All the countries in this study (with the possible exception of Brazil) face threats from transnational (often radical Islamic) armed groups and individuals.

Not all the signs point to peace. Russia, for example, has not eschewed military means to advance its ambitions. This has been particularly true in Central Asia, the Middle East, and Eastern Europe, where Russia has intervened repeatedly in recent years. Moscow has not been focused on a development strategy, but has used its resources to maintain a sizable military establishment. Nor has Russia been hesitant to employ its forces in areas such as Georgia and the Crimea. Russia, moreover, has not been shy about using its diplomatic and military leverage in countries where it sees a strategic interest—for example, in Syria. The fact that Russia does not prize economics above politics—or is seemingly more willing to deploy military power to achieve its interests—means that Russia is not a country that easily fits the profile of a "peaceful riser." As Lukyanov notes, "Instead of focusing on patient economic engagement, integrating itself into global economic and trade networks, and using interdependence to strengthen its position relative to other great powers, Russia reverted to traditional geopolitics and the use of force" (p. 116, this volume). President Putin has sought domestic legitimacy through an activist and nationalist foreign policy rather than a renewed economic dynamism. This serves as a potent source of future conflict, especially to the degree that Russian leaders use nationalism and external threats to maintain internal legitimacy and control.

The image of rising peaceful powers may be a myth or an outdated conventional wisdom. China, after all, seems to be slowly shedding its "peaceful rise" banner in favor of a China ready to protect its interests in the East and South China Sea—with the use of force if needed. China has asserted a "no fly zone" in the East China Sea and has constructed man-made islands in the South China Sea. It is developing its military power at a relatively rapid pace. This behavior is not unusual for a rising great power, especially for one that does not have the backing of a larger country, as Japan and Germany had from the United States after World War II. Despite China's efforts at reassurance as explained by Men Honghua, these maritime policies have worried its neighbors.[23]

India may want to focus on development, but it cannot ignore security challenges on its borders nor can it forget historical grudges that exacerbate tensions. According to Raghavan, nuclear-armed neighbor Pakistan remains a physical and existential threat as a result of "deep-seated drivers such as historical memory and identity." From nuclear posturing to subconventional skirmishing in Kashmir, conflict is a daily reality for India. And potential disputes with China along their shared border could also impel India to use force—as could unstable political situations on its frontiers with Nepal, Bangladesh, Burma, and Sri Lanka. India does not seek to promote its economic well-being through force, but war is a constant concern.

Israel must also weigh the centrality of hard power in its strategy. Surrounded by potentially hostile neighbors, no permanent borders, and with a high level of development already achieved, Israel has relied on military means as much as diplomacy. Violence is a daily possibility for most Israelis; their use of force typically provides immediate security, but does not resolve long-term issues and in some cases makes them more intractable. Levite notes that "Israel's territorial gains in 1967, inspired by fear and a hope to safeguard its security, have complicated peacemaking, accentuated divisions within Israel, and made coherent strategic planning far more difficult than it was at Israel's inception" (p. 99, this volume).

A source of potential conflict for the shapers is the potent blend of regional ambition and strategic insecurity. In Asia, fear and opportunity mix between China and Japan in the east and India and China in the west. As Men stresses in his chapter, countries maneuvering for "defensive purposes" may seem like aggressors to their regional competitors, unleashing unexpected hostility. And some may have intentional plans for exerting broader influence. Most of the shaping powers aspire to leadership, if not hegemony, in their neighborhoods; those aspirations often constitute a challenge to others. Regional, not global, dynamics will be the cockpit of international competition in coming decades.

The Shapers and the United States

James Steinberg points out "good strategy must take into account the strategies pursued by others" (p. 138, this volume). Likewise, it would be foolish to consider the anticipated impact of the strategies of the shapers on world politics without considering how they interact with the policies of other states, particularly those of the most powerful contemporary nation, the United States. Scholars and policymakers alike debate whether the United States is in decline in terms of capabilities and willingness to lead. Yet, as Steinberg asserts, "[the United States] may lack the means to order the world unilaterally, but it most certainly can shape it" (p. 141, this volume). What will this impact look like? How will the strategies of the United States and those of emerging countries intersect?

The United States has been the undisputed leader of the international system since the end of the Cold War. It has developed military power that has dwarfed the combined capabilities of other major countries. Governments abroad focus on the United States; consider Spektor's stunning point that Brazilians fear the United States as a threat to the Amazon and the recently discovered oilfields under the Brazilian seabed. Outsiders complain that the United States tends to strike out on its own with too little consultation and too few constraints on its actions.

Rather than defending the existing order, the United States seems to have been a leader in changing it—at least from the perspective of other countries. As one of the central principles in its founding, the United Nations Charter stated: "Nothing contained in the present Charter shall authorize the United Nations to intervene in matters which are essentially within the domestic jurisdiction of any state."[24] Yet, in recent years, the United States has been one of the leading proponents of intervention in other countries in order to protect human rights and to prevent massacres and genocide, thereby fulfilling its "responsibility to protect" ("R2P").[25] Such interventions appear threatening to regimes that fear they are being accused of human rights violations and targeted for intervention. Defense of sovereignty has been a defining concern of many countries, including China, India, Russia, and Israel.

Shaping powers are also rattled by the U.S. tendency and capability to go it alone, whether in the 2003 invasion of Iraq (justified by the "Global War on Terrorism") or the U.S.-India nuclear deal. As Spektor relates:

From the Brazilian perspective, upon the end of the Cold War, the United States became the single greatest threat to the status quo. Its pattern of interventionism, its use of force, its extraterritorial application of U.S. laws, its emphasis on regime change, its conditional embrace of the norms of sovereignty, and its eagerness to differentiate between "civilized" states and "barbarian" threats made the United States seem especially menacing to international order in the aftermath of 9/11.

Likewise, critics denounce the drone attacks of the Obama administration and resent the United States' global surveillance as exposed by Edward Snowden and others.

In recent years, a different kind of unilateralism has taken shape as the United States has hesitated to bear the costs of global leadership. Israel, Levite explains, sees the United States "pivoting away from the Middle East" (p. 101, this volume). U.S. hesitancy was epitomized by its initial failure to support the "moderate" insurrectionists in Syria and by its reliance on risk-free drone strikes. Reflecting the frustration from past interventions, President Obama has asked, "Why is it that everybody is so eager to use military force after we've just gone through a decade of war at enormous cost to our troops and to our budget?"[26] Yet the Obama administration has embraced the need for limited intervention in Iraq and Syria against ISIS. This shift has been encouraged by changing circumstances on the ground, but it reflects vacillation and uncertainty in the eyes of friends and foes. Washington's failure to act, or sometimes its temptation to overreact in the service of "stability" may portend "systemic transformation."

The impact of shaper strategies in some ways may enhance U.S. influence, even if U.S. capabilities decline. If uncertainty is rampant, a steady U.S. role could give it an advantage in making enduring commitments. If states are free-riding on the U.S. global security role by not building their military capabilities, they will also be in no position to challenge Washington. This has sometimes been the case in Germany's and Japan's foreign policies since World War II. If regions remain the focus of shaper governments, Washington may be in the catbird seat. Only one country is present in all the regions and able to exercise leverage across them: the United States. The regionalization of world politics may increase U.S. sway.

The outcomes of specific interactions between countries that define world politics will be determined by how and how much the U.S. interacts with the shapers—and the reverse: much is contingent. As Steinberg points out in his call for a "hybrid" U.S. strategy, poor choices may lead to unnecessary conflict or undercut the prospect of mutual gains. States could focus on issues where views clash—such as Washington insisting that economic liberalization is the only way forward or shapers refusing to contribute at all to environmental solutions. Yet there is also room for mutual gains (for example, containing terrorism) as each power selects tactics suited to its particular circumstances and promotes inclusive, rather than exclusive institutions, be they global (for example, the UN Security Council) or regional (for example, Asian free trade agreements). Steinberg is accurate that not all shapers are alike: U.S. strategies should be crafted accordingly and the interactions in each case will vary. In recent years, the United States has cut deals with rising countries such as India (nonproliferation) and China (climate change). It remains to be seen how these deals will affect global governance and the management of common problems.[27] How the world will be remade by shapers and the United States together is not easily foretold, except for this: both will be important in what happens.

※ ※ ※

Though predictions are difficult, several trends are apparent in the strategies reviewed in this volume. Overwhelmingly, the environment of this emerging group of countries is one of significant uncertainty. Though international affairs is often akin to William James's description of a newborn's world—"all blooming buzzing confusion"—the fragmentation of national identity and authority, shifts in power, ambiguous and volatile policies, and weakened institutions all have created a climate of unpredictability. It is a world in which rising countries will stay most focused on their own development rather than pay attention to shared problems that might divert precious resources. And it is a world where states will be focused much more on regional than on global order. These states want to master their neighborhoods; if successful, they may or may not search for bigger targets.

At a minimum, since these states have nuclear weapons on their territory and/or the ability (or the capacity to get the ability) to deploy nuclear weapons, they matter a great deal for the future of global security. There is good news and bad news in terms of the prospects for peace. Because many of the shapers are focused on development, and because most of them see the path to development through economic engagement with the world, there are few incentives for atavistic global aggression. However, the picture is less clear in those regions where these rising giants are neighbors, harbor historical gripes, and/or where ambition transcends borders. And it is also less clear in countries where economic advancement is not the main goal or where economic gains are considered most achievable by conquest versus commerce.

In a turbulent world coupled with diminished state authority, the role of leaders will grow. The world that the shapers are making will depend on the quality of those at the helm. Leaders really could make all the difference as they maneuver for influence and power in their respective regions yet operate in a global arena beckoning for more collective goods and institutional rules in the face of pandemics, terrorism, climate change, and economic turbulence. And the mix of circumstance and personality will be heavily influenced by the interactions between the shapers and the United States.

The conventional wisdom about what determines international relations is not wrong: the balance of power along with the level of economic interdependence in the international system, as well as the choices of a declining hegemon, will be important. Yet if the story ended there it would be a faulty guide to the future. World politics will also be made by the shaping powers discussed in this volume. The shapers represent a new trend in the international arena—most will not define world politics, but they will affect their individual regions, and regional dynamics could reshape global politics. Collectively, they will have a significant impact on the twenty-first century: we would be wise to pay attention to the factors driving their decisions and actions. And it would be prudent to consider the consequences of their strategies for the nature of international order and disorder.

NOTES

Introduction

1. Robert Chase, Emily Hill, and Paul Kennedy, "Pivotal States and U.S. Strategy," *Foreign Affairs* 75, no. 1 (January/February 1996), 33–51.
2. See "World Development Indicators," The World Bank, http://databank.world-bank.org/data/download/GDP.pdf.
3. For more information, see the Frederick S. Pardee Center for International Futures, http://www.ifs.du.edu/ifs/frm_MainMenu.aspx.
4. Carl von Clausewitz, *On War*, trans. by Michael Howard and Peter Paret, abridged by Beatrice Heuser (New York: Oxford University Press, 2008), 74, 133–35.
5. Lawrence Freedman, *Strategy: A History* (New York: Oxford University Press, 2013), xi. For an elegant introduction to the concept of grand strategy, see Paul Kennedy, "Grand Strategy in War and Peace: Toward a Broader Definition," in *Grand Strategies in War and Peace*, ed. Paul Kennedy (New Haven, CT: Yale University Press, 1991), 1–7. See also Basil Liddell Hart, *Strategy* (London: Faber and Faber, 1967), 322.
6. Perhaps the classic study of the making of grand strategy over the *longue durée* is Paul Kennedy, *The Rise and Fall of the Great Powers: Economic Change and Military Conflict from 1500 to 2000* (New York: Random House, 1987).
7. Peter Paret, introduction to *Makers of Modern Strategy from Machiavelli to the Nuclear Age*, ed. Gordon Craig Paret and Felix Gilbert (Princeton, NJ: Princeton University Press, 1986), 3.
8. Williamson Murray and Mark Grimsley, "Introduction: On Strategy," in *The Making of Strategy: Rulers, States, and War*, ed. Williamson Murray, MacGregor Knox, and Alvin Bernstein (London: Cambridge University Press, 1994), 1–23.

9. See an excerpt from Bismarck's memoirs: "The Nightmare of Coalitions: Bismarck on the Other Great Powers (1879/1898)," GHDI, http://germanhistorydocs.ghi-dc.org/sub_document.cfm?document_id=1855.

10. Thucydides, *History of the Peloponnesian War,* trans. Rex Warner (New York: Penguin, 1954), I: 23, 49.

11. Kennedy quotes British statesman and imperial enthusiast Leo Amery as asserting that "those people who have the industrial power and the power of invention and science will be able to defeat all the others." Kennedy writes that "much of the international affairs during the following half-century turned out to be a fulfilment of such forecasts." *Rise and Fall,* 196–197. A nuanced study of whether economic interdependence leads to war is found in Dale C. Copeland, *Economic Interdependence and War* (Princeton, NJ: Princeton University Press, 2014).

12. For Steinberg's further work on this topic, see James B. Steinberg and Michael O'Hanlon, "Keep Hope Alive: How to Prevent U.S.-Chinese Relations from Blowing Up," *Foreign Affairs* 93 no. 4 (July/August 2014), 107–117; Steinberg and O'Hanlon, *Strategic Reassurance and Resolve: U.S.-China Relations in the Twenty-First Century* (Princeton, NJ: Princeton University Press, 2014). For a range of views on the U.S.-China relationship, see, for example, Ted Galen Carpenter, *America's Coming War with China: A Collision Course over Taiwan* (New York: Palgrave Macmillan, 2006); Michael Vlahos, "History's Warning: A U.S.-China War Is Terrifyingly Possible," *National Interest,* June 26, 2014, http://nationalinterest.org/print/feature/historys-warning-us-china-war-terrifyingly-possible-10754. China's 2015 defense strategy white paper struck many China-watchers as bellicose. See "China Unveils Plans for Greater Naval Role beyond Its Coasts," *Bloomberg News,* May 25, 2015, http://www.bloomberg.com/news/articles/2015-05-26/china-unveils-strategy-for-greater-naval-role-beyond-its-coasts. An interesting effort to extrapolate lessons from the past is found in Richard N. Rosecrance and Steven E. Miller, eds., *The Next Great War? The Roots of World War I and the Risk of U.S.-China Conflict* (Cambridge, MA: MIT Press, 2014).

13. See "National Accounts Main Aggregates Database," United Nations Statistics Division, http://unstats.un.org/unsd/snaama/resQuery.asp.

14. Barry Posen, *The Sources of Military Doctrine: France, Britain, and Germany between the World Wars* (Ithaca, NY: Cornell University Press, 1984), 13.

1. Brazil

1. Miles Kahler, "Negotiating the Rise of New Powers," *International Affairs* 89, no. 3 (2013): 711–729; Andrew Hurrell, "Lula's Brazil: A Rising Power, but Going Where?," *Current History* 107, no. 706 (2008): 51–57; Stewart Patrick, "Irresponsible Stakeholders: The Difficulty of Integrating Rising Powers," *Foreign Affairs* 89, no. 6 (2010): 44–53; Randall Schweller, "Emerging Powers in the Age of Disorder," *Global Governance* 17, no. 3 (2011): 289–299.

2. Fátima Anastasia, Christopher Mendonça, and Helga Almeida, "Poder Legislativo e Política Externa No Brasil: Jogando Com as Regras," *Contexto Internacional* 34, no. 2 (2012): 617–657; Simone Diniz and Cláudio Oliveira Ribeiro, "The Role of the Brazilian Congress in Foreign Policy: An Empirical Contribution to the Debate," *Brazilian Political Science Review* 2, no. 2 (2008): 10–38.

3. Timothy Power, "Brazilian Democracy as a Late Bloomer: Reevaluating the Regime in the Cardoso-Lula Era," special issue, *Latin American Research Review* 45, no. 4 (2010): 218–247; Timothy Power and Cesar Zucco Jr., "Estimating Ideology of Brazilian Legislative Parties, 1990–2005: A Research Communication," *Latin American Research Review* 44, no. 1 (2009): 218–246; Jason Cason and Timothy Power, "Presidentialization, Pluralization, and the Rollback of Itamaraty: Explaining Change in Brazilian Foreign Policy Making in the Cardoso-Lula Era," *International Political Science Review* 30, no. 2 (2009): 117–140.

4. Fernando Henrique Cardoso, "Relações Norte-Sul no Contexto Atual: Uma Nova Dependência," in *O Brasil e a Economia Global,* ed. Renato Baumann (Rio de Janeiro: Campus, 1996); Cardoso, *O Presidente Segundo o Sociólogo. Entrevista de Fernando Henrique Cardoso a Roberto Pompeu de Toledo* (São Paulo: Companhia das Letras, 1998); Cardoso, *The Accidental President of Brazil: A Memoir* (New York: Public Affairs, 2006).

5. See Perry Anderson, "Lula's Brazil," *London Review of Books* 33, no. 7 (2011): 1–23; Werner Baer and Joseph L. Love, eds., *Brazil under Lula: Economy, Politics, and Society under the Worker-President* (New York: Palgrave Macmillan, 2009); Celso Amorim, *Conversas com Jovens Diplomatas* (São Paulo: Benvirá, 2011).

6. Cardoso, "Remarks Before the French National Assembly" (speech, Paris, France, October 30, 2001, http://www1.folha.uol.com.br/folha/brasil/ult96 u26254.shtml.

7. Philip Nel and Ian Taylor, "Bugger Thy Neighbour? IBSA and South–South Solidarity," *Third World Quarterly* 34, no. 6 (2013): 1091–1110.

8. André Singer, *Os sentidos do Lulismo no Brasil—Reforma Gradual e Pacto Conservador* (São Paulo: Companhia das Letras, 2012); Singer, "Rebellion in Brazil," *New Left Review* 85 (January/February 2014): 19–37.

9. On future trends, see Cesar Zucco and David J. Samuels, "Lulismo, Petismo, and the Future of Brazilian Politics" (paper presented at the "Le Brésil de Lula: Héritage et Défis" conference, Montréal, Canada, October 11–12, 2012).

10. Peter Trubowitz, *Politics and Strategy: Partisan Ambition and American Statecraft* (Princeton, NJ: Princeton University Press, 2011); Candice Eleanor Moore, "Governing Parties and Southern Internationalism: A Neoclassical Realist Approach to the Foreign Policies of South Africa and Brazil, 1999–2010" (PhD diss., The London School of Economics, 2011).

11. Kenneth Waltz, "Structural Realism after the Cold War," *International Security* 25, no. 1 (2000): 29.

12. Cardoso, "Relações Norte-Sul no Contexto Atual," 12.

13. This section draws on Matias Spektor, *18 Dias: Quando Lula e FHC se Uniram para Conquistar o Apoio de Bush* (Fortaleza, Brazil: Objetiva, 2014).

14. Marcelo de Paiva Abreu, *Comércio exterior: interesses do Brasil* (Rio de Janeiro: Elsevier, 2007).

15. Stephen Walt, *Taming American Power* (New York: W. W. Norton, 2005).

16. Celso Amorim, Interview with Folha de S. Paulo, May 16, 2005, http://onpoint. wbur.org/2015/09/28/anne-marie-slaughter-work-life-balance.

17. Andrew Cooper, "Squeezed or Revitalised? Middle Powers, the G20 and the Evolution of Global Governance," *Third World Quarterly* 34, no. 6 (2013): 963–984; Philip Golub, "From the New International Economic Order to the G20: How the 'Global South' Is Restructuring World Capitalism from Within," *Third World Quarterly* 34, no. 6 (2013): 1000–1015.

18. Spektor, *18 Dias;* João Augusto de Castro Neves and Matias Spektor, "Obama and Brazil," in *Shifting the Balance: Obama and the Americas,* ed. Abraham F. Lowenthal, Theodore J. Piccone, and Laurance Whitehead (Washington, DC: Brookings Institution Press, 2011), 43–54.

19. For a discussion of why emerging nations may choose to free-ride, see Randall Schweller and Xioyu Pu, "After Unipolarity: China's Vision of International Order in an Era of US Decline," *International Security* 36, no. 1 (2011): 41–72.

20. Spektor, *18 Dias;* Carlos Poggio Teixeira, *Brazil, the United States, and the South American Subsystem: Regional Politics and the Absent Empire* (Lanham, MD: Lexington Books, 2014).

21. This section on world order is based on Sean Burges, "Building a Global Southern Coalition: The Competing Approaches of Brazil's Lula and Venezuela's Chávez," *Third World Quarterly* 28, no. 7 (2007): 1343–1358; Steve Ellner, "Leftist Goals and the Debate over Anti-Neoliberal Strategy in Latin America," *Science and Society* 68, no. 1 (2004): 10–32; Andrés Malamud, "A Leader without Followers? The Growing Divergence between the Regional and Global Performance of Brazilian Foreign Policy," *Latin American Politics and Society* 53, no. 3 (2011): 1–24; Diana Tussie, "Latin America: Contrasting Motivations for Regional Projects," *Review of International Studies* 35, suppl. S1 (2009): 169–188; and Matias Spektor, "The State of Brazil's South America Project" (working paper, The Inter-American Dialogue, Washington, DC, 2014, http://www.thedialogue.org).

22. Oliver Stuenkel, "Rising Powers and the Future of Democracy Promotion: The Cases of Brazil and India," *Third World Quarterly* 34, no. 2 (2013): 339–355.

23. Brigitte Weiffen, Leslie Wehner, and Detlef Nolte, "Overlapping Regional Security Institutions in South America: The Case of OAS and Unasur," *International Area Studies Review* 16 (December 2013): 370–389.

24. Marco Cepik, "Regional Security and Integration in South America: What UNASUR Could Learn from the OSCE and the Shanghai Cooperation Organization," in *The United States and Europe in a Changing World. Dordrecht, Netherlands: Republic of Letters,* ed. Roger Kanet (Dordrecht, Netherlands: Republic of Letters Publishing, 2009); Adriana Erthal Abdenur and Danilo Marcondes de

Souza Neto, "Region-Building by Rising Powers: The South Atlantic and Indian Ocean Rims Compared," *Journal of the Indian Ocean Region* 10, no. 1 (2014): 1–17.

25. For a discussion focusing on naval power dynamics, see Érico Duarte, "South American Strategic Condition and Implications for Brazilian National Defense" (paper presented at the IPSA-ECPR Joint Conference, São Paulo, Brazil, February 16–19, 2011); Duarte, "Securing the South Atlantic: In Favour of a Revised Brazilian Maritime Strategy," in *Enduring NATO, Rising Brazil: Managing International Security in a Recalibrating Global Order*, ed. Brooke A. Smith-Windsor (Rome: NATO Defence College, 2015).

26. Oliver Stuenkel, *The BRICS and the Future of Global Order* (Lanham, MD: Lexington Books, 2015).

27. Oliver Stuenkel, *India-Brazil-South Africa Forum (IBSA): The Rise of the Global South* (London: Routledge, 2014).

28. Celso Lafer, "Brazilian International Identity: Past, Present and Future," *Daedalus* 129, no. 2 (Spring 2000): 207–238.

29. Tullo Vigevani and Gabriel Cepaluni, *Brazilian Foreign Policy in Changing Times: The Quest for Autonomy from Sarney to Lula* (Lanham, MD: Lexington Books, 2009); Samuel Pinheiro Guimarães, *Quinhentos Anos de Periferia* (Rio de Janeiro: Contraponto, 2007); Pinheiro, *Desafios Brasileiros na Era dos Gigantes* (Rio de Janeiro: Contraponto, 2006).

30. See for instance Celso Amorim, *Teerã, Ramala e Doha: memórias de uma política externa ativa e altiva* (São Paulo: Saraiva, 2015).

31. Antonio de Aguiar Patriota, *Política Externa Brasileira: Discursos, Artigos e Entrevistas* (Brasilia: FUNAG, 2013).

2. China

1. Men Honghua, *China's Grand Strategy: A Framework Analysis* (Beijing: Peking University Press, 2005), 41.

2. Information Office of the State Council, *Defense White Paper: The Diversified Employment of China's Armed Forces* (Beijing: Xinhua, 2013). These generalizations were repeated in a May 2015 official document from the Chinese Ministry of National Defense, "China's Military Strategy," May 26, 2015, http://news.usni. org/2015/05/26/document-chinas-military-strategy.

3. Ministry of National Defense, "China's Military Strategy."

4. Ralph Sawyer, trans., "T'ai Kung's Six Secret Teachings," in *The Seven Military Classics of Ancient China* (Boulder, CO: Westview, 1993), 19–106.

5. Ralph Sawyer, trans., "Sun-tzu's Art of War," in *The Seven Military Classics of Ancient China*, 157–186.

6. Zhu Yuanzhang quoted in Wang Gungwu, "Ming Foreign Relations: Southeast Asia," in *The Cambridge History of China*, Vol. 8: *The Ming Dynasty, 1368–1644, Part 2*, ed. Denis Twitchett and Frederick Mote (Cambridge: Cambridge University Press, 1998), 311–312.

7. Mao Tsetung, "Be Concerned with the Well-Being of the Masses, Pay Attention to Methods of Work," in *Selected Works of Mao Tsetung*, Vol. 1 (Beijing: Foreign Languages Press, 1967), 150.

8. Ministry of National Defense, "China's Military Strategy," 3.

9. Carlyle Thayer, "Vietnam Sends High-Level Military Delegation to China," Chennai Centre for China Studies, October 17, 2014, http://www.c3sindia.org/uncategorized/4571.

10. Honghua, *China's Grand Strategy*, 2–6.

11. Justin Lin, *Demystifying the Chinese Economy* (New York: Cambridge University Press, 2012).

12. Åsa Johannson et al., *Looking to 2060: Long-Term Growth Prospects* (Paris: OECD, 2012), http://www.oecd.org/eco/outlook/2060%20policy%20paper%20FINAL.pdf.

13. Jessica Mathews, "Power Shift," *Foreign Affairs* 76, no. 1 (1997): 50–66.

14. Men Honghua, "Remedial Measures for Failed States: A Strategic Dimension of Sino-American Security Cooperation," *American Studies* 18, no. 1 (2004): 7–32; Ashraf Ghani and Clare Lockhart, *Fixing Failed States: A Framework for Rebuilding a Fractured World* (New York: Oxford University Press, 2009).

15. Dennis C. Blair and John T. Hanley Jr., "From Wheels to Webs: Reconstructing Asia-Pacific Security Arrangements," *The Washington Quarterly* 24, no. 1 (2001): 7–17; Jean-Marie Guehenno, "The Impact of Globalization on Strategy," *Survival* 40, no. 4 (1998/1999): 5–19.

16. Joseph Grieco, Robert Powell, and Duncan Snidal, "The Relative-Gains Problem for International Cooperation," *American Political Science Review* 87, no. 3 (1993): 727–743.

17. See especially the section "Military and Security Cooperation" in Ministry of National Defense, "China's Military Strategy."

18. Xi Jinping, "New Asian Security Concept for New Progress in Security Cooperation" (remarks presented at the Fourth Summit of the Conference on Interaction and Confidence Building Measures in Asia, Shanghai, China, May 21, 2014), http://www.fmprc.gov.cn/mfa_eng/zxxx_662805/t1159951.shtml.

19. "Why China Is Creating a New 'World Bank' for Asia," *The Economist*, November 11, 2014, http://www.economist.com/blogs/economist-explains/2014/11/economist-explains-6.

20. Men Honghua, *Open-Up and China's National Strategic System* (Beijing: People's Press, 2008), 11–22.

21. Deng Xiaoping, *Deng Xiaoping Anthology*, Vol. 3 (Beijing: People's Press, 1993), 328, 349; Men Honghua, "Reconstruction of China's Strategic Culture: A Research Agenda," *Education and Research* 40, no. 1 (2006): 57–63.

22. Xiaoping, *Deng Xiaoping Anthology*, 374.

23. Dai Bingguo, "Stick to the Path of Peaceful Development," *China Daily*, December 10, 2010, http://www.chinadaily.com.cn/opinion/2010–12/13/content_11690133.htm.

24. Ministry of National Defense, "China's Military Strategy," 4.

25. Yu Keping, *Democracy Is a Good Thing* (Washington, DC: Brookings, 2009).

26. "Xinhua Insight: China's Xi Points Way for Arts," *Xinhua*, October 16, 2014, http://news.xinhuanet.com/english/china/2014–10/16/c_133719778.htm.

27. Patti Waldmeier and Clive Cookson, "China Sends Thousands of Doses of Anti-Ebola Drug to Africa," *Financial Times*, October 15, 2014, http://www.ft.com/intl/cms/s/0/33012186-539a-11e4-929b-00144feab7de.html#axzz3GnN3BoI.

28. "China's Military Vows to Show More Muscle," *Washington Post*, May 27, 2015, A8.

29. Yan Xuetong, "From Keeping a Low Profile to Striving for Achievement," *Chinese Journal of International Politics* 7, no. 2 (2014): 153–184.

30. Qin Yaqing, "Continuity through Change: Background Knowledge and China's International Strategy," *Chinese Journal of International Politics* 7, no. 3 (2014): 285–314.

31. Ezra Vogel, *Deng Xiaoping and the Transformation of China* (Cambridge, MA: Harvard University Press, 2011).

32. Ezra F. Vogel, *One Step Ahead in China: Guangdong under Reform* (Cambridge, MA: Harvard University Press, 1989).

33. Chen Yawei, *Shanghai Pudong: Urban Development in an Era of Global-Local Interaction* (Amsterdam: IOS Press, 2007).

34. David Lampton, "China's Foreign and Security Policy-Making Process: Is It Changing and Does it Matter?," in *The Making of Chinese Foreign and Security Policy in the Era of Reform*, ed. David Lampton (Stanford, CA: Stanford University Press, 2001), 1–38.

35. Shi Yinhong, "'Triumphalism' and Decision Making in China's Asia Policy," *Economic and Political Studies* 1, no. 1 (2013): 107–119.

36. Wen-Hsuan Tsai and Nicola Dean, "The CCP's Learning System: Thought Unification and Regime Adaptation," *China Journal* 69 (January 2013): 87–107.

37. Men Honghua et al., "The Evolution of China's Diplomacy Decision-Making Mechanism: 1949–2009," *World Economy and Politics* 11 (November 2009): 44–54.

38. "中国共产党十八届三中全会公报发布(全文)" (Third Plenary Session of the Communist Party of China communique), *Xinhua*, November 12, 2013, http://news.xinhuanet.com/house/suzhou/2013–11–12/c_118113773.htm.

39. Qin Yaqing, "Continuation and Evolution of the International System," *Foreign Affairs Review*, no. 1 (2010): 7; Yu Zhengliang, "Transformation of Current International System: Basic Characteristics," *Forum of World Economy and Politics* 6 (2010): 1–8.

40. Le Yucheng, "International Relations and China's Diplomacy," *Foreign Affairs Review*, no. 6 (2010): 1–10.

41. Calculated from the World Bank, *World Development Indicators 2014* (Washington, DC: World Bank, 2014), doi:10.1596/978-1-4648-0163-1.

42. Alastair Iain Johnston, "How New and Assertive Is China's New Assertiveness?," *International Security* 37, no. 4 (Spring 2013): 7–48; Bjorn Jerden, "The Assertive China Narrative: Why It Is Wrong and How So Many Bought Into It," *Chinese*

Journal of International Politics 7, no. 1 (2014): 47–88; Brantly Womack, "China and Vietnam: Managing an Asymmetric Relationship in an Era of Economic Uncertainty," *Asian Politics and Policy* 2, no. 4 (November 2010): 583–600.

43. Zalmay Khalilzad, Abram N. Shulsky, Daniel Byman, Roger Cliff, David T. Orletsky, David A. Shlapak, and Ashley J. Tellis, *The United States and a Rising China: Strategic and Military Implications* (Santa Monica, CA: Rand Corporation, 1999).

44. These concerns are evident in Ministry of National Defense, "China's Military Strategy."

45. "Joint Communique of the United States of America and the People's Republic of China 1982," American Institute in Taiwan, August 17, 1982, http://www.ait.org.tw/en/us-joint-communique-1982.html; for U.S. arms sales to Taiwan, see Shirley A. Kan, *Taiwan: Major U.S. Arms Sales since 1990* (Washington, DC: Congressional Research Service, 2014), http://www.fas.org/sgp/crs/weapons/RL30957.pdf.

46. See, for example, "China (Hong Kong)," National Endowment for Democracy (U.S.), http://www.ned.org/where-we-work/asia/china-hong-kong.

47. Ministry of National Defense, "China's Military Strategy," 11.

48. Information Office of the State Council The People's Republic of China, "China's Foreign Aid," 2011, http://english.gov.cn/archive/white_paper/2014/09/09/content_281474986284620.htm; Information Office of the State Council The People's Republic of China, "China's Foreign Aid," 2014, http://english.gov.cn/archive/white_paper/2014/08/23/content_281474982986592.htm.

49. Charles Wolf Jr., Xiao Wang, and Eric Warner, "China's Foreign Aid and Government-Sponsored Investment Activities: Scale, Content, Destinations, and Implications," Rand National Defense Research Institute, 2013, http://www.rand.org/pubs/research_reports/RR118.html.

50. "The BRICS Bank: An Acronym with Capital," *The Economist*, July 19, 2014, http://www.economist.com/news/finance-and-economics/21607851-setting-up-rivals-imf-and-world-bank-easier-running-them-acronym.

51. Reid Standish and Bethany Allen-Ebrahimian, "Interactive Map: Follow the Roads, Railways, and Pipelines on China's New Silk Road," *Foreign Policy*, May 7, 2015, http://foreignpolicy.com/2015/05/07/interactive-map-follow-the-roads-railways-and-pipelines-on-chinas-new-silk-road/; "China's Initiatives on Building Silk Road Economic Belt and 21st Century Maritime Silk Road," *Xinhua*, May 31, 2015, http://www.xinhuanet.com/english/special/silkroad/; Camille Brugier, "China's Way: the New Silk Road," European Union Institute for Security Studies, May 2014, http://www.iss.europa.eu/uploads/media/Brief_14_New_Silk_Road.pdf.

52. Ministry of National Defense, "China's Military Strategy," 7.

53. Calculated from the World Bank, *World Development Indicators 2014*. The World Bank uses data from the Stockholm International Peace Research Institute (SIPRI).

54. "Total Aircraft Carrier Strength by Country," GFP, February 17, 2015, http://www.globalfirepower.com/navy-aircraft-carriers.asp.

55. David Sanger and William Broad, "China Makes Missiles More Potent in Move Seen as Message to U.S.," *New York Times*, May 16, 2015, http://www.nytimes.com/2015/05/17/world/asia/china-making-some-missiles-more-powerful.html?_r=0.

56. Simon Denyer, "China's Military Vows to Show More Muscle," *Washington Post*, May 27, 2015, A8.

57. Daniel Bell, *Beyond Liberal Democracy: Political Thinking for an East Asian Context* (Princeton, NJ: Princeton University Press, 2006); Peter Nolan, *China at the Crossroads* (Cambridge: Polity Press, 2004).

58. Details from the Confucius Institute Headquarters can be found at http://english.hanban.org/.

59. Ministry of National Defense, "China's Military Strategy," 7.

60. David Kang, "Getting Asia Wrong: The Need for New Analytical Frameworks," *International Security* 27, no. 4 (2003): 57–85.

61. Men Honghua, "East Asian Order Formation and Sino-Japanese Relations," *Indiana Journal of Global Legal Studies* 17, no. 1 (2010): 47–82.

3. Germany

1. Recent studies on post-reunification German foreign and security policy include Stephan Böckenförde, ed., *Deutsche Sicherheitspolitik: Herausforderungen, Akteure und Prozesse* (Opladen, Germany: Budrich, 2009); Hanns W. Maull, ed., *Germany's Uncertain Power* (New York: Palgrave MacMillan, 2006); Eric Gujer, *Schluss mit der Heuchelei: Deutschland ist eine Großmacht* (Hamburg: Körber-Stiftung, 2007); Helga Haftendorn, *Deutsche Außenpolitik zwischen Selbstbeschränkung und Selbstbehauptung 1945–2000* (Stuttgart: Deutsche Verlags-Anstalt, 2001); Gunther Hellmann, Daniel Jacobi, and Ursula Stark Urrestarazu, eds., *"Früher, entschiedener und substantieller"? Die neue Debatte über Deutschlands Außenpolitik* (Wiesbaden, Germany: Springer-VS, 2015); "The Sick Man of the Euro," *The Economist*, June 3, 1999, http://www.economist.com/node/209559.

2. Rose Jacobs, "On Top of the World: This Could Be the Start of a Century of German Success," *Newsweek*, July 17, 2014, http://www.newsweek.com/2014/07/25/top-world-could-be-start-century-german-success-259410.html.

3. In 2011, Polish foreign minister Radosław Sikorski said in a memorable speech in Berlin: "I fear German power *less* than I am beginning to fear her inactivity." See Sikorski, "Poland and the Future of the European Union" (speech, Berlin, Germany, November 28, 2011), http://www.mfa.gov.pl/resource/33ce6061-ec12-4da1-a145-01e2995c6302:JCR; Zanny Minton Beddoes, "Germany: Europe's Reluctant Hegemon," *The Economist*, June 15, 2013, http://www.economist.com/news/special-report/21579140-germany-now-dominant-country-europe-needs-rethink-way-it-sees-itself-and.

4. At the 2014 Munich Security Conference, Germany's president, foreign minister, and defense minister all gave speeches calling for greater German responsibility. Hans Joachim Gauck, "Germany's Role in the World: Reflections on Responsibility, Norms, and Alliances" (speech, Munich, Germany, January 31, 2014), http://www.bundespraesident.de/SharedDocs/Downloads/DE/Reden/2014/01/140131-Muenchner-Sicherheitskonferenz-Englisch.pdf?__blob=publicationFile; Frank-Walter Steinmeier, "Speech at the 50th Munich Security Conference" (speech, Munich, Germany, February 2, 2014), http://www.auswaertigesamt.de/DE/Infoservice/Presse/Reden/2014/140201-BM_M%C3%BCSiKo.html; Ursula von der Leyen, "Speech at the 50th Munich Security Conference" (speech, Munich, Germany, January 31, 2014), https://www.securityconference.de/fileadmin/MSC_/2014/Reden/2014-01-31-SpeechMinDef_von_der_Leyen-MuSeCo.pdf.

5. Germany is the only member state to have committed all its forces to the alliance.

6. Eberhard Sandschneider, "Deutsche Außenpolitik: eine Gestaltungsmacht in der Kontinuitätsfalle," *Aus Politik und Zeitgeschichte,* March 1, 2012, http://www.bpb.de/apuz/.

7. For a useful overview, which shares the view that Germany could do more to preserve and protect the international order, see Georg Nolte, "Deutschlands Rolle bei der Weiterentwicklung des Völkerrechts," *Vereinte Nationen* 6 (2013): 243.

8. For a thought-provoking discussion, see Daniel M. Kliman and Richard Fontaine, *Global Swing States: Brazil, India, Indonesia, Turkey, and the Future of International Order* (Washington, DC: Center for a New American Security, 2012), http://www.cnas.org/files/documents/publications/CNAS_GlobalSwingStates_KlimanFontaine.pdf.

9. The German term is *Gestaltungsmacht;* it was first introduced to refer to emerging non-Western powers (in connection with the largely unfulfilled expectation that they would contribute their own normative concepts), but is now also used to refer to Germany as well—usually in conjunction with the adjective "potential." See Bundesregierung, "Globalisierung gestalten—Partnerschaften ausbauen—Verantwortung teilen," Deutscher Bundestag, February 8, 2012, http://dip21.bundestag.de/dip21/btd/17/086/1708600.pdf.

10. A comprehensive study of current German international order policies would be very useful, but has yet to be written. See Ian Bremmer and Mark Leonard, "US-German Relationship on the Rocks," *Washington Post,* October 18, 2012, http://www.washingtonpost.com/opinions/us-german-relationship-on-therocks/2012/10/18/ed6a9f1c-13c2-11e2-be82-c3411b7680a9_story.html. This critique is somewhat strident and not accurate in all respects—but it captures the key issue well. The author would like to thank Thorsten Benner, director of the Global Public Policy Institute in Berlin, for key insights that helped shape this section.

11. Statistisches Bundesamt, "Außenhandel. Rangfolge der Handelspartner im Außenhandel der Bundesrepublik 2013," Destatis, 2014, https://www.destatis.de/

DE/ZahlenFakten/GesamtwirtschaftUmwelt/Aussenhandel/Handelspartner/
Tabellen/RangfolgeHandelspartner.pdf?_blob=publicationFile.

12. A revealing indicator of the importance attached to the EU as a power maximizer by Germany is the fact that Berlin—usually far less adept at inserting German diplomats into leadership positions in international organizations than its Western peers—has put many of its best civil servants into key euro area policy slots.

13. Daniela Schwarzer and Guntram Wolff, "Memo to Merkel: Post-election Germany and Europe," *Bruegel Policy Brief*, September 24, 2013, http://www.bruegel. org/publications/%C2%ACpubli%C2%ACca%C2%AC%C2%ACtion-detail/ publication/794-memo-to-merkel-post-election-germany-and-europe/. See also Daniela Schwarzer, "Germany in the Euro Area Crisis," in *The New Palgrave Dictionary of Economics*, online edition, ed. Steven N. Durlauf and Lawrence E. Blume (London: Palgrave Macmillan, 2014), 14, http://www.dictionaryofeconomics.com/ article?id=pde2014_G000225&edition=current&q=Schwarzer&topicid=&resu lt_number=1. Schwarzer points out that the next-largest country, with 20 percent of the Eurozone's GDP, is France and that "Germany's economy is more or less the same size as the combined economies of the 20 smaller member states."

14. This section is greatly indebted to conversations with Daniela Schwarzer, the German Marshall Fund's director of research and head of its Europe program.

15. This was the "ordoliberalism" or Freiburg School of economics, which dominated German economic policy and discourse in the postwar period, displaced today by what is referred to as "New Classical Economics." See Sebastian Dullien and Ulrike Guérot, "The Long Shadow of Ordoliberalism: Germany's Approach to the Euro Crisis," *European Council on Foreign Relations* 49 (July 27, 2012), http:// www.ecfr.eu/article/commentary_the_long_shadow_of_ordoliberalism.

16. Schwarzer, *Germany in the Euro Area Crisis*, 7. Schwarzer notes that while the Germans saw the Agenda 2010 reforms as the precondition for their country's later resilience in the crisis, others felt they had acted as "beggar-thy-neighbor" policies which had contributed to the worsening of the crisis elsewhere in Europe.

17. A multitude of German and international polls support this, from Allensbach to the Eurobarometer and Pew polls, as well as the German Marshall Fund's *Transatlantic Trends*.

18. The constitutional court has insisted on drawing thick red lines for German sovereignty transfers to the European Union, with key judgments on the Maastricht and Lisbon Treaties in 2004 and 2009; in the latter decision, it scolded the Bundestag for abrogating its rights to Brussels and decreed that it would have to be given greater co-decision-making powers in any similar sovereignty transfers in the future.

19. Schwarzer, *Germany in the Euro Area Crisis*, 9.

20. Ibid., 11–12.

21. Ibid., 13.

22. Some German policymakers (most importantly Finance Minister Wolfgang Schäuble) and economists have welcomed this. See Glienicker Group, "Towards the Euro Union," *Die Zeit,* October 17, 2013, http://www.glienickergruppe.eu/ ZEIT_Artikel%20der%20Glienicker%20Gruppe.pdf.

23. Chancellor Merkel invariably refers to the partnership with Israel as *deutsche Staatsraison,* which translates to a vital national commitment to Israel's security for the German state.

24. The term was coined by Hans Kundnani. See Kundnani, "Germany as a Geo-Economic Power?," *The Washington Quarterly* 34, no. 3 (2011): 31.

25. In 2014, ten months into the Ukraine crisis, German policymakers and politicians were increasingly questioning whether their country's relationship with Russia could still be described as strategic. The term is maintained here because of the unquestionable impact of Russian strategies on Germany and Europe.

26. Constanze Stelzenmüller, *Transatlantic Power Failures—America and Europe, Seven Years after 9/11: Hard Power Humbled, Soft Power Delusions Exposed, and a Looser, More Pragmatic Relationship* (Washington, DC: German Marshall Fund, 2008), http://www.gmfus.org/brusselsforum/2008/doc/constanzeWEB.pdf.

27. And, of course, the United States is Germany's third-largest trade partner, after the euro area and China.

28. See Daniela Schwarzer and Constanze Stelzenmüller, *What Is at Stake in Ukraine* (Washington, DC: German Marshall Fund, 2014), http://www.gmfus.org/wp-content/blogs.dir/1/files_mf/1401287286Schwarzer_Stelzenmueller_Ukraine_Mar14_web.pdf.

29. On June 3, 2014, the monthly ARD Deutschlandtrend poll reported that 57 percent of respondents felt that the United States is not a trustworthy partner. See "ARD Deutschlandtrend," *Tagesschau,* July 3, 2014, http://www.tagesschau.de/ multimedia/bilder/crbilderstrecke-110.html. The German media have covered the issue extensively and soberly, but in an increasingly exasperated tone. See Stefan Kornelius, "Im freien Fall," *Süddeutsche Zeitung,* July 17, 2014, 4.

30. Statistisches Bundesamt, "Außenhandel."

31. For details and background, see Constanze Stelzenmüller, "Germany's Russia Question: A New Ostpolitik for Europe," *Foreign Affairs* 88, no. 2 (March/April 2009): 89.

32. Hence the speech made on June 5, 2008, in Berlin by Russia's then-president Dmitry Medvedev, which outlined a pan-European security architecture. The proposal was seen as a "non-starter" by senior German policymakers because it would have forced NATO out of Europe. See Dmitry Medvedev, "Meeting with German Political, Parliamentary and Civic Leaders" (speech, Berlin, Germany, June 5, 2008), http://archive.kremlin.ru/eng/speeches/2008/06/05/ 2203_type82912type82914type84779_202153.shtml.

33. Jakob Mischke and Andreas Umland, "Germany's New Ostpolitik," *Foreign Affairs Snapshot,* April 9, 2014, http://www.foreignaffairs.com/articles/141115/ jakob-mischke-and-andreas-umland/germanys-new-ostpolitik; Markus Kerber,

"German Industry Should Speak Hard Truths to Putin," *Financial Times*, May 7, 2014, http://www.ft.com/intl/cms/s/0/3f73efe6-d5cf11e383b200144feabdco. html#axzz3H5l2cpG5; Rolf Mützenich, "Rapprochement Reloaded: Why Détente with Russia Is Not Appeasement," *Foreign Affairs*, February 25, 2015, https://www.foreignaffairs.com/articles/eastern-europe-caucasus/2015-02-25/rapprochement-reloaded; Karsten Voigt, "Collaboration, as Far as Possible; Defense, as Far as Necessary," *AICGS Blog*, April 14, 2015, http://www.aicgs.org/issue/collaboration-as-far-as-possible-defense-as-far-as-necessary/.

34. For a comprehensive review of the challenges raised by the conflict in Ukraine, see Andreas Schockenhoff and Karl-Georg Wellmann, "Für eine Neubestimmung der Beziehungen zu Russland: Positionspapier" (paper presented to the German Bundestag, Berlin, Germany, July 1, 2014), http://schockenhoff.de/download/140701_Russia_Paper_EN.pdf.

35. Felix Haiduk, "Conflicting Images? Germany and the Rise of China," *German Politics* 23, no. 1–2 (2014): 118, 119. Haiduk notes that German-Chinese trade has grown nearly tenfold since the mid-1990s. In July 2014, Merkel made her seventh trip to China as chancellor.

36. Thomas Heberer and Anja Senz, "Die deutsche Chinapolitik," in *Deutsche Außenpolitik*, ed. Thomas Jäger et al. (Wiesbaden, Germany: VS Verlag für Sozialwissenschaften, 2010), 673–692.

37. Nowhere is this more apparent than in China's ambiguous response to the Ukraine conflict. See Andrew Small, *Ukraine, Russia, and the China Option: The Geostrategic Risks Facing Western China Policy* (Washington, DC: German Marshall Fund, 2014).

38. See the German Marshall Fund's annual survey "Transatlantic Trends," http://trends.gmfus.org/transatlantic-trends/; "Involvement or Restraint?," Körber Foundation, 9, http://www.koerber-stiftung.de/en/international-affairs/special-topics/survey-foreign-policy.html; Heberer and Senz, "Die deutsche Chinapolitik," 681–683.

39. For an analysis of current policy and discourse, as well as its evolution, see Haiduk, "Conflicting Images?"; Heberer and Senz, "Die deutsche Chinapolitik."

40. Rem Korteweg, *A Presence Farther East: Can Europe Play a Strategic Role in the Asia-Pacific Region?* (London: Center for European Reform, 2014), 10, http://www.cer.org.uk/publications/archive/policy-brief/2014/presence-farther-east-can-europe-play-strategic-role-asia-pac.

41. Josef Janning, "Germany's Summer of Discontent on Foreign Policy," *European Council on Foreign Relations Blog*, July 30, 2014, http://www.ecfr.eu/blog/entry/Germanys_summer_of_discontent_on_foreign_policy; Sebastian Heilmann, "Chinesische Erschütterungen," *Frankfurter Allgemeine Zeitung*, July 4, 2014.

42. This thinking is rooted in Germany's understanding of parliamentary democracy. See Basic Law for the Federal Republic of Germany, Article 65, "Power to Determine Policy Guidelines-Department and Collegiate Responsibility," July 11, 2012, http://www.gesetze-im-internet.de/englisch_gg/englisch_gg.html#p0297.

Clause one provides that the chancellor defines the "general guidelines" of policy, whereas clause two states that ministers are responsible for the articulation and implementation of policy by their departments.

43. Federal Ministry of Defense, *White Paper 2006 on German Security Policy and the Future of the Bundeswehr* (Berlin: Bundesministerium der Verteidigung, 2006); Ministry of Defense, *Defense Policy Guidelines 2011: Safeguarding National Interests—Assuming International Responsibility—Shaping Security Together* (Berlin: Bundesministerium der Verteidigung, 2011).

44. Patrick Keller, "German Hard Power: Is There a There There?," *AEI National Security Outlook*, October 8, 2013, http://www.aei.org/outlook/foreignanddefense-policy/defense/nato/german-hard-power-is-there-a-there-there/. For a more detailed account of the transformation of the German armed forces, see Sven Bernhard Gareis, "Militärische Auslandseinsätze und die Transformation der Bundeswehr," in Jäger et al., *Deutsche Außenpolitik*, 148–170. The requirement of previous authorization by the legislature, not explicitly set down in the Basic Law, was construed by the court in its landmark decision on July 12, 1994, in the context of German participation in NATO operations in Yugoslavia. Given public opposition to deployments of the Bundeswehr, this decision was critical to domestic acceptance of Germany's participation.

45. According to the court's jurisprudence, Germany's federal armed forces are a *Parlamentsarmee* (parliamentary army), meaning that all governmental decisions to use force must be authorized by the legislature (*Parlamentsvorbehalt*); the details of the process were laid down in a 2005 law. The report of the Rühe Commission was published on June 16, 2015. https://www.bundestag.de/blob/385166/6f6e52130e6436b7462da1c9c6093899/bericht-kom-englisch-data.pdf.

46. For more information, see the website of the German Ministry of Defense, http://www.bmvg.de/portal/a/bmvg/!ut/p/c4/04_SB8K8xLLM9MSSzPy8x-Bz9CP3I5EyrpHK9pNyydL3y1Mzi4qTS5Az9gmxHRQBg2ftX/.

47. See Hilmar Linnenkamp and Christian Mölling, "Rüstung und Kernfähigkeiten," *SWP-Aktuell* 45 (2014), http://www.swpberlin.org/fileadmin/contents/products/aktuell/2014A45_lnk_mlg.pdf; Claudia Major and Christian Mölling, *German Defense Policy: Is the Change for Real?* (Washington, DC: German Marshall Fund, 2014), http://www.gmfus.org/wpcontent/blogs.dir/1/files_mf/1403712892Major_Moelling_GermanDefensePolicy_Jun14.pdf; Sarah Brockmeier, "Will Berlin Clear the Way for More Common Defence?," *IISS Survival Editor's Blog*, January 9, 2014, http://www.iiss.org/en/politics%20and%20strategy/blogsections/2014d2de/january1f44/german-common-defence-2846.

48. German politicians have occasionally—notably former foreign minister Guido Westerwelle—tried to elevate this attitude to the status of a doctrine, calling it *Kultur der militärischen Zurückhaltung* (culture of military restraint).

49. In May 2014, Foreign Minister Steinmeier set in motion a year-long review of German foreign and security policy, including an extended series of public

diplomacy outreach events in Germany itself; the final report, which set in motion changes that are intended to significantly enhance the foreign ministry's crisis management capabilities as well as its contributions to global order, was published on February 25, 2015. The report and publications related to the review can be found at http://www.auswaertiges-amt.de/cae/servlet/contentblob/699442/publicationFile/202977/Schlussbericht.pdf.

4. India

1. See for instance, George K. Tanham, *Indian Strategic Thought: An Interpretive Essay* (Santa Monica, CA: RAND, 1992). For a more recent account see Harsh V. Pant, *The China Syndrome: Grappling with an Uneasy Relationship* (New Delhi: Harper Collins, 2010).

2. For works in this vein, see Rudra Chaudhuri, *Forged in Crisis: India and the United States since 1947* (New York: Oxford University Press, 2014); Baldev Raj Nayyar and T. V. Paul, *India in the World Order: Searching for Major Power Status* (Cambridge: Cambridge University Press, 2003); C. Raja Mohan, *Crossing the Rubicon: The Shaping of India's New Foreign Policy* (New Delhi: Penguin, 2003).

3. This was suggested in the work of Samuel Huntington. See especially Huntington, *The Common Defense: Strategic Programs in National Politics* (New York: Columbia University Press, 1961).

4. Sunil Khilnani, *The Idea of India* (New York: Farrar, Straus & Giroux, 1997); Ramachandra Guha, *India after Gandhi: The History of the World's Largest Democracy* (New York: Ecco/HarperCollins, 2007).

5. The best overview is Francine Frankel, *India's Political Economy: The Gradual Revolution* (New Delhi: Oxford University Press, 2005). Also see Vijay Joshi and I. M. D. Little, *India: Macroeconomics and Political Economy, 1964–1991* (Washington, DC: The World Bank, 1994); Dani Rodrik and Arvind Subramanian, "From 'Hindu Growth' to Productivity Surge: The Mystery of Indian Growth Transition" (Working Paper 04/77, International Monetary Fund, March 2004).

6. Arvind Panagariya, *India: The Emerging Giant* (New Delhi: Oxford University Press, 2008); Atul Kohli, *Poverty amid Plenty in the New India* (Cambridge: Cambridge University Press, 2012).

7. David Scott, "India's 'Extended Neighborhood' Concept: Power Projection for a Rising Power," *India Review* 8, no. 2 (2009): 107–143.

8. Shivshankar Menon, "India's National Security: Challenges and Issues" (speech, P. C. Lal Memorial Lecture, New Delhi, India, April 2, 2012).

9. Devesh Kapur, "Public Opinion and Indian Foreign Policy," *India Review* 8, no. 3 (2009): 286–305.

10. Paul Kapur, *Dangerous Deterrent: Nuclear Weapons Proliferation and Conflict in South Asia* (Stanford, CA: Stanford University Press, 2007).

11. Rajesh Basrur, *Minimum Deterrence and India's Nuclear Security* (Stanford, CA: Stanford University Press, 2006).

12. Srinath Raghavan, "A Coercive Triangle: India, Pakistan, the US, and the Crisis of 2001–02," *Defence Studies* 9, no. 2 (2009): 242–260.

13. Walter C. Ladwig III, "A Cold Start for Hot Wars? The Indian Army's New Limited War Doctrine," *International Security* 32, no. 3 (Winter 2007/2008): 158–190.

14. Lawrence Freedman, *Deterrence* (Cambridge: Polity Press, 2004), 60–74.

15. Excerpts of his speech on January 5, 2015, can be found at https://www.youtube.com/watch?v=N7ESR5RU3X4.

16. Manmohan Singh, "Statement at the Inaugural Sessions of the XVIIth SAARC Summit" (speech, Addu City, Maldives, November 12, 2011), SAARC, http://www.saarc-sec.org/statements/Statement-by-Prime-Minister-of-India-Dr.-Manmohan-Singh-at-the-Inaugural-Session-of-the-XVIIth-SAARC-Summit/15/.

17. Ibid.

18. K. Natwar Singh, *My China Diary 1956–1988* (New Delhi: Rupa, 2009).

19. The best treatment so far is George J. Gilboy and Eric Heginbotham, *Chinese and Indian Strategic Behavior: Growing Power and Alarm* (Cambridge: Cambridge University Press, 2012).

20. You Ji, "Dealing with the Malacca Dilemma: China's Effort to Protect its Energy Supply," *Strategic Analysis* 31, no. 3 (2007): 467–489.

21. For a lively treatment see Sunanda K. Datta-Ray, *Looking East to Look West: Lee Kuan Yew's Mission India* (New Delhi: Penguin, 2009).

22. Nirupama Rao, "India and the Asia-Pacific: Expanding Engagement" (speech, Berkeley, CA, December 5, 2011), https://www.indianembassy.org/archives_details.php?nid=1690.

23. The best available treatment of this is C. Raja Mohan, *Samudra Manthan: India-China Rivalry in the Indo-Pacific* (Washington, DC: Carnegie Endowment, 2012).

24. "Agreement on Strategic Partnership between Islamic Republic of Afghanistan and the Republic of India," Ministry of Foreign Affairs, Islamic Republic of Afghanistan, October 4, 2011, http://mfa.gov.af/en/page/3381.

25. Shyam Saran, "A Premature Power?," *Outlook,* November 2, 2010, http://www.outlookindia.com/article.aspx?267750.

26. For a recent account, see Adam Tooze, *The Great War and the Remaking of the Global Order* (London: Allen Lane, 2014).

5. Israel

1. "The Declaration of the Establishment of the State of Israel," Israel Ministry of Foreign Affairs, May 14, 1948, http://www.mfa.gov.il/mfa/foreignpolicy/peace/guide/pages/declaration%20of%20establishment%20of%20state%20of%20israel.aspx.

2. For Israel's grand strategy, see, for example, Yehezkel Dror, *Grand Strategy for Israel* (Jerusalem: Academon, 1989); Dror, "Grand Strategy for an Era between Peace and War," *Ma'arachot,* no. 377 (2001): 2–15; Isaac Ben Israel, *Israel's Defence*

Doctrine (Tel Aviv: Modan, 2013); Avner Yani, ed., *National Security and Democracy in Israel* (Boulder, CO: Lynne Rienner, 1993).

3. Lieberman first elaborated on his swap concept at the fifth Herzliya conference in 2004. See Avigdor Lieberman, "A Land Swap between Israel and the Palestinian Population" (presentation at the annual Herzliya conference, Herzliya, Israel, December 13–16, 2004), http://www.herzliyaconference.org/?CategoryID=228& ArticleID=1687.

4. For a recent analysis of the huge economic opportunities for Israel inherent in peacemaking, see Eytan Avriel, "The Dove of Peace is Worth 67 Billion to the State Coffers," *Markerweek,* July 4, 2014, http://www.themarker.com/ markerweek/1.2366553.

5. An original perspective on the evolution of the Israeli-Palestinian conflict and its consequences is provided in Ari Shavit, *My Promised Land* (New York: Spiegel & Grau, 2013).

6. Uri Friedman, "Martin Indyk Explains the Collapse of the Middle East Peace Process," *The Atlantic,* July 3, 2014, http://www.theatlantic.com/international/ archive/2014/07/indyk-netanyahu-and-abbas-loathe-each-other/373922/.

7. Systematic tracking of the shifting Israeli public preferences over peacemaking is provided by the Peace Index project. See the Israeli Democracy Peace Institute, "The Peace Index: September 2014," September 23, 2014, http://www.peaceindex. org/defaultEng.aspx.

8. Minister of Defense Moshe Ya'alon presents the most lucid formulation of this approach. See "Ya'alon: Zero Chance of Palestinian Reconciliation, Hamas Is More Likely to Take Control of the West," *Nana,* June 10, 2014, http://news. nana10.co.il/Article/?ArticleID=1061591.

9. Prime Minister Netanyahu has implied as much in a recent speech at the Institute for National Security Studies. See Benjamin Netanyahu, "Speech at the Institute for National Security Studies" (Tel Aviv, Israel, June 29, 2014), https:// www.youtube.com/watch?v=DPtQQ5t11LY&list=PLCapdZwzDpNnYultApP pGDjy-OGwGGOFT&index=7'.

10. Former Finance Minister Yair Lapid was the most formidable representative of this viewpoint. See Yair Lapid, "Address by the Minister of Finance," *News1,* June 8, 2014, http://www.news1.co.il/Archive/004-D-93101-00.html.

11. For a historical overview of the evolution of Israel's military doctrine, see Ariel E. Levite, *Offense and Defense in Israeli Military Doctrine* (Boulder, CO: Westview Press, 1989).

12. Prime Minister Netanyahu has repeatedly addressed the risks and opportunities to Israel inherent in the cyber domain, as well as Israel's determination to be among the five top world leaders in this field. See Benjamin Netanyahu, "Remarks at the International Cyber Headquarters and Yuval Ne'eman Workshop" (speech, Tel Aviv, Israel, June 9, 2013), http://www.pmo.gov.il/MediaCenter/ Speeches/Pages/speechcyber090613.aspx.

13. The best studies on these issues remain Yehuda Ben Meir, *National Security Decision-Making: The Israeli Case* (Boulder, CO: Westview Press, 1986); Ben

Meir, *Civil-Military Relations in Israel* (New York: Columbia University Press, 1995).

14. Amichai Cohen, "The Israeli Supreme Court's Political Role in Matters of National Security," Social Science Research Network, February 3, 2014, http://dx.doi.org/10.2139/ssrn.2390411.

15. Ronen Medelkern, "The Interaction of Ideas and Institutions and Its Impact on the Responses of the Bank of Israel and the Budgets Division to the Recession," *Economic Quarterly* 58, no. 2 (2011): 67–90, http://www.academia.edu/2414064/The_Interaction_of_Ideas_and_Institutions_and_its_Impact_on_the_Responses_of_the_Bank_of_Israel_and_the_Budgets_Division_to_the_Recession_in_Hebrew_.

16. The Israeli Democracy Peace Institute, "The Peace Index: May 2014," June 5, 2014, http://www.peaceindex.org/indexMonthEng.aspx?num=275&monthname=May.

17. Uri Savir, "President Peres," *The Jerusalem Post*, September 6, 2014, http://www.jpost.com/landedpages/printarticle.aspx?id=355811; Yossi Beilin, "Peres Was to Speak," Mako, August 19, 2012, http://www.mako.co.il/video-blogs-yossi-beilin/Article-fd809d00c8d3931006.htm.

18. Yehoshafat Harkabi, *Israel's Fateful Hour* (New York: Harper and Row, 1988).

6. Russia

1. "Generals 'Clashed over Kosovo Raid,'" *BBC News*, August 2, 1999, http://news.bbc.co.uk/2/hi/europe/409576.stm.

2. Sergei Karaganov, "Russia and the U.S.: A Long Confrontation?," *Rossiya v global'noy politike*, no. 3 (2014), http://eng.globalaffairs.ru/number/Russia-and-the-US-A-Long-Confrontation-16990.

3. John J. Mearsheimer is very right when he identifies this thinking: "A huge expanse of flat land that Napoleonic France, imperial Germany, and Nazi Germany all crossed to strike at Russia itself, Ukraine serves as a buffer state of enormous strategic importance to Russia. No Russian leader would tolerate a military alliance that was Moscow's mortal enemy until recently moving into Ukraine." See John J. Mearsheimer, "Why the Ukraine Crisis Is the West's Fault: The Liberal Delusions That Provoked Putin," *Foreign Affairs* 93, no. 5 (September/October 2014): 77–89.

4. Mikhail Gorbachev, "Address to the 43rd U.N. General Assembly Session" (speech, New York, December 7, 1988), Wilson Center, http://digitalarchive.wilsoncenter.org/document/116224.pdf?v=f866824e174083f0e3ff46fc6af64891.

5. Mikhail Gorbachev, "Address to the Council of Europe" (speech, Strasbourg, France, July 6, 1989), CVCE, http://www.cvce.eu/content/publication/2002/9/20/4c021687-98f9-4727-9e8b-836e0bc1f6fb/publishable_en.pdf.

6. Mikhail Sergeevich Gorbachev, *Perestroika: New Thinking for Our Country and the World* (New York: Harper & Row, 1987).

7. Vladimir Putin, "Speech in the Bundestag of the Federal Republic of Germany" (speech, Berlin, Germany, September 25, 2001), http://archive.kremlin.ru/eng/speeches/2001/09/25/0001_type82912type82914_138535.shtml.

8. Sergei Karaganov, "Confrontation or Cooperation? The New Russia Is No Longer a Crippled Giant," IP-Journal, July 1, 2008, https://ip-journal.dgap.org/en/ipjournal/regions/confrontation-or-cooperation.

9. Pavel Felgenhauer, "Putin Serious about NATO," The Moscow Times, November 29, 2001, http://www.themoscowtimes.com/opinion/article/putin-serious-about-nato/249944.html.

10. Vladimir Putin, "Presidential Address to Parliament over Crimea," RT, March 19, 2014, http://on.rt.com/x9p95c.

11. Vladimir Putin, "Russia and the Changing World," Ria Novosti, February 27, 2012, http://en.ria.ru/analysis/20120227/171547818.html.

12. Mearsheimer, "Why the Ukraine Crisis Is the West's Fault," 86.

13. Vladimir Putin, "Presidential Address to the Federal Assembly" (speech, the Kremlin, Moscow, April 25, 2005), http://archive.kremlin.ru/eng/speeches/2005/04/25/2031_type70029type82912_87086.shtml.

14. Putin, "Russia and the Changing World."

15. For one of the characteristic examples, see Alexander Dugin, "Mikhail Gorbachev's Betrayal," YouTube (video posted by "Ulaghchi"), July 29, 2014, https://www.youtube.com/watch?v=XR3JozlmG4g.

16. Putin, "Russia and the Changing World."

17. Ibid.

18. Ibid.

19. Vladimir Putin, "Opening Remarks at the Security Council Meeting" (speech, the Kremlin, Moscow, July 22, 2014), http://eng.kremlin.ru/transcripts/22714.

20. Vladimir Putin, "A New Integration Project for Eurasia: The Future in the Making," Izvestia, October 3, 2011, http://www.russianmission.eu/en/news/article-prime-minister-vladimir-putin-new-integration-project-eurasia-future-making-izvestia-3-.

21. Ibid.

22. Ibid.

23. Vladimir Putin, "Presidential Address to the Federal Assembly" (speech, the Kremlin, Moscow, December 12, 2013), http://eng.kremlin.ru/news/6402.

24. Putin, "Presidential Address to Parliament over Crimea."

25. Igor Zevelev, "Russia's Future: Nation or Civilization?," Russia in Global Affairs, no. 4 (2009), http://eng.globalaffairs.ru/number/n_14246.

26. Vladimir Putin, "Presidential Address to the Federal Assembly" (speech, the Kremlin, Moscow, July 8, 2000), http://archive.kremlin.ru/eng/speeches/2000/07/08/0000_type70029type82912_70658.shtml.

27. See Vladimir Putin, "Russia at the Turn of the Millennium," Intellectual Takeout, December 30, 1999, http://www.intellectualtakeout.org/library/primary-sources/russia-turn-millennium. This was published on the eve of Boris Yeltsin's resignation.

28. Ibid.

29. Putin, "Presidential Address to the Federal Assembly" (2013).

30. Cynthia A. Robert, "The Czar of Brinkmanship: A Classic Cold War Strategy Makes a Comeback in the Kremlin," *Foreign Affairs Snapshot,* May 5, 2014, http://www. foreignaffairs.com/articles/141390/cynthia-a-roberts/the-czar-of-brinkmanship.

7. Turkey

I would like to thank Gencer Özcan, William Quandt, and Sabri Sayarı for their suggestions on previous versions of this chapter.

1. For general information on Turkish strategy and its determinants, see Günter Seufert, *Foreign Policy and Self-Image: The Societal Basis of Strategy Shifts in Turkey* (SWP Research Paper) (Berlin: German Institute for International and Security Affairs, 2012); Karabekir Akkoyunlu, Kalypso Nicolaïdis, and Kerem Öktem, *The Western Condition: Turkey, the US and the EU in the New Middle East* (Oxford: SEESOX, 2013); Ramazan Erdağ and Tuncay Kardaş, "Türk Dış Politikası ve Stratejik Kültür," in *Türk Dış Politikası Yıllığı 2012,* ed. Burhanettin Duran, Kemal İnat, and Ufuk Ulutaş (Ankara: SETA, 2013), 65–90; and the collection of articles published as a special issue in Tarık Oğuzlu and Emel Parlar Dal, eds., "Turkey's Rise and the West: Conceptual Lenses and Actors," *Turkish Studies* 14, no. 4 (2013): 617–811.

2. Recep Tayyip Erdoğan became the first popularly elected president of Turkey in August 2014. Minister of Foreign Affairs Ahmet Davutoğlu replaced Erdoğan as the prime minister and the official leader of the Justice and Development Party.

3. Murat Yeşiltaş, "The Transformation of the Geopolitical Vision in Turkish Foreign Policy," *Turkish Studies* 14, no. 4 (2013): 663–666.

4. For the military's role in foreign policy decisions, see Gencer Özcan, "The Military and the Making of Turkish Foreign Policy," in *Turkey in World Politics: An Emerging Multiregional Power,* ed. Barry Rubin and Kemal Kirişçi (London: Lynne Rienner, 2001), 13–30.

5. Eric S. Edelman, Svante E. Cornell, Aaron Lobel, and Michael Makovsky, *The Roots of Turkish Conduct: Understanding the Evolution of Turkish Policy in the Middle East* (Washington, DC: Bipartisan Policy Center, 2013), 16–18.

6. Ali Karaosmanoğlu, "The Evolution of the National Security Culture and the Military in Turkey," *Journal of International Affairs* 54, no. 1 (2000): 199–216.

7. Barry Rubin, "Understanding Turkey's New Foreign Policy," in *Turkey in World Politics,* 251–252.

8. Yeşiltaş, "The Transformation," 666–668.

9. For a detailed analysis of the relations between Turkey and the EU, see Birol Yeşilada, *EU-Turkey Relations in the 21st Century* (Abingdon, Oxon: Routledge, 2013).

10. "Avrupa Birliği'yle Gizli Mektup Trafiği," *Hürriyet,* March 20, 2000, http://hurarsiv.hurriyet.com.tr/goster/haber.aspx?id=-141273.

11. İsmail Cem wrote a series of articles on strategy in the daily *Sabah*, September 1–6, 1998. For example, see Cem, "Son Bir Yıldan, Önümüzdeki Yüzyıla," *Sabah*, September 1, 1998, http://arsiv.sabah.com.tr/1998/09/01/r11.html; Sem, "Ortadoğu'ya Yeniden Döndük," *Sabah*, September 2, 1998, http://arsiv.sabah.com.tr/1998/09/02/r21.html.

12. For a concise summary of Davutoğlu's ideas, see Ahmet Davutoğlu, "Turkey's Foreign Policy Vision: An Assessment of 2007," *Insight Turkey* 10, no. 1 (2008): 77–96. Although in the article Davutoğlu lists five principles of foreign policy, here they are substantially reframed and there is no one-to-one correspondence between his description and the one in this chapter.

13. Ibid., 81–82.

14. Ibid., 79–80.

15. For a biography of Recep Tayyip Erdoğan, see M. Hakan Yavuz, *Secularism and Muslim Democracy in Turkey* (Cambridge: Cambridge University Press, 2009), 118–134.

16. Haldun Gülalp, "Globalization and Political Islam: The Social Bases of Turkey's Welfare Party," *International Journal of Middle East Studies* 33, no. 3 (2001): 435–441.

17. Marvine Howe, *Turkey Today: A Nation Divided over Islam's Revival* (Boulder, CO: Westview, 2000), 187–188.

18. Fethullah Gülen was acquitted in Turkish courts in 2006. For an account of the Gülen movement, see Joshua D. Hendrick, *Gülen: The Ambiguous Politics of Market Islam in Turkey and the World* (New York: New York University Press, 2013).

19. For a concise list of the conditions under which liberals had supported the JDP, see İhsan Dağı, "Limits of Liberal Support for the AKP," *Today's Zaman*, October 11, 2007, http://www.todayszaman.com/columnist/ihsan-dagi_124383_limits-of-liberal-support-for-the-ak-party.html.

20. For the gradual dismantling of the military's influence in Turkish politics, see Yaprak Gürsoy, *Türkiye'de Sivil-Asker İlişkilerinin Dönüşümü* (Istanbul: Bilgi University Press, 2013). The 2013 court decision on the *Balyoz* plot was canceled by the Constitutional Court in June 2014 and all of the suspects were acquitted in April 2015 after a retrial. In March 2014, the Constitutional Court also released *Ergenekon* suspects from prison. In 2015, a new trial of this case was pending.

21. Edelman et al., *The Roots of Turkish Conduct*, 77–78.

22. Mustafa Kutlay, "Economy as the 'Practical Hand' of 'New Turkish Foreign Policy': A Political Economy Explanation," *Insight Turkey* 13, no. 1 (2011): 67–88.

23. Senem Aydın-Düzgit and E. Fuat Keyman, "Democracy Support in Turkey's Foreign Policy," Carnegie Endowment for International Peace, March 25, 2014, http://carnegieendowment.org/2014/03/25/democracysupportinturkeysforeignpolicy/h5ne?reloadFlag=1.

24. For the activities of IHH in Africa, see Mehmet Özkan and Birol Akgün, "Turkey's Opening to Africa," *The Journal of Modern African Studies* 48, no. 4 (2010): 525–546.

25. Sabri Sayarı, "New Directions in Turkey-USA Relations," *Journal of Balkan and Near Eastern Studies* 15, no. 2 (2013): 129–142.

26. For a detailed analysis of the Turkish government's reactions to the Arab uprisings, see Ziya Öniş, "Turkey and the Arab Uprising: Between Ethics and Self-Interest," *Insight Turkey* 14, no. 3 (2012): 45–63.

27. "Başbakan: Darbeler Kötüdür," *Hürriyet*, July 5, 2013, http://www.hurriyet.com.tr/gundem/23661500.asp; "Egypt Asks Turkish Ambassador to Leave over Support for Muslim Brotherhood," *The Guardian*, November 23, 2013, http://www.theguardian.com/world/2013/nov/23/egypt-turkey-ambassador-muslim-brotherhood-mohamed-morsi.

28. Oytun Orhan, "Reyhanlı Saldırısı ve Türkiye'nin Suriye İkilemi," *Ortadoğu Analiz* 5, no. 54 (2013): 10–16.

29. Stephen J. Flanagan, "The Turkey-Russia-Iran Nexus: Eurasian Power Dynamics," *The Washington Quarterly* 31, no. 1 (2013): 167–171; Kadri Gürsel, "Iran-Turkey Rivalry Worsens over Patriot Deployment," *Al-Monitor*, January 4, 2013, http://www.almonitor.com/pulse/originals/2013/01/turkey-patriot-missiles-iran.html#.

30. "Kürt Petrolü Türkiye'ye Gönderildi," *Milliyet*, December 15, 2013.

31. Tim Arango and Clifford Kraus, "Kurds' Oil Deals with Turkey Raise Fears of Fissures in Iraq," *The New York Times*, December 2, 2013, http://www.nytimes.com/2013/12/03/world/middleeast/kurds-oil-deals-with-turkey-raise-fears-of-fissures-in-iraq.html?pagewanted=all&_r=0.

32. Morton I. Abramowitz and Eric S. Edelman, *From Rhetoric to Reality: Reframing U.S. Turkey Policy* (Washington, DC: Bipartisan Policy Center, 2013): 35, 39–40.

33. Tim Arango, "Turkish Liberals Turn Their Backs on Erdoğan," *The New York Times*, June 19, 2013.

34. Joe Lauria, "Reclusive Turkish Imam Criticizes Gaza Flotilla," *The Wall Street Journal*, June 4, 2010.

35. "Başbakan Erdoğan'dan İsrail'e: Alçak Bir Pervasızlıktır," *Radikal*, June 1, 2010, http://www.radikal.com.tr/politika/basbakan_erdogandan_israile_alcak_bir_pervasizliktir-1000071.

36. Glen Johnson and Richard Spencer, "Turkey's Politicians, Gold Dealer and the Pop Star," *The Telegraph*, December 29, 2013.

37. Fevzi Kizilkoyun, "Hatay'da Silah Yüklü TIR," *Hürriyet*, January 2, 2014, http://www.hurriyet.com.tr/gundem/25484247.asp.

38. For reports on the chief of the MİT, see Adam Entous and Joe Parkinson, "Turkey's Spymaster Plots Own Course on Syria," *The Wall Street Journal*, October 10, 2013; David Ignatius, "Turkey Blows Israel's Cover for Iranian Spy Ring," *Washington Post*, October 17, 2013, http://www.washingtonpost.com/opinions/david-ignatius-turkey-blows-israels-cover-for-iranian-spy-ring/2013/10/16/7d9c1eb2-3686-11e3-be86-6aeaa439845b_story.html.

39. For a study that adopts this definition of populism, see, for example, Cas Mudde and Cristobal Rovira Kaltwasser, "Exclusionary vs. Inclusionary Populism:

Comparing Contemporary Europe and Latin America," *Government and Opposition* 48, no. 2 (2013): 150, 147–174.

40. Benjamin Moffitt and Simon Tormey, "Rethinking Populism: Politics, Mediatisation and Political Style," *Political Studies* 62, no. 2 (2014): 391–392.

41. The significance Erdoğan assigned to the United States was apparent when he implicitly accused the ambassador to Ankara, Francis Ricciardone, of involvement in the graft inquiry and threatened to oust him from the country. Semih Idiz, "US-Turkey Crisis Averted over Corruption Probe," *Al-Monitor*, December 24, 2013, http://www.almonitor.com/pulse/originals/2013/12/united-states-losing-patience-erdogan.html.

42. From Erdoğan's speech to the party's provincial heads on December 25, 2013, available online at https://www.akparti.org.tr/site/haberler/basbakan-erdoganin-25-aralik-tarihli-genisletilmis-il-baskanlari-toplantisi/57147.

43. Aylin Ş. Görener and Meltem Ş. Ucal constructed Erdoğan's leadership profile based on a content analysis technique and concluded that Erdoğan had a "dichotomizing tendency," which saw "politics as a struggle between right and wrong, just and unjust, villains and victims." See Aylin Ş. Görener and Meltem Ş. Ucal, "The Personality and Leadership Style of Recep Tayyip Erdoğan: Implications for Turkish Foreign Policy," *Turkish Studies* 12, no. 3 (2011): 377.

44. Giray Sadık, "Magic Blend or Dangerous Mix? Exploring the Role of Religion in Transforming Turkish Foreign Policy from a Theoretical Perspective," *Turkish Studies* 13, no. 3 (2012): 301–305.

8. United States

1. "X" (George Kennan), "The Sources of Soviet Conduct," *Foreign Affairs*, July 1947, http://www.foreignaffairs.com/articles/23331/x/the-sources-of-soviet-conduct.

2. This is not a novel insight. For example, see Melvyn Leffler and Jeffrey Legro, introduction to *To Lead the World: American Strategy after the Bush Doctrine*, ed. Melvyn Leffler and Jeffrey Legro (New York: Oxford University Press, 2008), 5. "When US policymakers have not been . . . attuned to the evolving international landscape, the result has been doleful."

3. Francis Fukuyama, *The End of History and the Last Man* (New York: Free Press, 1992).

4. See, for example, Christopher Layne, "The End of Pax Americana: How American Decline Became Inevitable," *The Atlantic*, April 26, 2012, http://www.theatlantic.com/international/archive/2012/04/the-end-of-pax-americana-howwestern-decline-became-inevitable/256388/. "Given America's relative loss of standing, emerging powers will feel increasingly emboldened to test and probe the current order with an eye toward reshaping the international system in ways that reflect their own interests, norms and values."

5. For contrasting views on the implications of emerging powers, compare Walter Russell Mead "The Return of Geopolitics," *Foreign Affairs*, May/June 2014; G. John Ikenberry, "The Illusion of Geopolitics," *Foreign Affairs*, May/June, 2014.

6. See the essays in Richard Rosecrance and Steven Miller, eds., *The Next Great War? The Roots of World War I and the Risk of US-China Conflict* (Cambridge, MA: MIT Press, 2014).

7. "The growth of the power of Athens and the alarm which this inspired in Lacedaemon, made war inevitable." Thucydides, *The Peloponnesian Wars*, trans. Richard Crawley and T. E. Wick (New York: Modern Library, 1982), I: 30. See also Graham Allison, "Thucydides's Trap Has Been Sprung in the Pacific," *Financial Times*, August 21, 2012, http://www.ft.com/cms/s/0/5d695b5a-ead3-11e1-984b-00144feab49a.html#axzz37RNzmJ54.

8. See, for example, Christopher Clark, *The Sleepwalkers: How Europe Went to War in 1914* (New York: HarperCollins, 2013). Clark chronicles compellingly the role of judgment and misjudgment in triggering the First World War.

9. Both Matias Spektor (Brazil) and Srinath Raghavan (India) note the importance of domestic political rivalries in shaping foreign policy debates.

10. For example, Srinath Raghavan observes: "India is not a revisionist power: it seeks not to alter the system radically in accordance with a particular strategic vision but to uphold and enhance these institutions." During the Lula administration in Brazil, Matias Spektor states: "There was no sense inside Brazil that the country was willing or able to be a spoiler. There was no desire to attack the existing order with a view to design an alternative one." Similarly Men Honghua argues that China "no longer constitutes a challenge to the international system. In fact, China seeks to integrate itself into international society and to participate in the evolving international order as a responsible stakeholder." Others have argued that China has more revisionist goals. See, for example, Aaron Friedberg, *A Contest for Supremacy* (New York, W. W. Norton, 2011).

11. Raghavan writes: "[India's] approach . . . is conditioned by the recognition that India has been a prime beneficiary of the open global economic as well as political order that currently prevails."

12. See, for example, Men Honghua: "China wants to assume a larger role in refashioning the multilateral institutions that uphold the global order." Spektor argues that Brazil's efforts to create new institutions in Latin America "was a conscious attempt to counter U.S. hegemony in the region."

13. Israel is a possible exception here; at least some Israeli leaders and strategists believe that Israel benefits from U.S. freedom of action on the international stage.

14. It is notable that few of the authors in this volume discuss at length the importance of "BRICS" or other anti-Western coalitions.

15. In the case of Japan, the desire for more independence stems from a fear of abandonment vis-à-vis China ("Japan passing") as well as from historic pride and a desire to become a more "normal" state.

16. See Robert Kagan, "End of Dreams, Return of History," in Leffler and Legro, *To Lead the World,* 45. "The alternative to American regional predominance, in short, is not a new regional stability. . . . Difficult as it may be to extend American predominance into the future, no one should imagine that a reduction of

American power or a retraction of American influence and global involvement will provide an easier path." A more recent version of this argument, focused on China, can be found in Robert Blackwill and Ashely Tellis, *Revising US Grand Strategy toward China* (New York: Council on Foreign Relations, 2015). On page 4, they write, "Because the American effort to 'integrate' China into the liberal international order has now generated new threats to U.S. primacy in Asia—and could result in a consequential challenge to American power globally—Washington needs a new grand strategy toward China that centers on balancing the rise of Chinese power rather than continuing to assist its ascendancy."

17. This argument is elaborated in James Steinberg and Michael O'Hanlon, *Strategic Reassurance and Resolve: US-China Relations in the 21st Century* (Princeton, NJ: Princeton University Press, 2014).

18. See, for example, Christopher Layne, "The (Almost) Triumph of Offshore Balancing," *The National Interest,* January 27, 2012, http://nationalinterest.org/commentary/almost-triumph-offshore-balancing-6405; Stephen M. Walt, "Offshore Balancing: An Idea Whose Time Has Come," *Foreign Policy,* November 2, 2011, http://www.foreignpolicy.com/posts/2011/11/02/offshore_balancing_an_idea_whose_time_has_come.

19. See, for example, Hugh White, "Australia's Choice," *Foreign Affairs,* September 4, 2012, http://www.foreignaffairs.com/articles/139902/hugh-white/australias-choice. "In essence China and the United States would need to find a way to share power as equals." For a longer version of the argument, see Hugh White, *The China Choice: Why America Should Share Power* (Collingwood, Australia: Black Inc., 2012). In the case of Russia, a number of analysts have criticized U.S. willingness to offer the prospect of including countries of the former Soviet Union as members of NATO, instead arguing that the United States (and Western Europe) should accept a de facto Russian veto over such association—for example, with regard to Ukraine. See Graham Allison, "A Belgian Solution for Ukraine?," *The National Interest,* March 15, 2014, http://nationalinterest.org/commentary/%E2%80%9Cbelgian-solution%E2%80%9D-ukraine-10062. See also, for example, Hans Morgenthau, *Politics among Nations,* 4th ed. (New York: Knopf, 1967), 11: "Judge other nations as we judge our own and having judged them in this fashion, [pursue] policies that respect the interests of other nations while protecting and promoting those of our own." In the case of China, see "U.S.-China Joint Statement," Office of the Press Secretary, November 17, 2009, http://www.whitehouse.gov/the-press-office/us-china-joint-statement: "The two sides agreed that respecting each other's core interests is extremely important to ensure steady progress in U.S.-China relations."

20. This is both a "collective action" and institutional efficacy problem.

21. The debate over whether the United States should join China's proposed Asian Infrastructure Development Bank is illustrative of this problem.

22. See Robert J. Art, "Selective Engagement in the Era of Austerity," in *America's Path: Grand Strategy for the Next Administration,* ed. Richard Fontaine and Kristin Lord (Washington, DC: Center for a New American Security, 2012),

http://www.cnas.org/files/documents/publications/CNAS_AmericasPath_Fon-taineLord_o.pdf.

23. See the extended discussion of how to implement this approach vis-à-vis China in Steinberg and O'Hanlon, *Strategic Reassurance and Resolve.*

24. A creative example of this kind of engagement on the security front is the U.S. "Western Hemisphere Defense Policy Statement," adopted in 2012, which emphasizes the importance of bilateral and regional security cooperation among the Western Hemisphere nations. See Alejandro Garcia, "The Future of Western Hemisphere Defense Cooperation," *International Affairs Review,* January 13, 2013, http://www.iar-gwu.org/node/451.

25. See "China's Xi Calls for Asia Security Framework at Summit," *Bloomberg News,* May 21, 2014, http://www.bloomberg.com/news/2014-05-21/china-s-xi-calls-for-asia-security-framework-at-summit.html. An earlier manifestation of this approach was the East Asia Economic Caucus advocated by former Malaysia prime minister Mahatir.

26. See "Fifth Ministerial Plenary," Global Counterterrorism Forum, September 23, 2014, http://www.thegctf.org/web/guest/home.

27. The chapters in this volume on Turkey and Brazil illustrate clearly the domestic political benefits from challenging U.S. foreign policy.

28. See the Open Government Partnership website, http://www.opengovpartnership. org.

29. The expression (and the concept) has been used in varying forms by both Chinese and American leaders in recent years. During a visit to the United States in February 2012 (while he was still vice president), Xi Jinping called for "a new type of relationship between major countries," and the idea has been echoed in the United States by former Secretary of State Hillary Clinton and National Security Advisors Tom Donilon and Susan Rice. See David M. Lampton, "A New Type of Major Power Relationship: Seeking a Durable Foundation for U.S.-China Ties," *Asia Policy* 16 (July 2013), http://www.nbr.org/publications/element. aspx?id=650.

30. Steinberg and O'Hanlon, *Strategic Reassurance and Resolve.*

31. For example, George Kennan claimed that NATO enlargement would be "a strategic blunder of potentially epic proportions." Strobe Talbott, *The Russia Hand: A Memoir of Presidential Diplomacy* (New York: Random House, 2002), 220.

Conclusion

1. Robert Jervis, "The Future of World Politics: Will It Resemble the Past?," *International Security* 16, no. 3 (Winter 1991/1992): 39–73. More recently compare W. R. Mead, "The Return of Geopolitics: Revenge of the Revisionist Powers," *Foreign Affairs* (May/June 2014): 69–79; G. J. Ikenberry, "The Illusion of Geopolitics: The Enduring Power of the Liberal Order," *Foreign Affairs* (May/June 2014): 80–90. In the policy world, see National Intelligence Council, *Global Trends 2030: Alternative*

Worlds (Washington, DC: National Intelligence Council, 2012), http://www.dni. gov/index.php/about/oranization/national-intelligence-council-global-trends.

2. Paul Kennedy, *The Rise and Fall of the Great Powers: Economic Change and Military Conflict from 1500 to 2000* (New York: Random House, 1987); Robert A. Pastor, ed., *A Century's Journey: How the Great Powers Shape the World* (New York: Basic Books, 1999); John Mearsheimer, *The Tragedy of Great Power Politics* (New York: Norton, 2001); Jeffrey Legro, *Rethinking the World: Great Power Strategies and International Order* (Ithaca, NY: Cornell University Press, 2005); Dale Copeland, *Economic Interdependence and War* (Princeton, NJ: Princeton University Press, 2014).

3. Works that do speak to the topic include Robert Chase, Emily Hill, and Paul Kennedy, eds., *The Pivotal States: A New Framework for U.S. Policy in the Developing World* (New York: W. W. Norton, 2000); Stewart Patrick, "Irresponsible Stakeholders?: The Difficulty of Integrating Rising Powers," *Foreign Affairs* 89 (November/December 2010): 44–53; Henry R. Nau and Deepa Mary Ollapally, eds., *Worldviews of Aspiring Powers: Domestic Foreign Policy Debates in China, India, Iran, Japan and Russia* (New York: Oxford University Press, 2012); Charles Kupchan, *No One's World: The West, the Rising Rest, and the Coming Global Order* (Oxford: Oxford University Press, 2012); Amrita Narlikar, "Introduction: Negotiating the Rise of New Powers," *International Affairs* 89, no. 3 (May 2013): 561–577.

4. Fractured identities and distributed authority is not limited to emerging states— for example, consider the extreme polarization of contemporary American politics.

5. Pierre F. Landy, *Decentralized Authoritarianism in China: The Communist Party's Control of Local Elites in the Post-Mao Era* (New York: Cambridge University Press, 2008); William Antholis, *Inside Out, India and China: Local Politics Go Global* (Washington, DC: The Brookings Institution, 2013).

6. Sumantra Bose, *Transforming India: Challenges to the World's Largest Democracy* (Cambridge, MA: Harvard University Press, 2013). Consider, for example, how difficult it has been for India to pass legislation on multi-retail foreign direct investment or involving external partnerships in higher education.

7. "Who's Afraid of the Activists?," *The Economist*, May 9, 2015, http://www.economist.com/news/asia/21650548-democratic-asian-governments-well-authoritarian-ones-crack-down-ngos-whos-afraid.

8. A. F. K. Organski and Jacek Kugler, *The War Ledger* (Chicago: University of Chicago Press, 1980); Robert Gilpin, *War and Change in World Politics* (Cambridge: Cambridge University Press, 1981); Dale Copeland, *The Origins of Major Power War* (Ithaca, NY: Cornell University Press, 2000); Douglas Lemke, *Regions of War and Peace* (Cambridge: Cambridge University Press, 2002).

9. Charles Kindleberger, *The World In Depression, 1929–39* (Berkeley: University of California Press, 1974); Stephen D. Krasner, "State Power and the Structure of International Trade," *World Politics* 28, no. 3 (1976): 317–347; Gilpin, *War and*

Change in World Politics; Robert Keohane, *After Hegemony: Cooperation and Discord in the World Political Economy* (Princeton, NJ: Princeton University Press, 1984); David A. Lake, *Power, Protection, and Free Trade: International Sources of U.S. Commercial Strategy, 1887–1939* (Ithaca, NY: Cornell University Press, 1988). More recently see Michael Mandelbaum, *The Case for Goliath: How America Acts as the World's Government in the Twenty-First Century* (New York: Public Affairs, 2005).

10. G. John Ikenberry, *Liberal Leviathan: The Origins, Crisis, and Transformation of the American World Order* (Princeton, NJ: Princeton University Press, 2010).

11. Paul Belkin, Derek Mix, and Stephen Woehrel, *NATO: Response to the Crisis in Ukraine and Security Concerns in Central and Eastern Europe* (Washington, DC: Congressional Research Service, 2014), http://fas.org/sgp/crs/row/R43478.pdf.

12. Jakob Vestergaard and Robert Wade, *Out of the Woods: Gridlock in the IMF, and the World Bank Puts Multilateralism at Risk* (Copenhagen: Danish Institute for International Studies, 2014), http://www.diis.dk/files/media/publications/import/extra/rp2014-06_gridlock-imf-wb_jve_wade_web_2.pdf.

13. See Ian Goldin, *Divided Nations: Why Global Governance Is Failing, and What We Can Do About It* (Oxford: Oxford University Press, 2013); Stewart Patrick, "The Unruled World: The Case for Good Enough Global Governance," *Foreign Affairs* (January/February 2014): 58–73. For an argument that institutions did work in the 2008 financial crisis, see Daniel Drezner, *The System Worked: How the World Stopped Another Great Depression* (Oxford: Oxford University Press, 2014).

14. Yun Sun, *Africa in China's Foreign Policy* (Washington, DC: Brookings Institution, 2014), http://www.brookings.edu/~/media/research/files/papers/2014/04/Africa%20china%20policy%20sun/africa%20in%20china%20web_cmg7.pdf.

15. Jane Perlez, "China and Russia Reach 30-Year Gas Deal," *New York Times*, May 21, 2014, http://www.nytimes.com/2014/05/22/world/asia/china-russia-gas-deal.html?_r=0; Andrew Roth, "Russia and China Sign Cooperation Pacts," *New York Times*, May 8, 2015, http://www.nytimes.com/2015/05/09/world/europe/russia-and-china-sign-cooperation-pacts.html?_r=0.

16. Christopher Bodeen, "China, 21 Other Countries Initiate New Asian Bank Opposed by US as Rival to Existing Lenders," *US News and World Report*, October 24, 2014, http://www.usnews.com/news/business/articles/2014/10/23/china-21-other-countries-initiate-new-asian-bank.

17. One study of uncertainty and investor behavior argues "if volatility rises for a long period, the prolonged uncertainty leads us to subconsciously conclude that we no longer understand what is happening and then cortisol scales back our risk taking. In this way our risk taking calibrates to the amount of uncertainty and threat in the environment." John Coates, "The Biology of Risk," *The New York Times*, June 7, 2014. See, too, John Coates, *The House between Dog and Wolf: How Risk Taking Transforms Us, Body and Mind* (London: Penguin, 2012).

18. Richard Rosecrance, *The Rise of the Trading State: Commerce and Conquest in the Modern World* (New York: Basic Books, 1986).

19. There is a large literature on the rise of regionalism. For example, see Louise Fawcett and Andrew Hurrell, eds., *Regionalism in World Politics—Regional Organization and International Order* (Oxford: Oxford University Press, 1995); David Lake and Patrick Morgan, eds., *Regional Orders—Building Security in a New World* (University Park: Pennsylvania State University Press, 1997); Barry Buzan and Ole Waever, *Regions and Powers: The Structure of International Security* (Cambridge: Cambridge University Press, 2004); Peter Katzenstein, *A World of Regions: Asia and Europe in the American Imperium* (Ithaca, NY: Cornell University Press, 2005).

20. See Henry Kissinger, "The Future of U.S.-Chinese Relations Conflict Is a Choice, Not a Necessity," *Foreign Affairs* (March/April 2012), http://www.foreignaffairs. com/articles/137245/henry-a-kissinger/the-future-of-us-chinese-relations.

21. Susanne Gratius and Miriam Gomes Saraiva, "Continental Regionalism: Brazil's Prominent Role in the Americas" (CEPS Working Document No. 374, Centre for European Policy Studies, Brussels, February 13, 2013), http://aei.pitt.edu/40231/1/ WD_No_374_Brazil's_Continental_Regionalism.pdf; Michael Shifter, "The Shifting Landscape of Latin American Regionalism," *Current History* 111, no. 742 (February 2012): 55–61.

22. Elizabeth C. Economy, "How Xi Jinping Is Consolidating Power in China and Expanding Influence Abroad," *Foreign Affairs* (November/December 2014), https:// www.foreignaffairs.com/articles/china/2014-10-20/chinas-imperial-president.

23. Alastair Iain Johnston argues that China has shown aggressiveness on maritime issues but not overall behavior. See Alastair Iain Johnston, "How New and Assertive Is China's New Assertiveness?," *International Security* 37, no. 4 (2013): 7–48.

24. UN General Assembly, Charter of the United Nations, Article 2.7, http://www. un.org/en/documents/charter/chapter1.shtml.

25. Alex J. Bellamy, *Responsibility to Protect: The Global Effort to End Mass Atrocities* (Cambridge: Polity, 2009).

26. Quoted in Mark Landler, "Obama to Detail a Broader Foreign Policy Agenda," *New York Times*, May 25, 2014, A4.

27. Harsh V. Pant, *The U.S.-India Nuclear Pact: Policy, Process, and Great Power Politics* (New Delhi: Oxford University Press, 2011); Quirin Schiermeier, "What Does the US-China Climate Deal Mean?," *Nature*, November 12, 2014, http:// www.nature.com/news/what-does-the-us-china-climate-deal-mean-1.16335.

CONTRIBUTORS

Yaprak Gürsoy is a scholar and associate professor in the Department of International Relations at Istanbul Bilgi University. Her areas of interest include regime change, civil-military relations, politics in Southern Europe, and foreign policy. She is the author of *The Transformation of Civil-Military Relations in Turkey* (in Turkish, 2013). Her scholarly publications have also appeared in *Political Science Quarterly, Democratization, South European Society and Politics, Journal of Modern Greek Studies,* and *Turkish Studies,* among others.

William I. Hitchcock is professor of history at the University of Virginia and Randolph P. Compton Professor and Director of Research and Scholarship at the Miller Center. His work and teaching focus on the international, diplomatic, and military history of the twentieth century, in particular the era of the world wars and the Cold War. His book *The Bitter Road to Freedom: A New History of the Liberation of Europe* (2008) was a finalist for the Pulitzer Prize, a winner of the George Louis Beer Prize, and a *Financial Times* bestseller in the UK. His most recent book is *The Human Rights Revolution: An International History* (coedited with Petra Goedde and Akira Iriye, 2012), which features an essay by Hitchcock on the Geneva Conventions of 1949 and the evolution of the laws of war. He is now at work on a book called *The Age of Eisenhower: America and the World in the 1950s.*

Men Honghua is the deputy director of the International Strategic Studies Center and KF Chair Professor at the Party School of the CPC Central Committee in China (CCPS), the institution that trains the highest-level officials of the Communist Party of China. Honghua was the recipient of a Kimsey Fellowship from the Carnegie Endowment for International Peace in 2003 and in 2011 received an Eisenhower Fellowship in the Northeast Asia Regional Program. He has written six books on Chinese grand strategy, U.S. strategy, and international security, including

China's Grand Strategy: A Framework Analysis (2005, 2006), *The Wings of Hegemony: U.S. Institutional Strategy* (2005), and *Men Honghua: A Journey of Field Studies* (2012). He has edited twelve books on international relations and translated fourteen classic English academic books into Chinese.

Melvyn P. Leffler is Edward Stettinius Professor of History and Miller Center faculty associate at the University of Virginia. He won the Bancroft Prize for *A Preponderance of Power: National Security, the Truman Administration, and the Cold War* (1992) and the George Louis Beer Prize for *For the Soul of Mankind: the United States, the Soviet Union, and the Cold War* (2007). In 2010, he and Odd Arne Westad edited the three-volume *Cambridge History of the Cold War*. Leffler was Harmsworth Professor at the University of Oxford in 2002–2003 and was president of the Society for Historians of American Foreign Relations in 1993. He is the author of several articles and essays seeking to put U.S. national security policy after 9/11 in historical perspective.

Jeffrey W. Legro is Taylor Professor of Politics, vice provost for Global Affairs, and Miller Center faculty associate at the University of Virginia. A specialist on international relations, Legro is the author of *Rethinking the World: Great Power Strategies and International Order* (2005) and *Cooperation under Fire: Anglo-German Restraint during World War II* (1995). He is the coeditor (with Melvyn Leffler) of *To Lead the World: U.S. Strategy after the Bush Doctrine* (2008) and *In Uncertain Times: American Foreign Policy after the Berlin Wall and 9/11* (2011). Legro chaired the American Political Science Association (APSA) Task Force on U.S. Standing in the World and is past president of the APSA's International History and Politics section. He has taught at China Foreign Affairs University in Beijing and was a Fulbright-Nehru Senior Researcher at the Institute for Defense and Strategic Analyses in New Delhi.

Ariel E. Levite is a nonresident senior associate in the Nuclear Policy Program at the Carnegie Endowment for International Peace. He is a member of the board of directors of the Fisher Brothers Institute for Air and Space Strategic Studies. From 2002 to 2007, Levite was the principal deputy director general for policy at the Israeli Atomic Energy Commission. He also served as the deputy national security advisor for defense policy and was head of the Bureau of International Security and Arms Control in the Israeli Ministry of Defense. Before his government service, Levite worked for five years as a senior research associate and head of the project on Israeli security at the Jaffee Center for Strategic Studies at Tel Aviv University.

Fyodor Lukyanov is a research professor in the School of World Economy and World Politics at the National Research University Higher School of Economics in Moscow and editor-in-chief of *Russia in Global Affairs* (founded in 2002), a journal published in Russian and English with the collaboration of *Foreign Affairs*. Lukyanov is a Russian foreign policy analyst who has worked for multiple Russian newspapers and TV and radio stations. He is chairman of the Presidium of the Council for Foreign and Defense Policy and a member of the Russian Council for International

Affairs. He is also the recipient of a Laureate of the Russian Government Award for his contributions to international journalism.

Srinath Raghavan is a senior fellow at the Centre for Policy Research in New Delhi and is a lecturer in Defense Studies at King's College London. Previously, he was an associate fellow at the National Institute of Advanced Studies, Bangalore. Raghavan has been associated with the King's College's e-learning program "War in the Modern World" and was a visiting lecturer at the Royal Air Force College, Cranwell. Prior to joining academia, Raghavan spent six years as an infantry officer in the Indian army. His book *War and Peace in Modern India: A Strategic History of the Nehru Years* was published in 2010.

Matias Spektor is an associate professor and scholar at the Center for International Relations at Fundação Getulio Vargas in Brazil. Previously, he was a visiting fellow at the Woodrow Wilson International Center for Scholars, the Council on Foreign Relations, and the London School of Economics, and he worked as an official for the United Nations and as a consultant for the Tavistock Institute in London. His first book, *Kissinger and Brazil* (2009), is forthcoming in English, and he is now completing *18 Days*, a history of U.S.-Brazil relations under President George W. Bush and President Lula da Silva.

James B. Steinberg is dean of the Maxwell School of Syracuse University and University Professor of Social Science, International Affairs, and Law. Previously, he was a deputy secretary of state, serving as the principal deputy to Secretary Hillary Clinton. From 2005 to 2008, Steinberg was dean of the Lyndon B. Johnson School of Public Affairs; previously he was vice president and director of Foreign Policy Studies at the Brookings Institution, where he supervised a wide-ranging research program on U.S. foreign policy. He has also served as a deputy national security advisor to President Clinton from 1996 to 2000. Steinberg's latest book is *Strategic Reassurance and Resolve: US-China Relations in the 21st Century* (2014), with Michael O'Hanlon. He has also authored *Difficult Transitions: Foreign Policy Troubles at the Outset of Presidential Power* (2008), with Kurt Campbell.

Constanze Stelzenmüller is the inaugural Robert Bosch senior fellow with the Center on the United States and Europe at the Brookings Institution. Previously she was a senior transatlantic fellow with the German Marshall Fund of the United States in Berlin, where she also served as the director of the Berlin office from 2005 to 2009. Stelzenmüller was an editor in the political section of the Hamburg weekly *Die Zeit* from 1994 until 2005. Essays and articles by Stelzenmüller have appeared as German Marshall Fund publications, as well as in *Foreign Affairs, Internationale Politik*, the *Financial Times*, the *International Herald Tribune*, and *Süddeutsche Zeitung*. She chairs the academic advisory board of the German Foundation on Peace Research (DSF), is chairwoman of the German section of Women in International Security, is a member of the advisory board of the Protestant Academy of Berlin-Brandenburg, and is a governor of the Ditchley Foundation.

ACKNOWLEDGMENTS

The chapters in this volume began as conference papers for a roundtable event at the Miller Center in Charlottesville, Virginia, held in April 2014. The editors would like to offer our sincere thanks to many people who have made this volume possible.

Our first debt is to the Stevenson family, who created the William and Carol Stevenson Conference at the Miller Center. The endowment allows the Miller Center to host a biennial conference on a pressing issue of national and international importance. We are deeply grateful to Carol Stevenson for her support of our work, and we hope this volume is a worthy tribute to the memory of William Stevenson.

We wish to thank the staff of the Miller Center, including its director, Bill Antholis, and former director, Gerald Baliles, both of whom gave strong support to this project. Every conference requires a great deal of unseen preparatory work, and we are deeply thankful for the efforts of Anne Carter Mulligan, who did an outstanding job overcoming the many challenges such conferences invariably create. Mike Greco and Rob Canevari gave us their outstanding technical support to allow for remote videoconferencing for some of the participants. We also want to offer our special thanks to Brantly Womack for his invaluable assistance.

At the conference itself, three people provided commentary on the papers: Philip Zelikow, William Quandt, and Kimberly Marten. We thank them for their thoughtful interventions.

Stefanie Georgakis Abbott has been truly invaluable in transforming the rough manuscript into a final product. Her attention to detail and her superb organizational skills kept us all on track in the final editorial stages of the project.

INDEX

www.ingramcontent.com/pod-product-compliance
Lightning Source LLC
Chambersburg PA
CBHW051727260326

41914CB00031B/1782/J